THE PROPHETS
AND
OUR TIMES

By

R. GERALD CULLETON

"It shall come to pass in the last days, says the Lord, that I will pour forth of my Spirit upon all flesh; and your sons and your daughters shall prophesy, and your young men shall see visions, and your old men shall dream dreams. And moreover upon my servants and upon my hand-maids in those days will I pour forth of my Spirit, and they shall prophesy."
(Acts 2:17-18)

"In all ages men have been divinely instructed in matters expedient for the salvation of the elect . . . and in all ages there have been persons pos-sessed of the spirit of prophesy, not for the purpose of announcing new doctrines, but to direct human actions."
(St. Thomas: Summa: 2:2:174:Res. et ad 3)

TAN BOOKS AND PUBLISHERS, INC.
Rockford, Illinois 61105

NIHIL OBSTAT:
 L. Arvin
 Censor Deputatus

IMPRIMATUR:
 Philip G. Scher
 Bishop of Monterey-Fresno, California
 November 15, 1941

The imprimatur indicates merely negative approval, that is
to say that no errors against faith or morals have been noted
in the book. But it does not mean that any approval is given
to any private oracle or any opinion expressed in the work.

Originally published by the author, Rev. R. Gerald Culleton in 1941 and 1943.

Copyright © 1941 and 1943 by R. Gerald Culleton

Copyright © 1974 by TAN Books and Publishers, Inc.

ISBN: 0-89555-050-4

TAN BOOKS AND PUBLISHERS, INC.
P.O. Box 424
Rockford, Illinois 61105

1974

CONTENTS

THE PROPHETS AND OUR TIMES

Preface 5

Part One: Has this Century been foreseen 9

Part Two: Topical Index to the Prophecies . . . 53

Part Three: The Prophetic Texts 83

Bibliography 249

Index to the Prophecies 252

PUBLISHER'S PREFACE

A few words need to be said about reissuing Father Gerald Culleton's *The Prophets and Our Times*. First of all it is now thirty-three years since the book was first published, and Father Culleton had an idea the world was then witnessing the events foretold by the prophecies he had recorded, the colossal occurence of that time being of course, World War II, the greatest struggle the world has ever known. Yet, from our view we realize those prophecies he presented and interpreted have *not* been fulfilled. Then too, there appeared in 1970 Mr. Yves Dupont's *Catholic Prophecy—The Coming Chastisement,* which for its brevity and command of the significance of the prophecies' meaning, has no equal in any book that I am familiar with, and certainly the present volume will not replace his nor eliminate the need of students interested in this subject reading *Catholic Prophecy* as well. Father Culleton's work traces many of the same prophecies as Mr. Dupont's and in general restricts itself to the same era; however, Father's book is considerably larger and more comprehensive in its coverage, for which reason, mainly, we have thought to reprint it. Added to this, however, is the general accuracy of *The Prophets and Our Times,* despite Father's penchant for interpreting the prophecies as being fulfilled by the events of his day.

Probably the most provocative characteristic of this book, especially to readers who have had no introduction to the subject, is the cohesiveness of the various prophecies—how they coalesce, dovetail, agree, and complement one another—this despite the fact that they were made in different centuries, from the fourth down to our own, and at times generally when transportation and communication were very poor, a factor which would preclude collusion (this is virtually unthinkable, given the conditions). The question arises then, do these prophecies, taken together, form a body of knowledge, or even a quasi body of knowledge? The author certainly treats them as if they do. Still the contemporary reader will ask: "Well, do they?" This, I believe, each person will have to answer for himself, based largely upon the interior evidence of the prophecies themselves. For my own part, I think they do. This judgment, however, is more mature than perhaps most readers will be able to make and comes from having read in various books prophecies other than those appearing here or in any recent editions, all of which prophecies I feel fit the general pattern laid down by Father Culleton in *The Prophets and Our Times*. Moreover, it has been my good fortune to come across a number of books from which he draws his material, some of these over a hundred years old. The impression which a reading of these older books gives, most decidedly, is that people in those days were just as interested in the prophecies as we are today, and the writers of those books were extremely careful to cite their sources and would be judged by their work as sane, sensible and careful academicians, giving most scrupulously *their own* sources and filling in many details about the lives of the various saintly prophets. In this regard I am thinking especially of *The Christian Trumpet*. The present author, moreover, has not exerpted *all* that he could from these books, but rather has selected only the most apropos material.

If we are to grant that this group of prophecies forms a sort of corpus of knowledge, what are the general outlines of this information? Here, I believe, we all owe a great debt to Father Culleton for his grouping of this information into two general categories, the first of which he covers in the present book and the second of which he treats in his *Reign of Antichrist* (1951), also being reissued concomitantly with the present book, and one which the reader, if he is interested in this subject at all will surely want to peruse, in order to flesh out his view or perspective of events. In general, the information covered by his two books concerns the time of Antichrist, on the one hand, and the time generally which precedes it, on the other. The time preceding Antichrist we might well refer to as the "dress rehearsal" period. Now the time of the Antichrist will be the most distressing the world has ever known, and the Bible is very explicit in specifying that his reign will last three and one-half years or forty-two months or 1,290 days. These figures are given in several different places in the Bible (*Daniel* 12:7; 12:11; *Apoc.* 11:2-3; 13:14), in order that, it would seem, we do not in any way understand them symbolically; the reason for this is obvious: God wishes to console the good people of that time with the knowledge of precisely when their great tribulation will end—in truly a touching measure of His mercy toward frail humanity. Shortly after the end of Antichrist comes the End of Time, the most prophesied event in the Bible, otherwise referred to as "the Day of the Lord," which is a time not to be longed for: "Woe to them that desire the day of the Lord" says the prophet Amos (5:18). In the view of St. Thomas Aquinas, the Day of the Lord immediately precedes the General Judgment. At that time Our Lord returns in triumph and in judgment as the Lord of lords and King of kings. Now, the whole affair is so important, it would seem, considering both the Biblical prophecies and the saintly prophecies (which Father Culleton concerns himself with here), that it is not sufficient for it simply to happen once. Rather it seems we are to have a foretaste of both the agony and the joys of that later set of events, during a time which serves very much as a warning to the world. This period is dominated by the personage of the Great Monarch; the world in his time enters a severe period of tension (social, political, and religious), which eventuates in terrific military struggles (none of which appear to be Armageddon, it might be added), the final result being the world-wide triumph of this Catholic prince, under whom and through whose influence virtually the entire world becomes Catholic. During his reign there is unprecedented peace, prosperity, and progress. But toward the end of his time, the stiff-necked, hard-hearted men of that day descend once more into widespread sin, and shortly after the Great Monarch, Antichrist makes his appearance. Just as Our Lord at His second coming, the Great Monarch is a king of kings and lord of lords, who rules in justice and who brings an unheralded *Pax Christiana,* thus it would seem, forming a "type of Christ" in His second coming. Such, then, is a rough delineation of the events recorded in Father Culleton's two books. Whether or not it is valid the reader can judge for himself.

A number of other questions arises in this regard which might be considered briefly. "Are we in the Great Apostacy mentioned by St. Paul in 2 *Thessalonians,* Chapter 2? One encounters among troubled Catholics today a good deal of mention about this. The answer is that it would seem we are not, but in view of the "dress rehearsal" concept elucidated above, we are most certainly experiencing a *serious* loss of faith on the part of a large portion of the Catholic population; yet many are still holding fast, despite the confusion rampant in the Church. When the reader has read the prophecies contained here, he will begin to see that most likely "the Great Apostacy" will come *after* the reign of the Great Monarch and refers to the general falling away after his time.

It might well be asked, "Are we close to the End of Time, or to the time of Antichrist?" Many authoritative writers think that we are. Personally, I would not discount the possibility, especially since some of the conditions are now fulfilled, and it takes little imagination to see how others could be. In this regard writers, and even saints, have been mistaken in the past, for which reason none of us should be too hasty to say yes to this question. Referring to the End of Time, Our Lord Himself told us, "But of that day or hour no man knoweth, neither the angels in heaven, nor the Son, but the Father." (*Mk.* 13:32). Nonetheless, we are certain that it will come and come "as a thief in the night." (1 *Thess.* 5:2). St. Paul tells us that Our Lord will return "in a very little while" (*Heb.* 10:37), and St. Peter tells us that "one day with the Lord is as a thousand years, and a thousand years as one day" (2 *Pet.* 3:8), from which we can safely infer that the present Christian era is not going to be all that long. If indeed we are close to the End of Time, or at least close to or beginning the "dress rehearsal" period, it would seem providential that these prophecies would be made known now on so widespread a basis, enabling those who thus desire to be advised on the matter.

"Have some of the prophecies about the first of these two periods in fact been fulfilled?" The answer to this question is yes, some of these prophecies seem to be coming true, notably the widespread loss of faith, confusion in the Church (even in matters of Faith), bankruptcy of the democracies in Western Europe (that is to say their inability to cope with problems of labor, inflation, political unrest, social justice, international finance, and simple "planning for the future"). Already, we are hearing more and more about an immenent eruption in Italy, which will be one of the hallmarks of the period of the Great Monarch. Given the space to develop the notion in a substantive way, and citing additional prophecies to this effect, I believe I could quite easily support this answer.

Despite the fact that these prophecies, taken together, form a compelling tract, we must remember that they are not dogma, that is, do not concern *de fide* pronouncements of the Church. They are simply given for our instruction, to help us, it would seem, in a trying time. If some good Catholics choose not to accept them or choose to lay little stock in them, it is not the duty of any one of us to coerce his mind into assent (as if that were possible). These prophecies are not needed for salvation, but they may indeed be needed for sanity, and certainly for hope, by some or many of us. Indeed, there is a great deal of hope in the personages of the Great Monarch and the Angelic Pastor (a holy Pope) mentioned here. They are truly romantic figures, in the best sense of the word, and so much after the style of God, who in His action among men tends to be both simple and surprising, subtle and irresistible; in His own good time surely something like the events predicted in this book are bound to occur—they are, as it were almost wrapped up part and parcel in the confusion of the world's current life. With the development of that confusion, so trying on us all, is bound to emerge the solution from a most unpredictable quarter. Hence, the enemies of God and of His Holy Church will not know where or how to prepare themselves to resist successfully the advent of the Great Monarch. God will nurture this man in His own manner, who, the prophecies seem to indicate, will not even be known to himself until a late moment. When that man finally takes the field, it will be all over for the enemies of God, despite their numerical superiority and seeming greater power.

With these thoughts in mind we are pleased to reissue *The Prophets and Our Times* and hope that it will bring enlightenment and consolation to those who read it.

Thomas A. Nelson
June 26, 1974
Feast of Ss. John and Paul

PREFACE

My modest attempt to put before modern readers many prophecies which their forefathers used to read has been very graciously accepted. As the orders for copies of the book have exceeded my supply I present this second edition. Readers of the first have expressed regret that the prophecies were not arranged chronologically nor indexed. I have been guided by this constructive criticism.

I am sure that there are still private prophecies which have escaped both me and my past readers. If any new reader knows of any such I would greatly appreciate a communication from him. This would make a third edition as complete as humanly possible.

There has been, of course, some destructive criticism. It has come chiefly from those who read only the title of the book. To those and to all I would say: "If we arrange our things spiritual on the presumption that we are dealing with true prophets and living in the times forecast, but our things material as though it were a waste of time to read this book, we shall find ourselves pleasing God and not making fools out of ourselves before sensible men."

There are many individuals and institutions to whom I am greatly indebted for their kind help with this work. On them I pray God to bestow appropriate blessings.

—Feast of Easter, 1943

The First Pentecost—The Coming Of The Holy Ghost

PART I

HAS THIS CENTURY BEEN FORE-SEEN?
(Signs to preceed the Reign of Anti-Christ)

Introduction 9

    The contents of this book 10

    Some notions on prophecy 11

    What we MUST versus what we MAY believe . . . 14

    Apology for this Book 18

    Estimates of the Prophecies 19

Chapter I: Evils of the Latter Days 23

Chapter II: Persecution of Christians 30

Chapter III: The Latter Day Jews 33

Chapter IV: Devotion to the Sacred Heart 36

Chapter V: Famine, Pest and War 40

Chapter VI: The Great Monarch and Angelic Pastor . 49

Come, Holy Ghost, Creator blest,
And in our hearts take up Thy rest.
Come with Thy grace and heav'nly aid
To fill the hearts which Thou hast made.

O Holy Ghost, through Thee alone,
Know we the Father and the Son.
Be this our never changing creed,
That Thou dost from them both proceed.

INTRODUCTORY CHAPTER

PREAMBLE

In all times of international or at least widespread strife a number of oracles are brought off musty shelves and the Scriptures are searched to learn, if possible, the divine reasons behind it and its likely outcome. In all such times there is a conflict, more or less pronounced, between good and evil hence often the question: Is this the time of Anti-Christ or at least is it a combat of such tremendous importance in the history of the Christian Church that it has merited pre-mention in the Scriptures[1] and the expressions of long buried wise or holy men?

In our days there progresses a war, the equal of which has never before disgraced the earth. Is it merely the natural development of war science and the interdependence of nations that makes each succeeding conflict more terrible and extended than its predecessor? Or is this war more sinister because it is a strife "par excellence" of error against truth?

We may feel quite sure that the present world engagement lacks the signs for the end of the world. There is no reason to suspect any modern war lord of being the Anti-Christ. Could the struggle be a type or symbol or even an announcement of the Anti-Christ? Scripture tells us to expect many an Anti-Christ before the real one comes. Many there have been, are, and doubtless will be. For a certainty there are anti Christian leaders and armies in the field today so we must admit that this war comes under the Scripture text: "There shall be many false Christs . . . but the end is not yet," but to go farther and say that this conflict is an announcement of the near approach of the Anti-Christ is another question.

---

[1] "We feel that the present hour is a phase of the solemn story of humanity predicted by Christ." Pius XII Radio Address, 11-24-40.

The Contents of This Book

There are gathered together between the covers of this book a number of Scripture texts. Some of them certainly and others probably refer to the latter (but not necessarily the last) days of the world. To these have been added many sayings of saints and sages which bear on things to come after their day, yet apparently before the appearance of Anti-Christ.

The author has divided the prophecies used herein into two groups: the public prophecies (Scripture and the Fathers) and the private prophecies as found in the Apocrapha and the works of pious or learned men. The whole collection quotes over 200 seers. The extracts are arranged more or less chronologically so that the development of the ideas concerning the latter days may be more apparent. The prophecies are prefaced by an exhaustive topical index and the author's concordance of them.

With this in mind the gentle reader will realize that the author possesses not the gift of prophecy, nor does he profess even reasonable certainty for his own interpretations or correlations. On the contrary, he furnishes his texts to the reader and reminds all that where the Universal Church is silent each may draw his own conclusions provided he draw with caution.

The prophetic texts recorded are of certain divine origin only in the instances where they form parts of Sacred Scripture or Tradition, and the interpretations of these are matters of faith only in those few instances where the Church has given the meaning.

All other oracles found herein are to be classed as private. Some of them are said by their authors to have been revelations from God either to the author himself or to one or other pious or saintly person known to the author. Others of them have come down in the tradition of one or other nation and no doubt represent what the national bards were given to understand by the early national saints. The remainder are rather commentaries on oracles. They are by authors who do not profess to have had revelations, but who were wise men and who based their ideas of the future on Scripture, the Fathers, the saints and an intimate knowledge of history, the effects of evil and the capabilities of human ingenuity.

Without going into the various arguments in favor of, or against the authenticity, either of the present documents which contain these private oracles, or the oraclces themselves, the writer has felt justified in using all those quotations which seem not to contradict the teaching of the Church, and which, at the same time, have merited acceptance in the works of other authors better equipped than he to pass on their merit. Let us say this: they are (unless otherwise noted) oracles which have for generations intrigued the children of earth.

SOME NOTIONS ON PROPHECY

In our day it is common, even among some men of faith, to pay little or no regard to any prophecy and to consider one who does pay heed, a relic from a dark age. Such an attitude is to some extent unreasonable as well as quite unchristian. Human reason teaches that God, and He alone, knows the future and that He can and may reveal it to His intelligent creatures. It is an article of faith, as well as historically established, that God did make certain revelations about the future to man and that some of them have not yet been fulfilled. Scripture teaches that there is a gift of prophecy which the Creator may bestow and has bestowed on whomsoever He pleases. A time limit was set and is passed for public revelations but none exists for private. No man may refuse to study public oracles, and, while a reasonable person may shut his ears to any particular private prophecy, he may not deny the value of all.

There are certain characteristics of prophecy which it is well to know. For example, events are portrayed as it were in a deep mist. Thus a prophecy may be in process of fulfillment before one's eyes and he may not be aware of it. Christ's birth, life and death are clearly forecast in the Old Testament;

yet, in all Judea scarce a hundred of His contemporaries recognized Him.

Then, too, a prophecy often reminds one of an Egyptian picture. There is no perspective. Events centuries apart may be forecast in one vision with divine disregard for time. The reason for this is to be found in a certain nontemporal relationship of spiritual events. One that happened in one century may be the type of another to come a thousand years later, or again an earlier may be the sign of a subsequent one. Thus St. John the Baptist was both a type of Christ and a sign of His near approach, whereas the destruction of Jerusalem was a type of the destruction of the world. In this connection it must be remembered that one prophetic utterance can portray even several types of a great spiritual event, as well as the event itself. The prophecy in the Apocalypse concerning Babylon refers to ancient Rome, its emperors and its fall, but the text is not exhausted with this. For a certainty the civil government of Anti-Christ is also spoken of and there is reason to believe that the words foretell the future of all cities or governments which substitute materialism for true Christianity.

This peculiarity of prophecy makes the oracle credible by virtue of reason, as well as by virtue of faith, for when the type or sign is verified it is reasonable to expect the main event.

On the other hand, one momentous event is often forecast by many separate prophecies, from various angles and often over many centuries. In these instances, as the generations go by and the individual utterances increase, man gradually gets a more recognizable picture. Yet even here the event may have come and gone before all of these separate references are recognized as facets of one majestic gem. This feature is best noted in the Old Testament prophecies concerning the Messiah.

Prophetic ideas are often conveyed in visions. The recipient may not understand the meaning of the picture which passes before his mind. Sometimes further divine aid enlightens his mind. This aid may come immediately after the vision, later on in his life or not to him at all but to some one else. The "someone else" may be a contemporary or may not come into being till hundreds or even thousands of years later. In some instances only the incomprehensible vision proceeds from God. Actual history, probably centuries later, gives the first inklings as to what the picture means. The seer may give his personal opinion as to the meaning of one of his visions but such remains merely his opinion. In scripture divine inspiration guarantees that the revelations and their interpretations, when given, are free from error. We have no such guarantees in the case of the private prophecies.

Prophecies are sometimes conditional. Such usually contain or imply "unless penance be done" such and such will follow. True prophets may be saints or sinners as is evident from the Old Testament. False prophecies are easiest detected by the false doctrine they contain or their failure to materialize. The devil and his votaries cannot forecast the contingent future, but some writers contend that the devil can bring to pass sometimes one or other forecast of his servants. Such events, however, may be curious but must be unimportant. Propagandists, necromancers and astrologers are often authors of false prophecies, nor would God use them for truth without manifesting his presence as He did in the case of the Witch of Endor.

In this regard it must be remembered that the phenomena of the subconscious is sometimes truly remarkable and that this psychological character differs greatly in different individuals. It is almost certain that there are persons who by purely natural means, for example, mental telepathy, can know what others have in mind and therefore can foretell what will happen if those persons carry out their plan. Such persons also in their sub-conscious minds work on all the information they have, and often not knowing whence their conclusions come, nevertheless draw them and find out in time they have been very accurate. These phenomena however are easily distinguished from genuine prophecy, for the latter deals also with a future unknown to any human (even thus hypothetically) and must be accurate in all its parts. Phenomena of the subconscious are sometimes correct, more often incorrect, and always related to an unknown but actual present or future event which is already in the process of unfolding.

In cases of doubt one should presume that phenomena are to be explained rather by natural means than by the preternatural or supernatural.

All true prophecy is from God for His glory and the sake of the "elect." As it becomes fulfilled it establishes its own divine origin and the reliability of the documents which convey it. It is a consolation to the faithful for it warns them what to expect as individuals and members of society, and at the same time assures them of the means for their personal salvation, the perpetuation of their Church, and the ultimate triumph of Christian civilization. Then, too, it instills into the hearts of sinners a salutary fear of divine vengeance.

WHAT WE MUST VERSUS WHAT WE MAY BELIEVE

One hesitates about printing a book like this; not because he has failed to make himself clear, but because despite the clarity many insist upon being so certain of the interpretation of oracles obscure in themselves that they work themselves into a depression of spirit. This is folly not only because they consider certain, and immediately before them, a danger they may never encounter, but also because God's revelations are intended for the comfort and strength of the good. So true is this that if a private revelation which supposedly comes from God terrifies and weakens a good man he must either dismiss his interpretation of it or if his interpretation be correct then he must dismiss the revelation. In the case of the sinner God's words are intended for his conversion. He need not wonder then, if knowing he be in sin and chooses not to repent, should the words of God terrify him.

To be more certain that the reader will clearly realize the

difference between what Christians should believe and what they may or may not believe, I recount here (based on Hermann: *Institutiones Theologiae*, vol. II, pg. 812 ss.) what seems to be the common teaching of approved theologians concerning Anti-Christ and the end of the world as illustrative of what we should believe. Then I will give a summary containing also what it seems to me Christian saints and sages add to this common teaching. As for these additions, the Christian is free to accept any of them or reject all.

A. The Common Teaching by Approved Theologians:

    I. There shall be certain signs which precede the end of the world, of these we may consider some remote and others proximate:

        (a) *Remote signs*:
1. The total abolition of the Roman Empire;
2. The coming of Anti-Christ (though before him there shall be other anti-christs)
3. The appearance on earth of two great prophets of the Lord;
4. The preaching of the gospel in the whole world;
5. The conversion of the Jews which would at least be begun by the two prophets;
6. A general apostasy from the faith.

    The order in which these signs are to occur is not given.

        (b) *Proximate signs*:
1. The sun, moon and stars shall be darkened;
2. Stars shall fall upon the earth;
3. There shall be other and grave commotions in the sky, air, sea and earth.

    II. There shall be the second coming of Christ, the resurrection of the body, and the universal judgment.

    III. The world shall be reduced to ashes, or otherwise transformed by fire.

No one may dare assert *as certain* anything concerning the time for the consummation of the world and the second coming of Christ (Leo X in the 5th Lat. Council cf. Matt. 24:3; I Cor. 13:13; I Tim. 6:14).[1]

B. THE ABOVE WITH MY CORRELATION OF THE IDEAS OF SAINTS AND SAGES ADDED:

I. There have been and will be types of Anti-Christ.

II. The life of mankind on earth is, as it were, divided into ages, and the last age may be considered divided into two stages. The first stage is to end with the overthrow of Anti-Christ, and the second with the second coming of Christ, Universal Judgment, etc.

III. During succeeding generations evils would multiply with individuals and nations drifting even farther from God, and ever increasing numbers losing all faith. Certain scourges would afflict various countries such as wars, revolutions, tyrannical rulers, class struggles, persecutions and the like, but none of these would bring in its wake peace, unity or mass conversions.

IV. It is unlikely that the first stage of the last age commenced with the apparently irreparable loss of unity among Christians which was consummated in the 16th century.

V. Towards the end of this first stage there would be a preview to or an event particularly typical of the reign of Anti-Christ and his overthrow. It would take the form of three powerful but evil rulers who would cause a "flesh hewing course of warfare" and persecute Jews and Christians. They are to overcome their enemies. Two of them, however, seem destined to be overcome by the third and he is to fall before a good ruler aided visibly by God. This visible

---

[1] Pastor Kerr: *The History of the Popes*, vol. VIII, pg. 404.

aid is to be in some way a type of three days darkness noted below.

VI. Peace and a notable return of Governments and individuals to God and Christian unity shall follow. A great Pope and a great civil leader shall be responsible. This good sign, although a preview or type of what may be expected after Anti-Christ will be of short duration for the forces of evil will not have been vanquished but only momentarily upset. (Here ends the subject matter of this volume.)

VII. This peace is to be followed by the end of the first stage of the last age; namely, the three and one-half years of almost universal domination by Anti-Christ. The persecutions of that time will exceed in cruelty and extent anything that the world has seen and in no other time shall evil have so triumphed. Very few will remain faithful to God and live. It will seem as though the Church has ceased to exist. On the other hand, Henoch and Elias, the prophets of the Lord, by word and deed shall combat Anti-Christ and his diabolical hoards. The two prophets shall be martyred shortly before the end of the period. During the last terrible battle when all seems lost, will come three days darkness with the exterminating angels. When the darkness lifts there will not remain alive on earth an unconvertible evil man.

VIII. There follows at once a millenium in a less strict sense. It is the peace previewed before Anti-Christ and in turn a type of the true millenium. It would seem that Christ would appear in the skies or at least that there would be some happening typical of His Second Coming, and that it would be apparent that there was a preview of the Last Judgment. Would the Just martyred by Anti-Christ then rise from the dead, this being the first resurrection spoken of in the

Apocalypse? Would an earthly reward symbolical of heavenly rewards be bestowed upon the confessors who had escaped the beast? This seems not too clear but we are led to expect at least this, that there follows the fall of Anti-Christ an interval during which there will be universal peace and union in one faith under one shepherd with Christian life marvelously exemplified in the individual and in society. How long this symbol of a millenium will last is not clear but the common opinion of the Fathers was that it would not be long.

(Here ends the subject matter of the Second Volume.)

IX. Near the very end of this last stage of the last age the powers of Hell would again be loosed. Evil would rule but for a short time only. This time upheavals in nature would announce approaching doom, and in the end all men would perish from the earth. This final and universal destruction is certainly to be by fire. The real Second Coming of Christ seems to be connected with this time.

X. Then follow the resurrection of the dead, the universal judgment and the new Jerusalem or true millenium. (Here ends the subject matter of the third and last volume.)

APOLOGY FOR THIS BOOK

Even if in one or other, or for that matter all instances, my tentative application of prophecy be not justified in the light of the future, it means merely that I am wrong. The private prophets may also have erred, but they may have had in mind other things than those which I have supposed. At any rate, it is the future alone that will praise or condemn both private commentators and private prophets. Some prophecies recorded here and applied by me to times before Anti-Christ may in whole or in part have been intended for his reign only.

We must also remember that many have, ever since the

beginning, thought or professed to think that they saw signs
of Anti-Christ and the rest in their generations. The future
contradicted them. What the sincere ones noted were rather
signs or types of Anti-Christ and the rest. Despite this, one
seems to err not when, despite the errors of the past, he tries
in his day to understand, for in one generation or other, what
true prophets have foretold must come to pass; and on the other
hand, God tells us that certain of these things will come as a
thief in the night and that we must ever be prepared.

The only apology one might have for thinking that our
age may be a critical one in Christian history is that in past
Christian times evil organizations were either among non-
Christians or Christians in circumscsribed localities, whereas in
our day the great anti-Christian forces and the anti-Christian
philosophies of materialistic secret societies are already widespread, well armed and in the field for world-wide domination.
On the other hand, their leaders and even the rank and file are
for the most part Christians by baptism, and even natives of
lands steeped in Christian traditions.

ESTIMATE OF THE PROPHECIES
It will be noted by the reader that the private oracles recorded herein do not always agree. This could mean that one
or other is not genuine, but it could also indicate that we err
in relating them to the same event.[1]

It is also worthy of remark that frequently there is a relationship between Scripture and private prophecies in that the
latter seem to make an effort at particularizing prophecies of
the Sacred Text which are in themselves quite general. Not
infrequently a private prophet assigns a date often vaguely but
now and again quite precisely. Some of these precise dates have
passed but so far as we can see the event has not occurred. Unless, there be reason to suppose such oracles conditional it seems
better to reject them.

---

[1]Prophetic texts are sometimes changed in transmission and in translating.

A great number of statements seem to fit persons, events and conditions today but very often there are in the very same oracle ideas which do not fit. While this might mean that two events are considered without temporal perspective, it could also mean that the whole text despite its partial description of the present may refer to events still far in the future.[1] As a matter of fact parts of many of these prophecies have in times past been referred to Napoleon or the French Republican disorders and one or other of them to the First World War.

This merely means that caution must be used about even the value of any particular private prophecy and that we should not be too hasty in interpreting beforehand even the oracles of Sacred Scripture.

Despite this there is true value for every generation in all genuine prophecy. The burden thereof is always the same, namely: Organized evil cannot truly harm the elect nor even bring them any sorrow but the sorrow of Christ which is joy; no human, natural or preternatural agency can destroy the Church or Christian civilization; when evil becomes unbearable to the individual who trusts God, or to society, God will work a miracle if necessary to overcome it; physical and mental suffering exists for the perfection of the good and the conversion or destruction of the wicked.

As has been evident to the reader, the prophecies of Sacred Scripture seem not to apply to our modern conflict any more than they do to any other in the past where the Christian cause has been involved.

With a bit of imagination on the other hand the private oracles can be marshalled into a fairly good description of the present war to date and then taking the unfulfilled portions we can make a forecast of the future which would seem quite logical in the circumstances. But we must remember, too, that without

---

[1] It is not improbable that in some instances contradictory sentences are interpolations.

prophecies and with a history of the combat to date we can also make a fairly logical estimate of the future course of events. At any rate the author is no better equipped than is the reader. Wishful thinking often plays so great a part in the application of prophecy that it is sometimes better for one to keep his own interpretations to himself.

Whether this war be a particularly crucial one in Christian history or not makes little difference, for this much is certain: if a powerful anti-Christian force should emerge victor from this or any other conflict and its victory be anything like universal it may take one of two courses: Either it will throw off its anti-christian character, which is unlikely, or it will endeavor by force to destroy Christianity. In this latter event, we may lay aside all private prophecy and use just Scripture and Tradition. These tell us with infallible truth that when universal control means Christianity or Anti-Christianity the victor is Christianity, and this irrespective of what miracles may be needed or what blood may be shed. "I am with you all days, even to the consummation of the world." "Thou art Peter and upon this rock I will build my Church and the gates of Hell shall not prevail against it."

Come, Thou Holy Spirit, come,
And from Thy celestial home
Shed a ray of light divine.
Come, Thou Father of the poor,
Come, Thou Source of all our store,
Come, within our bosoms shine.

Comforter art Thou the best,
Thou the soul's most welcome guest,
Sweet refreshment here below.
In our labor rest most sweet,
Grateful coolness in the heat,
Solace in the midst of woe.

CHAPTER I

Evils of the Latter Days

An important sign of the latter days is the prevalence of false teachings with the natural consequences: defections from religion, lack of faith even among Catholics and great moral degeneration.

Several prophecies written long before the time of Christ speak of an age when many Gentile nations would deny the existence of God, and their oppressive and unjust rulers unite against Christianity, while much of the populace would devise vain things instead of the truth.

Since it was the Gentiles who accepted Christ when the Jews rejected Him, any reference to the Gentiles as nations united against Christ would apply rather to the latter times than to any previous period in the history of the Christian world. It would seem that when the Jews begin to return to Palestine, which is the start of their return to God, that the time would have arrived when God begins to reject the Gentiles before accepting the returning Jews.

That the Gentiles have already begun to reject Christ is certainly evidenced in the recent events in Russia, Mexico, Germany, and for that matter in nearly every nation. Christ is rejected when ignored or spurned as well as when He is proscribed by law. In some countries God has been rejected entirely, while in others Christ has been made subservient to one or other form of nationalism or internationalism, which is merely another way of speaking. Both systems substitute the created for the Creator. Despite these modern evil symptoms, it would not be necessary to presume that the Church would not, in the ordinary course of events, be quite able, without miracles, to overcome them.

Some such rebellion against God and His Christ is to extend itself throughout the world shortly before the reign of Anti-Christ, with even Catholics in great numbers abandoning the true faith. Coincidental with this general indifference toward religion, in fact even actual hatred of it, there is to be the complete degeneration of the morals of the people, a degeneration similar to that which existed among the pagans before the dawn of Christianity and civilization as we have known it.

These signs of the approaching end have, of course, been true in varying degrees in earlier ages. The essential difference, however, between former defections and those which pressage the end, is to be found in the universality and sinister character of the latter apostasy. Men of the latter days are to set out, either to banish Christ from the memory of man, or in other instances to turn Christianity into a form of materialism and one to be used to gain unworthy objectives.

Several years before this general apostasy there were to be false teachers who would cause great confusion and darkness in the minds of the people, resulting in the loss of entire nations to the true faith. This would very effectually prepare the way for Anti-Christ. Some say that this has already been fairly well accomplished by the so-called Reformation with its consequent evils. Much more and far worse evils were to befall the world immediately before the reign of Anti-Christ.

We have also been warned against various prophets and those who claim to have had visions that foretold a sign or a wonder. Although those signs or wonders may actually occur as foretold, we will know the prophets are false because their doctrines are false. They will seem to make the people forget the True God even while claiming to be sent by Him, thus profaning His Holy Name. They will rob the poor, give and take bribes, and though preaching peace, will, if their greedy demands are not complied with, wage war. Thus they say: "Peace, Peace"; yet there is no peace. However, their time will come to an end because God merely permits this to happen to try our faith and increase our love for and dependence on Him.

There will also be those who will indulge in fruitless discussions of so-called learned things, and by so doing will miss the real truth and the real faith because the things which engage their attention are based on false knowledge instead of the truth. The reason for this, primarily, is the education without religion which will exist in those days, for this education will not really educate but will have as its basis vain works and false ideals. This so-called education will be one of the most effective means used by Satan to prepare the world for Anti-Christ.

After the birth of Anti-Christ and shortly before the rise of the Great Monarch, the false doctrines were to multiply and spread to such an extent that even Catholics would doubt many of the articles of faith, resulting in their perversion, this to apply not only to the laity but even to many priests and some of the hierarchy. The zeal of these latter will be greatly affected by this lack of faith. There will be dissentions among the clergy. Many will be proud, selfish, unjust, covetous, and even forgetful of vows made at ordination regarding chastity. Many will even offer Mass and confer the Sacraments sacrilegiously.

When the zeal of the clergy fails they will see the faithful leaving the churches and turning to the world. The House of God will be deserted, singing of hymns will cease, and the observance of festivals abandoned. The relics of saints will be considered powerless and any contributions the laity will make to the church will be made grudgingly.

In many religious houses humility and poverty will be forgotten, pride and desire for worldly luxuries will characterize the inmates instead of the spirit of simplicity which is the mark of a true religious.

Because of these defections Catholics will be severely punished, for only by chastisements can God bring back to the minds of His people, a realization of their dependence upon Him. As a consequence, widespread persecution of priests and people will come upon the Church in order that faith and love of God may be revived, for as surely as night follows day, so will civilization crumble and the world become steeped in the darkness of ignorance, hatred, misery and vice when God, who is the Light of the World, will no longer rule in the hearts of His people.

It is true that many people will seem to honor God but this will be chiefly lip service and not based on real faith and love. They will be unwilling to recognize evil because they will prefer to follow the easy path of pleasure. Truth will be deserted and in its stead false doctrines eagerly embraced, because it will seem the people even wish to be deluded. As the prophets say: "It will be a lying generation, given to covetousness, deceit and even blasphemy."

The wickedness of the people during these days will be multiplied. Iniquity will be so general throughout the world that scandalizers and betrayers will abound and hatred for one another will replace charity in the hearts of men. Every man will oppose his neighbor, the base man against the honorable, the few really good people will be opposed on all sides by the unrighteous, while the wicked alone will prosper. Laws will be ignored and personal possessions will become the property of the strong, since force alone will rule. If the one who sows has not the strength to defend his possessions, he will see another reap the fruit of his toil.

Even family life will be completely disrupted. There in the heart of the family group, where, above all, there should abound genuine love and loyalty, will be found only bitterness and betrayal. Children, lacking respect for their elders, will rise against their parents, and even the parents in turn, will be without a natural love for their offspring, resulting in mutual mistrust.

The lowly among the people shall overtake those rightfully in power. Treaties will be broken with less compunction than if they were mere scraps of paper, the chief consideration being selfish advancement.

Family unity and fidelity we find glaringly absent in Communistic Russia and by no means satisfactory in other lands,

our own being among the foremost offenders. Lack of respect
for treaties we find almost daily exemplified, and when a true
history of our times is written we will discover that many
modern rulers have conveniently disregarded solemn promises.
The dreaded "Secret Police" of some nations operates everywhere and for all one may know, relatives of his may be members sworn to betray even their own flesh and blood. Despite
this, however, the prophets seem to suppose times more universally evil than ours today.

In the last days before Anti-Christ there are to appear many
anti-christs. This is the sign by which we will know that
the hour of the great evil is at hand. Of course at this time
evil will abound more than at any other period in the history
of the world. However, as mentioned above, we can expect a
preview of this culmination of evil in the world. During the
preview we will observe pride, greed, intemperance, immorality,
hypocrisy, unjust laws, lack of natural affection and dissemin-
ation of false knowledge rampant in the world.

Another peculiar thing about some of the false teachers is
that they will teach doctrines more severe even than those laid
down by God, such as commanding abstinence from certain
foods and drinks, and certain innocent pleasures, which God
intended for our proper use. In these days fiction will be preferred to truth because the people of the world will wish to
be seduced.

There will not be many who will be really wise, the intelligent will be very few in number and even these will be in
great part silent, because they know that they would be either
not listened to, or laughed at. The prophets say also that evil
and falsehood will increase as the world grows weaker with age.

We are told that in remote preparation for Anti-Christ there
was to be the beginning of the loosing of devils upon the world,
and that many more would be loosed shortly before his reign.
During these days people were to become inhospitable toward
each other, willing to betray either for honor or personal gain,

the rich were to become poor and the poor rich, the land was to become less fruitful and the animals less prolific than of old. At this time there were to arise three oppressive rulers who would exceed in tyranny and injustice all who were before them. They would bring to a head, as it were, the wickedness of Satan. Secularization of church property was a sign to precede their reign, also the persecution of priests, especially on "trumped-up" charges. Many governments would strive to control the Church, however God will not abandon the Church entirely at this time, but will make use of the demons to whom these rulers have abandoned themselves.

Towards the end of the world the Jews are to commit some atrocious crime for which they will be gravely persecuted. Could the crime be a veering away of many Jews from the belief in a personal God and personal Messiah and all that such belief implies?

We have been warned in Holy Scripture against those who deceive with empty arguments. These are the platitudes so often heard in defense of evil and so willingly accepted everywhere today. They have for their premise presumption on God's mercy and an unwillingness to recognize the true nature of sin and its evil consequences. As a result, vice more often than not is made to appear as virtue.

Among other things to happen during these evil days is the changing of God's laws by unscrupulous leaders to suit their own convenience. This shall lead to universal sin and a gradual lack of obedience to all of God's commandments. The prophets here could well refer to the sanction of divorce by the various Protestant churches and national legislatures, as well as the tacit or actual approval of the practice of artificial birth control. In this latter respect, even Catholics, as individuals, have become greatly contaminated in recent years. It is obvious that it is but one step from easy divorce and artificial birth control to widespread immorality.

As a result of these evils, great social disturbances were to appear on every side. With the family, which is the basis of society, breaking up, the fate of society itself must hang perilously in the balance. Only God's hand can stay it. Throughout the history of the world, whenever these evils have infected any nation, they have eventually caused the destruction of that nation. That they will spread disastrously before the rule of Anti-Christ into every strata of society over the entire world, causing the malignant growth of complete moral degeneration, is a warning given us by many prophets. There will be no standard by which morals will be regulated. Marriages will be solemnized without witnesses, and many young women will cohabit with men without marriage and this unblushingly and without secrecy. The various forms of immortality will become so widespread and habitual that only some terrible punishment will be able to eradicate them, for in these times men will live according to their own lusts and desires and not according to God's will and commandments.

Finally, it has been foretold that by the time Anti-Christ is twenty years old, most of the world will have become atheistic and be oppressed by its rulers.

In concluding this chapter, I shall quote from a recent statement of the present Pope to the Lithuanian minister, in which he said that as Supreme Pastor he could not close his eyes "When precisely for the salvation of souls arise new incommensurable dangers—when on the face of Europe, (Christian in all its fundamental lineaments), the sinister shadow of thoughts and deeds of enemies of God casts itself closer and more threateningly every day. In such circumstances more than in any other period of its history, the preservation, care, and if necessary, the defense of the Christian patrimony acquires for the future destinies of Europe and the prosperity of its people, large or small, a decisive importance."

CHAPTER II

THE PERSECUTION OF CHRISTIANS

The persecution of Christians has always been a sign that the Catholic Church was the true church founded by Christ. However it is clearly stated in the prophecies that this persecution would be greatly intensified shortly before and during the reign of Anti-Christ. On this point we might, in passing, call the attention of our readers to the grave sufferings of Catholics during the last decade in Mexico, Spain, Germany, Russia and Poland. We would, however, expect to find more widespread persecution were it a sign of the latter ages.

We are told that in the latter days three kings will rule in the world. Their reigns will be notable especially for their oppression. The Church will suffer much and it would seem from the prophecies that a great deal of this persecution is to be instigated by members of secret societies. This is often interpreted as a reference to Freemasonry, but we would likely not err if we added secret agents similar to those of certain national and international modern movements.

During the days of the three kings the yoke of Christ's Church is cast aside and they will set up their own insignia instead of the cross, the sign of Christ. It is a strange coincidence that in our day such anti-christian movements as Communism, Nazism and the rest put up their symbols everywhere.

On all sides blood is destined to flow, churches will be closed or desecrated, the celebration of church festivals forbidden, and the clergy banished from many lands. The tyrants and other hostile people will attack with bitter venom those who have been consecrated to God, robbing them of their meager possessions and subjecting them to most inhuman treatment. However, because of these persecutions, the clergy and religious will be forced to lead an apostolic life. Indeed it has been said by some prophets that so many of the clergy will be martyred that the Pope, forced to flee from Rome with his cardinals to seek sanctuary elsewhere, will have to walk over the dead bodies of his priests, while one or other oracle ordains that the Pope is destined to suffer a cruel death in his exile. In the last year of his reign, it would seem, he is to be in exile, and apparently, for the last three months he will be subjected to cruel torture. Pope Pius X saw a successor of his, one bearing his name, as the Pope who would leave the Vatican and go into exile, and, after about a year, suffer a cruel death.

Other prophecies concering this point tell us many of the clergy will have lost their zeal for God's work and will have forgotten their divinely appointed mission of saving souls, thinking rather of their own selfish interests. By these chastisements God will eventually bring them back to the true realization of their sacred duties.

Regarding the great number of those who will give up their lives for Christ before the end of the world, there are references to a chalice half-filled with the blood of martyrs, which, before the end, will be filled to overflowing. Those holy souls who have already shed their blood for the Word of God must wait until the blood of their fellow martyrs has filled this chalice before they can rejoice in the resurrection of the body. To date there have been, it is estimated, over thirteen million martyrs for the faith of Christ, and it is the belief of some students of prophecy, that before the end of the world approximately the same number must suffer a like fate. In this regard, however, we may be pardoned for doubting that mathematics will be discernible.

In addition there are to be spiritual locusts who will burn and poison souls with false doctrines. These, however, will have no power to injure those who remain faithful to the graces received in Baptism and Confirmation. They will be permitted to harass and persecute without killing for a short time, but will be powerless to destroy the Church. At this time man will long for death, welcoming it as an escape from his many miseries, but death will be denied him.

An old Saxon prophecy foretold that Spain would be split asunder by civil war, while another prophesied her glorious triumph over the enemies of God. This, no doubt, has already at least begun to come to pass. In 1534 it was foretold that the Jesuits would be driven out of Spain like dogs, but at a later date would return like nobles. This has occurred twice, the second time in conjunction with the recent civil troubles.

Other oracles refer to a division of the German empire and the persecution of the Church of Christ by a German ruler. A great war was prophesied for Europe, following the secularization of Church property. The prophets also mention that the late Pope Pius XI was destined to suffer "terrible immolation from within and without"; from within, they no doubt meant, by excruciating physical sufferings, and from without, by the persecution of his many children in Mexico, Spain, Germany, etc.

Finally, a bloody revolution has been foretold as coming upon the world during which time the Church of Christ is to suffer grievously, and her servants and leaders mocked, tortured and martyred. This revolution for a time (three months?) will triumph, but shortly thereafter a marvelous event will take place which will fill the world with astonishment, as well as save the faithful from further persecution. Likely this marvel will be darkness similar to the three days darkness often spoken of by the prophets. It would thus come first, at the conclusion of the world distress here noted, and as a sort of preview, then as a final occurrence at the end of the reign of Anti-Christ. However, the prophets foretell that this marvel will occur only after great changes in many kingdoms throughout the world.

CHAPTER III

The Latter Day Jews

It has been foretold very definitely that the Jews are destined to return to Palestine toward the end of the world. According to Scripture, God did not cast the Jews off forever, nor was their dispersal intended by God to be everlasting. He promised them that in the latter times of the world's history the children of Israel, scattered throughout the world, would return to Palestine, that the temple would be rebuilt, and that God would make a new and everlasting covenant with His people.

As early as 1860 the Universal Israelite Alliance was formed for the purpose of promoting the emancipation of the Jews, their mental and moral improvement, and especially to encourage the Jewish colonization of Palestine. Following 1878, the year of the Russo-Turkish war, the trek of the Jews to Palestine really began, and after the establishment of the British Protectorate in 1917 they flocked there in considerable numbers. In 1920 the flag of Judah once more flew from the Tower of David, a symbol, as it were, of the prophet's words.

In the days in which these prophecies were to be fulfilled, the land of Israel was destined to become once more fertile so that the number of the Jewish inhabitants would increase and multiply. For ages the scarcity of rain in Palestine had made it impossible to raise crops in their former fullness, but between the years 1860 and 1900 the rainfall in Palestine increased over fifty percent, so that the land which had been arid for centuries is now much more fertile.

The Jewish population throughout the world is rapidly increasing. In the past two hundred years their numbers have grown from around three million to approximately twenty-four million. They have a high birth and very low death rate.

According to prophecies, the migration of the Jewish people to Palestine was to be brought about through their being persecuted at the hands of the Gentiles, while their final return to God will be effected directly through the chastisements of God.

Throughout all the centuries following their unfaithfulness to God, they have been reviled, persecuted, exiled, and dispersed, yet God has miraculously preserved them as a race for a purpose worthy of Himself. They were His chosen people originally, yet because of their sins, salvation came to the Gentiles—they became enemies of God, as it were, for the sake of the Gentiles. However, because of the fidelity of their forefathers, they remain dear to God, and it was promised them that "in fulness of the times of the Gentiles" their blindness would be taken from them and that God's curse would be lifted.

The partial fulfillment of this prophecy has been in evidence for the past one hundred years or more during which time the Jews have been steadily rising out of the depths of debasement and subjection in which they had lain for centuries. One of the most remarkable occurrences in the history of our age is the civil emancipation of the Jews. However, the complete bursting of the bonds of the Gentiles will not occur until the final overthrow of the Turks. After this, the Jews will return to godliness in the last days because of their fear of the Lord. They shall once more become a nation after they have repented and sought the mercy of God, and only then shall they attain peace.

It is at that time that the Tabernacle, the Ark, and the Altar of Incense, shall be found, which have remained hidden since Jeremias placed them in a hollow cave. Jeremias had told the people that they would remain hidden until God should gather together a congregation of the people and bring it to mercy.

The present war is causing great misery to the Jewish people. Its eventual effect upon Jewish aspirations in the Holy Land cannot well be forecast, but if its outcome opens up to them their ancient heritage, and we see at long last a Jewish state there, it means that interesting events in the history of the world are probably not too distant. The prophets do not necessarily forecast a universal Jewish migration but certainly a Jewish Palestine.[1]

---

[1]Hilaire Belloc: *The Jews* (3rd Edition, 1937) will be found the most valuable book extant on the modern situation of Jewry. The Introductory Chapter treats the Zionist movement.

David Goldstein: *The Jewish Panorama* (1941) is also of interest, especially from the American point of view.

CHAPTER IV

Devotion to the Sacred Heart

There is evidence that it was the will of Our Divine Lord that Devotion to the Sacred Heart be reserved for the last ages of the world, so that, in the last great struggle between Himself and Satan, the souls that He loves so dearly may be drawn to Him with renewed warmth, and thus stengthened against the final desperate attacks of the enemy.

In the times preceding the end of the world, Satan and his cohorts were to be loosed upon the earth in a mighty effort to draw as many souls as possible away from God, before the power of Hell would be remarkably restricted, if not completely broken. Satan's mission is one of hate. God wins souls through love. Our Blessed Savior knew that the hatred which would be rampant in those evil days could be best conquered by a devotion which would inspire love and charity in the hearts of men. It was to serve, as it were, as a magnet and a bulwark of strength by giving men a clearer knowledge of God's deep and abiding love and mercy. It would provide a harbor of peace and security in those days of confusion and anguish, when men's souls would be tried almost beyond endurance.

In all times of great distress or danger, God has provided men with the means of conquering evil, as evidenced by the history of the world, both before the time of Christ, but especially since the Redemption. To mention just one of the instances of Divine intervention when a special devotion was given to the world at a crucial period, let us consider the Rosary. In the 13th century when the Albigenses were preaching their vicious doctrines against marriage, and the spread of this heresy seriously endangered the morals of the people, St. Dominic began preaching against them. He had but little success until Our Blessed Lady appeared to him, and told him to encourage devotion to the Rosary. This was done and the heresy quickly disappeared.

St. Gertrude, in the 14th century, who often conversed with the Beloved Disciple St. John, on one occasion asked him why he, who loved our Blessed Lord so fervently, had never written anything about the love of the Sacred Heart of Jesus. He explained to her his mission was to expound the Doctrine of the Incarnation and that as for the Love of the Incarnate Word as exemplified by His Divine Heart, it was reserved for the last ages to make it known, "so that the world, carried away by follies, may regain a little of the warmth of early Christian charity by learning of the love of the Sacred Heart."

It was on the feast of St. John the Evangelist, three centuries later in 1647, that Our Lord appeared to St. Margaret Mary Alacoque and made certain promises to those who had a special devotion to His Sacred Heart, which promises were destined to become the means of salvation to so many countless Christians. Regarding this vision, the Saint explained, "I understand that this devotion to the Sacred Heart was a last effort of His love towards Christians of these latter times, by proposing to them an object and a means so calculated to persuade them to love Him."

In 1815 Mother Maria Rafols wrote concerning her own visions at the urgent insistence of Our Blessed Lord, in the hope that many, after reading what He told her, would turn from their evil ways, and have recourse to His Merciful Heart.

Much of what she has written is prophetic, and concerns itself, in part, with the destiny of Spain. Referring to her own Mother House, at Saragoza, Spain, Mother Rafols wrote that the Sacred Heart would perform such wonders there as to win many sinners away from their corrupted lives. It is worthy of note that although the Communists laid siege to the city of Saragoza, it was never captured, as foretold by Mother Rafols.

Our Lord promised her that no matter what means men might invent to destroy the faith in Spain, they would be unsuccessful and that He would reign there until the end of time, because of the love of the just and chaste souls who would always live in Spain. This prophecy, only recently unearthed, must have been of great comfort to the good Christians during the trying days of the Civil War.

So forgotten would be the Word of God in the days to come, that men would even scandalize and pervert innocent children, and endeavor to obliterate His Blessed Name from their memory. This was true in Spain, and is true in many other countries today.

There would be such moral corruption, not only in Spain, but in the entire world, that God would be forced to destroy entire cities, should they fail to reform, after His call. This is already being fulfilled and no doubt vastly greater destruction will befall the world before God is appeased.

It was written that these things would be taking place when the documents would be found. They were found in 1931. Our Lord further told Mother Rafols that there is one thing that hurts His Sacred Heart still more, and that is to be forgotten, offended and despised by souls consecrated to Him. They sometimes forget how dearly He loves His chosen ones, how eagerly He waits in the Tabernacle for them to come to Him for inspiration and assistance in the great mission of saving souls. He wants them to be humble and chaste, and to practice true charity towards one another, and thus, avoid giving scandal. He desires that His priests be living models of Himself and that they propagate devotion to His Sacred Heart.

He wishes that all men have greater love for one another so that there can be peace on earth, and greater love for Him. The Sacred Heart was very sad because of the sacrileges men would commit on account of their coldness toward Him. He said that many would not only not heed the commands of Holy Mother Church, but would actually persecute Her and seek to destroy Her. Priests and religious would be treated with great disrespect.

He desires that men perform acts of satisfaction to fore-

stall the wrath of Divine Justice, and that the Feast of the
Sacred Heart be made a Holy Day of Obligation, and that all
the Faithful receive Holy Communion on that day. (It is a
Holy Day of Obligation in Spain.)

To those who devoutly wear the image of His Sacred Heart,
He promised great graces and special protection at the hour of
their death. He said that in times to come, many souls would
propagate the devotion to His Sacred Heart.

Since these three holy women connect this devotion with
the latter days it seems significant that its spread is quite modern.
It was not extended to the entire world until 1856 by Pope
Pius IX; the whole human race was commended to the Sacred
Heart by Leo XIII only in 1899; and a special act of consecration was prescribed by the late Pope Pius XI just fourteen
years ago (1929) to be recited throughout the entire world
on the Feast of Christ the King.

In conclusion we may note that the prayers ordered by Pope
Leo XIII to be said after Low Mass, to "restrain" Satan, are
followed by the threefold repetition of the ejaculation invok-
ing the aid of the Sacred Heart for this purpose: "Most Sacred
Heart of Jesus, have mercy on us!"

CHAPTER V

FAMINE, PEST, AND WAR

These signs have special importance. Even the seers of Sacred Scripture clearly treat of them. Of course there always have been wars, famines and the like, but the specific occurrences which herald the latter days are distinguishable in two or three ways. These catastrophies are to be more universal, disastrous, and deadly. They are to be easily traceable to widespread moral evils in personal, family, social, national and international life. They are to occur when the world says "peace and security" while neither exists; when man plans without God, when the lowly rise against the mighty, children against parents; in a word when materialism and utter selfishness reigns. Lastly at the same time, persecution of Jews and Catholics must be involved and the former must be returning to Palestine.

There are various other associated signs, a few of which we might mention here, for instance, the unnatural movement of heavenly bodies, the unseasonal flight of birds, vast numbers of fish being cast up by the sea, the rule of an unexpected person, war being carried on in the clouds, and finally, that after the birth of Anti-Christ, nation shall rise up against nation. Another enlightening point as already noted is that in these latter days there are to arise three great and evil rulers.

These various troubles were destined to begin with the revolt of the lower classes which, however, in the final analysis would lose the victory. The apparent order in which events are to occur at this time is more or less as follows: the people will be dissatisfied with the various conditions under which they live, revolutions will follow, together with various assassinations of those in high places, primarily because of various tyrannical laws.

Wars will break out in various countries begun primarily by Germany. Whole cities and even kingdoms will be destroyed, and these wars will spread to practically all countries of the world. As a sign of the approaching end of these wars there shall be much famine in the world through lack of rain, and a superabundance, in many places, of snow and ice. The famine shall be accompanied by earthquakes and various other terrors in nature. Finally, some pain causing plague will visit the earth. It would also seem that various meteors are to fall on the earth and a great comet is to appear in the northern sky, presaging tidal waves throughout the world.

As a result of all these various punishments which God will send upon the world, heretical and political sects will be completely disorganized and vanish as factors to be dealt with, but the toll that mankind must pay for a purified world will be one-third of the race. The majority of the dead will be men. Europe, of course, will be the hardest hit, for there three-fourths of the population shall be wiped out. In Europe and elsewhere most of the priests shall die in defense of their faith, no doubt the majority of these towards the end and during a three months rule under a system described as we would describe Communism. According to Nostradamus this period in the world's history begins when "Spain is split asunder for want of government and when militaristic elements rule Germany and Pagan cults revive." The people of Germany will have been impoverished, freedom banished and various "alarms" (war of nerves?) created. Nostradamus also foretells the impotency of a line of forts and the destruction of Paris. He refers also to the flight of a great German captain to England and the division of France, adding that part of it would be ruled over for a time by an old man (Petain?) who would later be deprived of power by the "Conqueror."

As regards England, it is noted that many "castles on the Thames" will be destroyed and that in the same year there will be great fear over the entire world with many terrible battles among many kingdoms. These events, according to one prophecy, were to occur when "King George, the son of a King George, ruled England." (The present king of England is a George, as was his father.) One of the Irish seers dates

England's troubles from the time a Saxon king would renounce the throne. These woes, according to another oracle, were to come especially from the sky and be caused by "an eagle" with a "headless cross." (The only modern symbol which might fit here is the swastika.) Another ancient prophecy gives us a more or less definite date for the accomplishment of these events, for it says "when Our Lord shall lie in Our Lady's lap (that is when a feast of Our Lady—no doubt the Annunciation, March 25th—shall fall on Good Friday) then England will meet with a strange mishap. (According to the calendar in use at the time of this prediction, one such year would have been 1940.)

According to the prophecies, it would seem that Italy would be taken over by Germany, who in turn would relinquish it to Russia. Germany would be able to take over Italy through some sort of a ruse engendered especially by a deceptive speech delivered apparently at Milan. In this connection the Pope would have to flee Rome, and would die a cruel death in exile about a year later. (Some prophets say 90 days—others 200 days.) Whether or not this exile is forced or voluntary (so that he would be in a position to better rule the Catholic world) is not clear from the prophets. The time of his departure from Rome will come when Italy is without an "emperor" and France without a "ruler."

A schism of short duration is destined to break out, no doubt, because of the Pope's departure from Rome. An anti-pope, of German origin, is to be set up, and finally Rome itself will be destroyed, but rather from the inside through pillage, than from without. Words attributed to the late Holy Father speak of Italy being laid waste but Rome spared. This, of course, would not indicate the absence of pillage.

About the time of the Pope's flight, France and Spain would unite in opposition to Germany and would be fairly successful. It would be then that Russia coming from the north, and Japan and Mohammedans from the east, would cause no small damage in Europe. Japan would furnish the sea power, Turkey the infantry, and Russia the air force. The planes are to be so numerous as to obscure the sky and their damage so great as to leave behind them a solid mass of flame. The initial success of France and Spain would be nullified for a moment, but they would continue to battle for the Christian cause and would be in the field when, by a patent miracle, God would defeat the combined armies of atheism.

We will know that the "Conqueror" has reached the zenith of his power when the "hooked cross" glistens on the top of Church spires. At about this same time revolution will break out in England as well as in France. However, France's will be of rather short duration, and with her aid, England's internal strife will be terminated. The English King would seem destined to be assassinated.

If a prophecy of Saint Columbkille applies to this same time it would seem that Japan is to send an enormous battle fleet against the English, and, among other places, will encounter and defeat them in the Mediterranean. However, this will not be accomplished before the English have put up a gallant fight against vastly superior forces. After this defeat, England will cease as a major power in the world. The prophet gives the reason: "they did not observe justice and rectitude." Three warning signs of England's approaching doom are given: first, the burning of the tower of the great kings; secondly, the burning of the English dockyards; and thirdly, the burning of the Treasury. The first two have of course occurred in this war, but in times past they have also occurred. The Bank of England has not been destroyed. I might note here, however, that the prophet may refer to the destruction of capitalism, especially as known in England, rather than the building itself. London is to be utterly destroyed, so much so that the capitol will be transferred to York, and the country will be governed by three joint rulers, apparently appointed by the Great Monarch. Between the destruction and the resurrection, England is destined to be battered by tidal waves. As a result of these sufferings, England will once more become a good and even great country. It will return to the Church. Conversions, however, shall be one by one. There is to be no mass swing to the Church.

The Russians and other atheists after breaking German resistance, will conquer everything before them until they are vanquished by internal revolts and external rebellion. At the height of their success they will unite with other atheists who rule Europe, possibly most of the world, and for a short time, probably three months, terrorize the vanquished. The Bible will be banished and burned, the war will eventually turn into a religious war in its fourth year, during which period there will be a terrible persecution of Christians of both sexes and all ages. We will know that peace is near when Russia divides Europe, and when the true Pope and a black (anti?) pope[1] die in the same night.

Before peace will once more come upon Europe, two factions will arise in France, the smaller, or Christian, will eventually win out, but terrible times will exist during this short civil war. Toward the end of this period there will appear the "Great Monarch." After the miraculous defeat of the atheistic hordes he will rule all Europe and likely, indirectly, the rest of the world.

The last decisive battle between the Christian and Anti-Christian forces will be fought near Essen, Germany. The southern or Christian forces will win. Their leader, the future Great Monarch of Europe, will wear a white coat and a cross on the front of it. This decisive battle will take place on a feast of Our Lady. Shortly before, atheism will begin to be overthrown in its center, apparently Russia. Russia and Japan in the end will be severely punished for the shedding of so much innocent blood, so much so that never again will they be powers to reckon with in the world. A terrible earthquake in the east,

---

[1] The Superior General of the Jesuits is sometimes referred to as the "Black Pope."

likely in Japan itself, will be a sign that the ruin of the Oriental power is at hand.

When everything seems hopeless for the Christian forces God will work a "wonderful miracle," or as some prophets refer to it, "a great event" or "a terrible event," in favor of His own. During this phenomenon the truly holy will not be harmed, and terrible though it will be, yet we may take consolation in the fact that it will mark the end of God's chastisements. It would seem that the event mentioned vaguely by so many seers, is that specified by others as three days of darkness with the sun and the moon, as it were, turning to blood. The air will be poisoned, thus killing off most of the enemies of Christ's Church. During these three days the only light available to men will be blessed candles, and one candle will burn the entire period. However, even blessed candles will not light in the houses of the godless, yet once the candle is lit by one in the state of grace, it will not burn out until the three day's darkness is over. This "great event" will usher in peace to the troubled world. It would be a sort of reenactment of the three hours of darkness "over the whole earth" at Christ's crucifixion, and a preview of that which will mark the end of the reign of Anti-Christ.

Madeleine Porzat refers to the time of the three days darkness in a similar manner. She speaks of a concurrance of feasts which also happen to occur in the year 1943. Nostradamus in a like way indicates the same year.

The Abbot Werdin says that the Pope will cross the sea in a year when the Feast of St. George (April 23rd) falls on Good Friday, and St. Mark's feast (April 25th) falls on Easter Sunday, and the feast of St. Anthony (June 13th) falls on Pentecost, and the feast of St. John the Baptist (June 24th) falls on Corpus Christi—all these concurrances will take place in the year 1943 and not again till 2038.

According to the St. Odile prophecy, the "German Conqueror" will reach the "apogee" eighteen months after the war in question begins (war with Russia?). From that point on will be noted what is spoken of as the "diminution of his power" which will last for approximately nine months. Toward the end of this latter period there will be a revolt of the women of his own country at seeing so many of their men mercilessly slaughtered. During this same period the various conquered countries will clamor for peace but this will avail them nothing. Then will follow what is spoken of as a "period of invasion" which will last less than nine months. This would be three years of war. Others speak of an end in the 4th year. Russia seems destined to be the nemesis and invader of both Germany and the various other countries that Germany had previously occupied. At about this time Japan will begin to show her real power, especially at sea, Germany will be pillaged, the German conqueror defeated. Finally the Great Monarch and the Christian forces reuniting and with the help of God "through an unknown and frightful illness" will overthrow the Russians, Japanese, Turks, and all other atheistic elements. (This would imply some secret alliance between Russia, Japan, and Turkey.)

Devotion to the Precious Blood and Five Wounds will promote peace but the sense here seems to be that the peace will be extended either in time or more widely and effectively over the earth by reason of these devotions. Also, about this time devotion to the Holy Ghost will greatly increase (see frontispiece).

After the war, famines, earthquakes, darkness, etc., there will be left in the world several women to every man. The Dominicans, Franciscans, and the various nursing nuns, seem to be the only religious orders left to carry on the work of God. Secular priests, of course, will always minister in Christ's Church.

It would seem that there is nothing we can do to avert these various catastrophies. The prophets advise us to prepare ourselves and endeavor to the best of our ability to appease God's anger as much as possible. The only prayers that will be readily heard by God are those for dying sinners. The most effective prayers that can be said are the five sorrowful mysteries of the Rosary.

To sum up and considering all these prophecies as referring to one and the same great war, I would say that a German conqueror will continue his successes over a period of about two years (against Rusia). Then, from internal dissension and external "pressure" he will start his inevitable decline, culminating in his death and the loss of all his gains. His conqueror would be Russia, and possibly Turkey and Japan. England would be involved but doomed because of her past injustices. Among other disasters to befall her would be the loss of her fleet and with it her possessions, yet she would seem destined to continue a small but good, and likely influential nation. France would resurrect, but not as such; Poland would emerge free with St. Andrew Bobola as Patron. Russia, Japan and Turkey would be permanently weakened; all small nations of Europe freed, and Germany a smaller but peaceful and happy nation.

Regarding the United States, I have encountered only contemporary prophesies. One of these says that the United States west of the Rockies will be ruled for a short time by the Japanese who are to succeed because, due to sabotage or other reasons, American defenders will have, as it were, only "sticks and stones" to fight with. The rest of the United States would change its form of government as the result of a revolution, which would last only about three months. These events would occur concurrently with similar events in Europe. The United States is of course included in the countries of the world, all of which would be due for punishment during the short rule of evil.

In conclusion it is worthy of note that the miracle which brings peace will destroy organized evil and very many evil individuals, but by no means all. At a future date there will be a reorganization of the diabolical remnant and others who have fallen from grace, but this new organization is not a revival of any destroyed on the fields of Westphalia.

Whether events unfolding themselves in the present world war fit in with these pictures or not, it is a little premature to say.

Heal our wounds, our strength renew,
On our dryness pour Thy dew,
Wash the stains of guilt away.
Bend the stubborn heart and will,
Melt the frozen, warm the chill,
Guide the steps that else would stray.

On the faithful, who adore
And confess Thee evermore,
In Thy sevenfold gifts descend.
Give them virtue's sure reward,
Give them Thy salvation, Lord,
Give them joys that never end.

CHAPTER VI

THE GREAT MONARCH AND THE ANGELIC PASTOR

Peace and Spread of Catholicism

After the various wars and other disasters noted in the last chapter a good and great "lion monarch" will give the whole world peace and plenty. During his reign, which some say will last for approximately eight to ten years, the Church will make gains throughout the world. Christian fervor among both the clergy and the laity will be consoling. Priests will be esteemed as nobles. This great ruler will be called "a lion" because there will be a "rampant lion" on his shield (that is, a lion standing on bent hind legs with one foreleg raised above the other). He will have the sign of the cross on his breast and his flag will be emblazoned with a white lily.

The Great Monarch will be of French descent (a Bourbon). He will have been an archduke. Some moderns would identify him with Archduke Otto of Hapsburg. The full name of the Archduke includes all the various names by which the Great Monarch has been called in private prophecy (Franz, Joseph, Otto, Antoine, Karl, Maximillian, Heinrich, Sixtus, Xavier, Felix, Renatus, Ludwig, Gaetan, Pius, Ignace, Prince of Hapsburg-Lorraine). Besides this, Otto is a Bourbon, a Catholic, and not a German[1] as seems to be required by the seers. Such coincidents while interesting, need not be taken seriously. They have been noted in others who are now in eternity.

Some say the Great Monarch will come from the east, others say from the west. This apparent discrepancy may readily be explained, for some apparently refer to his origin, others to the place of his exile previous to his assumption of power. I might note here that England in some way or other is to be

---

[1]There are not wanting critics who claim that the prophecies which insist that the great monarch will be French and not German have been tampered with by Frenchmen.

instrumental in the original success of the Great Monarch.

This Lion Monarch is to be a descendant of Pepin, Constantine, St. Louis, Frances I (of France) and Charlemagne. He will be greater than Alexander and more successful than Cyrus. He will be acknowledged as Emperor across the sea from Europe. He will begin his mission in the Iberian Peninsula, coming into power during the last year of the war (referred to in the preceding chapter). He will appear in the fourth year of the war. He, together with the Great Pope or Angelic Pastor, shall appear after socialism and a brief but terrible persecution of priests, but both of their reigns will cease before the reign of Anti-Christ.

The selection of the true Pope, according to the prophets, will be: a) almost miraculous; b) soon after the terrible war and revolutions; c) the selectors will assemble under many difficulties; d) some prophets foretell the intervention of Saints Peter and Paul and angels (hence his name?); e) some say he will have temporal power over Rome itself; f) some say he will be a French pope; g) the Pope of unity and he will eradicate schisms and heresies.

During the reign of the Great Monarch and the Angelic Pastor the Catholic Church will spread throughout the world, conversions will be innumerable, even many Jews will become Christians. The Blessed Virgin will be the chief one in gaining victory over all heresy and schism because of her power over the demons in the last ages of the world will be especially great. This will be recognized by her enthronement as "Mistress and Queen of Men's Hearts." The Great Pope will reign for approximately four years and will be followed by three other popes rich in wisdom and virtue, who will continue his great work. The successor to the Pastor Angelicus, according to one prophet, will be a Sabinian. The prophets mentioned that although the war pope would suffer much, beginning with his successor, the Popes hereafter will not be oppressed. Even the Pope chosen to rule at the beginning of the reign of Anti-

Christ will not suffer, since he would die a sudden death by assassination before his coronation.

The Great Pope, according to some, will be dressed in red. Whether the prophets refer to him as a cardinal before his election, or that he will change the papal garb from white to red, is not clear. (Note: this may symbolize his great devotion to the Holy Ghost.) In the former case it might be worthy to note that it has been only in comparatively recent years that the Pope is chosen from the ranks of cardinals, and the prophecy was written long before this rule was put into effect. This Angelic Pastor is called by the Monk of Padua, "Gregory XVII." The present Holy Father, although crowned on the feast of St. Gregory, chose the name Pius. Yet if there be no gaps in St. Malachy's list, Pius XII is the Angelic Pastor. The Paduan commentary on St. Malachy makes the pope chosen at the beginning of the reign of Anti-Christ Pius XII. However, the seers seem to destine him for assassination immediately after his selection so that he is not to rule the Church. This need not discredit the monk for other prophecies indicate that the Pastor Angelicus is rather a succession of three, four, or even five pontiffs, one to die in exile just before the era of peace, another (who could be Gregory XVII) who would replace an Anti-Pope. Two glorious successors and then the fifth would be the man chosen pope at the advent of Anti-Christ but destined to die before occupying his throne.

Toward the end of the reign of the Great Monarch, because of wonderful inventions, etc., Christians will be living in peace and plenty. They will have very little work to do and therefore have much free time. This freedom and living in luxury, unfortunately, will be to their detriment. They will become lax in religious matters, many even refusing to receive the Sacrament of Confirmation, saying "it is unnecessary." At this time the precursor of Anti-Christ will gather these lax Christians to his cause (most of those having received Confirmation will not apostatize). Then will follow the terrible reign of Anti-Christ.

Blessed Spirit, one with God above,
Thou Source of life and holy love.
O cheer us with Thy sacred beams,
Refresh us with Thy plenteous streams.

O may our lips confess Thy Name.
Our holy lives Thy praise proclaim;
With love divine our hearts inspire,
And fill us with Thy holy fire.

PART II

TOPICAL INDEX TO THE PROPHECIES

CONTENTS

I. The Evils Which Bring God's Vengeance:
   A. The Time to expect them.
   B. Their Universality.
   C. Their Causes.
   D. The specific evils in the individual, the family, and society generally.

II. Punishments Resulting Without a Special Divine Intervention:
   A. Some General Principles.
   B. Time for special chastisements.
   C. Sufferings of a serious and prolonged, but minor nature.
   D. A very particular War.

III. Punishments Resulting from Special Divine Intervention:
   A. The Terrifying Events.
   B. The Consoling Events.

IV. Great Personages of These Latter Days:
   A. The Great Monarch.
   B. The Angelic Pastor.

V. The Age of the Church's Triumph:
   A. Church and State.
   B. Things Spiritual.

VI. The Sixth Epoc of Time.

VII. The Jews and These Latter Times.

VIII. Notions Specifically Referring to This Generation.

Holy Ghost, with light divine,
Shine upon this heart of mine;
Chase the shades of night away,
Turn the blackness into day.

Let me see my Saviour's face,
Let me all His beauties trace;
Show these glorious truths to me
Which are only known to Thee.

I.   EVILS WHICH CAUSE TROUBLE AND GOD'S VENGANCE

> A. *Time*: In the latter or last days (8d, 27,[1] 28, 31, 33, 38, 41, 47, 69, 84, 105, 111, 160d, 200); after the birth of Anti-Christ (36, 84, 106c, 119, 132, 188); near the second coming of Christ (20, 23, 32); or more precisely after 1931 (147b); and when the Jews begin to return to God or to Palestine (53b).

> B. *Extent*: Evil will so abound and be so widespread that it will appear unsuppressable and provocative of God's wrath. It will be a case of evil increasing from age to age so that at this time the good will be very few. Christians, of course, offend like the rest (8d, 19c, 27a, b, 38, 48b, 58, 69, 70, 106c, 111, 114, 118, 132, 147, 153, 188).

> C. *Causes*: False prophets,[2] false Christs, scandalizers and seducers abound and have many followers; hence false doctrines and fruitless discussions are numberless (5, 8d, 9b, f, h, 11, 16, 19d, 20, 26, 29, 30, 33, 53b, 58, 61, 111). These evil leaders seek to turn men from God with their shallow arguments (9c, 25, 141); nor is this difficult for men really prefer error, heresy and lies (4b, 27, 70, 89, 106c). Evil spirits play their part (24, 27, 61, 130, 135, 180, 185, 188b), and so does bad literature (44b, 70) and unholy enterprises (63). There is no human protection for wise men are few and silent since they would not be heeded (15, 41c, 70).

---

[1]When no letter follows the number appearing in this index, the letter "a" is meant if more than one oracle bears the number.

[2]Even if men work miracles or correctly forecast the future, they are false prophets if they seek to turn man from God, so test them (2b, 19d, 29)

D. *Specific Vices*: a) RATHER IN THE INDIVIDUAL:
Men will be uncharitable, unkind, inhospitable,
hard-hearted and stingy (33, 70, 149); proud,
selfish, conceited, arrogant, ungrateful, and treacherous (27, 31, 33, 38, 47d, 58, 60d, 69);
envious, avaritious, covetous, thieving, and para-
citical (5, 9, 15, 27, 31, 38, 60d, 70); liars,
slanderers, perjurers, deceivers, and betrayers (5,
8d, f, 9, 19e, 24, 38, 44b, 48b, 69, 70); lazy,
intemporate, degenerate, drunken (31, 36, 58,
60d, 149); murderers, pleasure mad materialists,
bribers (5, 15, 38, 58, 63, 89). Most people
will possess something stolen (38).

b) AS AFFECTING THE FAMILY: People will be
shamelessly immoral, even the women. Concubin-
age will flourish publicly and marriage be defiled
(5, 19b, 38, 69, 70). Natural affections shall
grow cold with innumerable family quarrels, be-
trayals, and even murders (19, 20d, 33, 41e, 53,
69, 70, 89). Apart from the notes on murders already given, abortion and birth control may be
intended in (5, 69a).

c) IN MATTERS RELIGIOUS: People will be impious, blasphemous, murmurers against God, Godless, and many even Anti-God (8d, 20, 27, 31,
36, 37, 38, 44, 47, 60d, 70, 89, 119, 147b, 188).
Christians will be hypocrites, disrespectful to relics,
adverse to feast days and Sunday observance (4c,
27, 60d, 70, 183). Children will be scandalized
and grow up ignorant of religion (15b, 47, 58,
147, 173). Many Catholics will doubt some of
the Church's teachings (84, 105). People will
mock and ridicule honesty, humility, and other
virtues (28, 70). The pious will be few, churches

empty, neglected and even defiled. Priests and religion will not be respected The defection from the church will be general (37, 60d, 73, 105, 132, 147, 149). Priests and religious will quarrel among themselves, lack zeal and be worldly, unjust, covetous, immoral.[1] They will err from their reading and some will be tyrannical (9, 37, 38, 60d, 69, 70, 93b, 132, 147).

d) IN MATTERS GOVERNMENTAL AND SOCIAL GENERALLY:

1. Governments will be evil and Godless; they will scheme against other governments and opress their own subjects (38, 47e, 84c, 171, 189). Rulers, becoming all powerful, commit murders, outrage justice themselves, and permit underlings to do like-wise. They persecute, rob, and seek to overthrow the Church. They blaspheme, lie, have no respect for treaties, and provoke their subjects to hate and war against their neighbors (8e, 15, 41c, d, 70, 78, 89, 95, 104, 106c, 147b, 159, 200).[2]

2. Society is confused. There will be no standard to judge morals by, so laws are evil, changed by whim, and despised, as is also order and discipline. People will do and say what they please[3] (5, 8c, 27, 28, 31, 38, 41c, 58, 60d, 63, 68, 70, 78, 106c, 110, 112, 189).

---

[1] It may be that this wide-spread evil among priests and religious describes conditions immediately before Anti Christ, that is after the great monarch (q. v.)

[2] Anti-God symbols (4c); Secret Societies (147, 153)

[3] This refers, also, to the attempts of religious sects to legislate.

The common people will envy their betters;
kings, nobles, and the wealthy will be
overthrown; there will be many poor,
much revolt and class hatred. Rulers will
be befuddled (8b, 41, 47e, 60b, 70, 74,
89, 98, 116, 129, 147, 149, 159). Lies
make the just mourn and strengthen the
wicked, while the violent possess all things
and the good smart under the lash (5, 8f,
11b, 19a, c, 20e, 21, 27b, 32, 38, 44, 63,
70, 147b). And worst of all, the people
will call these evils and ignorances, peace
(5, 8d, 9, 11b, 16, 23).

II. PUNISHMENTS WHICH MAN INFLICTS ON HIMSELF,
     i.e., which result without special divine inter-
     vention—

   A. *Some General Principles*: False prophets preach
      peace but wage war if they don't get their way
      (16). Darkness and destruction is the lot of
      sinners. While God proves the good with trials,
      he judges therewith the wicked. Falsehood and
      its consequences fall and ill-gotten goods vanish
      under God's lash (5, 9h, 15, 16, 25, 45, 59b,
      61, 70). When a land, but especially when the
      nations generally rise up against God, he visits
      them in his anger with famine, war, and pestilence
      on man and beast (4, 11c, 57, 150).

   B. *Time for special chastisement*: Same as above in
      I A, with the additional note that it will be in
      the 3rd age and before the comet (3, 4, 9h, 11c,
      14a, c, 20c, 38, 41, 45, 47c, d, 57, 59, 60, 65,
      70, 84b, c, 95, 116, 159).

   C. *Sufferings to occur over some period of time and in
      various places*: There will be affliction, terror,
      tumult, confusion, commotion, rumor, and car-

nage. Man will cause wars, revolutions, persecutions, and upsets in rulers and governments;
and God will add earthquake, flood, drought,
fire, bad seasons and consequent famine, pestilence
and disease (3, 5, 19, 20, 32, 34, 38, 41, 45,
47, 57, 59, 60, 63, 65, 69, 70, 72, 81, 84, 92,
95, 98, 111, 116, 122, 129, 138, 153, 155, 156,
157, 168). There will be discord even in the
Church (173).

D. *A very particular war or series of wars:*
   a. *Time:* Same as above in II B, with these
      changes and additions: After the Comet,
      (some time after 1800, in the 20th cen-
      tury), specifically, after 1938 (84c, 98,
      112, 147, 155); after the invention of
      moving pictures, submarine, airplane, tele-
      graph, etc. (85, 122b, 126); after an Eng-
      lish King resigns and George son of George
      rules, more than 700 years after England
      takes Ireland, and when various English
      buildings are destroyed and British power
      wanes (69b, 82, 85b, 70d, 137).

   b. *Preliminaries to the conflict:* One war ends
      in a false peace (75, 86, 115, 149). The
      Kaiser leaves Germany; troubled peace fol-
      lows; a low born leader replaces royalty,
      makes Germany strong, persecutes Jews and
      Christians and starts the war (76, 88).
      The conflict in Europe starts in Poland
      (81b, 123a, b) but has come out of Asia
      (200, 201). When France has been rav-
      aged by one five year's war (1914-1918)
      she still has two blood purges to endure
      (102, 122c, 163, 167, 173).

   c. *General notions and extent:* This conflict

is described as Universal or nearly so; as a combination of war, revolution and persecution; as an era of no peace on earth, no trust or security with nation against nation, person against person; confusion, misery, terrible taxes, a dispoiled earth is seen on all sides and war is kindled on war (3, 8, 11, 14, 20, 23, 33, 38, 41, 47, 49, 57, 59, 60, 65, 88, 95, 98, 101, 122, 126, 137, 149, 150, 153, 159, 168c).

d. *Duration*: Five years (32b, 86, 102, 168, a, e).

e. *Some particular features*:

1. The South and West is against the North and East. Jews are involved and loose. The North is victor, but on dividing the South it is decisively defeated. The last battle continues three days; two armies of the North—East are wiped out, the third flies to the far east (12b, 89, 98, 122c, 133, 139, 162, 173, 174). Yellow and Red warriors are against Europe (184).

2. Of three evil rulers who oppress the earth, one dies in bed, a second is killed by the third, and the third falls by the sword. They who raise the armies perish with them. A whole eastern nation fights for an evil man. Ten kings are involved. These nations have mighty fleets (9i, 41c, 47f, 60b, 92, 126, 155).

3. The battlefield is half the earth. Death from the sky, poison gas, cities evacuated, cities and even whole provinces

and nations destroyed; a northern nation has great air power; great battles
on sea and in the air; blockades, injured
food resources, etc. All are featured in
this conflict. The Godless governments
of Europe tear each other and the con-
tinent to pieces (59, 65, 85a, b, 86c,
88b, 92, 98, 116, 157, 171, 176).

4. In 70d is what appears to be a description of a modern fleet and combined sea
and air bombardment. This is a war
where the weak must be strong (14c).
Emblems and atmosphere are described
thus: a headless, disgraced or hooked
cross (85b, 175, 184); a hammer,
red destroyers of the wealthy, yellow
warriors (146, 168, 175, 184). It is
a war of falsehood and enforced caution
of speech (60b, 86, 102).

f. *Various nations involved*:

1. The German leader is at first victorious,
then for half as long, while twenty nations clash, he holds his own, but in
far less time, having been weakened in
the East, his country is invaded, completely defeated, and the ruler crushed.
Soldiers of seven nations are in the last
battle which is in Westphalia. Russia
seems to fall at the same time. It will
take seven generations for Russia and
Prussia to recoup the losses (65, 71,
76, 89b, 104, 108, 125, 140, 155,
162, 167, 175).

2. England in alliance with France is helped
by a nation and fleet from the west

but defeated at sea by a fleet from the east (this may refer to a later date). London is destroyed. France will aid when revolt breaks in England. Many lords and the king perish. The English casualties will be nearly as great as the Prussian. In Europe England "pays the piper."[1] (69b, 70d, 84c, 85, 86c, 87, 98, 122, 128, 129, 137, 155, 201).

3. France falls as a result of her alliance with England. She will have a triple blood purge (two wars and a revolt?) (87, 98, 122, 137, 173). Her leader will be destroyed (98). Paris, Marseilles, and many other cities will be destroyed, but the good will escape death in Paris. There will be civil war in which the communists control three-fourths of France. The result, however, is quelled, and France aids England suppress a similar uprising there (65, 67b, 100, 102, 112, 137, 144, 156b 163, 167, 173, 176, 201). Paris will be oppressed for a little more than three years (158) (This may refer to time of Anti-Christ). It is France that will have started all this anti-religion trouble (141).

4. Italy suffers terribly, chiefly during the persecution noted below. Many cities are ruined in northern Italy, but also Naples and Palermo. Her islands are

---

[1]Tidal waves real or typical are spoken of as one of England's punishments.

evacuated. Lombardy is laid waste. Armies of the North, West, and East fight there. Rome is probably pillaged but not destroyed (65, 93b, 111, 123i, 139, 168e, 173, 184).

5. Russia outrages and murders nobles, wealthy, and the clergy (157, 188). She seems to be on the side of Prussia in the Battle of Westphalia with France, Spain, Poland, Italy, and apparently Austria on the opposite side (104b, 106, 163, 167, 175). She causes many exiles and fugitives (149).

6. Greece will not be secure till she returns to Christian Unity (106b). Spain survives civil war and trouble from the Godless (85, 87, 147, 184). Vienna is destroyed (157).

g. *The Persecution:*[1]

1. In the fourth year of the war it becomes a religious conflict, with men and women fighting for the faith. The church will lack a protector for 25 months but the actual persecution lasts 400 days (85b, 100, 101, 123h, 140, 173) (This may refer to time of Anti-Christ). The persecution will be terrible and directed chiefly against priests and religious. Many priests die not only for the faith but also for the country (19, 59b, 72, 84, 97, 111, 129, 134, 147a, b, 157b, 161, 164, 169b, 170).

---

[1]This is often equivalent to civil war (147b, 157, 159, 165, 170).

2. The persecution will be widespread. In France it is connected with civil war. In Italy it is especially severe and Russia and Prussia are responsible. The martyrs there are numerous (65, 111, 159, 168e), but the terror will spread even to where it is thought impossible (141). While a few Catholics, even some bishops, fall away, the clergy on the whole stand firm. Church and other Catholic property will be confiscated (67b, 139, 141, 153, 159).

3. Because of three powers the pope will have to leave Rome. He will depart with four Cardinals, suffer much, and die in exile (65, 88, 100, 101, 104, 124, 139, 142, 143, 147, 153, 156c, 164). He will leave Rome 200 days after the persecution starts (173b). Confusion and schism result (100, 124, 153), with German, Italian, and Greek Anti-popes (65, 72, 139).

4. This persecution rather becomes acute and starts in the fourth year of the war. It started long before in France and is stepped up in 1931 (141, 147b). The pest foretold for Russia, Italy, Spain, Prussia, and Westphalia may mean a persecution (172 and cf. 173a for communism).

h. *Evils concomitant with the War*: drought, floods, tidal waves, famine, and plague with terrible mortality (41a, e, 59, 76, 84c, 128, 138, 167, 168e).

III. PUNISHMENTS ADDED BY GOD OR THE DIVINE INTER-
VENTION TO END THE WAR AND EVIL.

    A. *The Terrifying Event:*—

        a. *Time:* When War and confusion reign su-
preme, when disorder and confusion is at
its height in France, when Rome is about to
fall to the enemies of religion; after famine,
pestilence, war, fraud, and communism
have left Italy in anarchy; when the humiliation of Sion (the Church and/or the
Jews) is complete; when in France, at least,
public prayer ceases and the churches close
for 24 hours; when the white and the
black (true and false?) pope die the same
night (47c, g, 93, 144, 158, 165, 168e,
173). Further, it will be at the end of a
terrible war, after one awful night in the
midst of persecution in France, in the age
which preceeds the universal preaching of
the Gospel, at the beginning of the third
period of time and more precisely in or near
a year when Easter falls on April 25th (19a,
106b, 113, 123h, 144, 168b, d).

        b. *Surprise:* The Day the Lord comes as a thief
in the night, when they (the forces of evil)
say peace and security, then suddenly comes
destruction upon them (23, 161, 174);
when all appears lost for the Church, just
then all is saved (118, 137, 138, 141, 144,
147b, 151, 152, 163, 168c, 169b, 173,
183).

        c. *Purpose:* God will cleanse the world and re-
turn it to its ancient state (34, 44a, 149,
164, 166, 191). It will be a case of Him
adding to the destruction of man (65,

156). It is His Judgment on the Nations (8a, c, 24, 41b, 122), the time for the mountain of the Kingdom of God to destroy all kingdoms and establish itself (12a). All that preceeds has not made man repent (32c).

d. *General description of the event:* a great, terrible, and most certainly and evidently miraculous happening (70b, 76, 129, 137, 144, 150, 152, 153, 158, 160, 168b, d, 169b, 171, 173, 194). Nothing like it before or after (14a, 161). It will be world wide but probably more severe in Europe (84b, 130, 137, 146, 150, 161, 174). A sorry event for those not truly holy (70b, 153). Fear, the snare, and the pit consume man (8c, 41f).

e. *More specific descriptions:*

1. A whirlwind of God's fierce anger scatters and destroys high and low (8a, c, 9d, 14, 24, 41b, 122); hurricanes (70a, 150, 173); winds, strong winds or storms (12a, 32, 63b, 65, 84c, 150, 155, 194).

2. A darkness (14a, c, 32, 45, 60b, 63b, 72b, 86b, 98, 162, 173b, 176) as the sign of Jonas (19b) will last three days and three nights (154, 156, 159, 162, 165, 170, 174). The heavens will be moved with frightful clouds, lightning and thunder. There will be earthquakes and tidal waves. (14a, c, 63b, 150, 174). A yellow fog, dust, flame, and smoke from the north (14c, 41c, 63c, 84c, 92, 184). Pest

in the air, an unknown and frightful illness (76, 156). Demons infest the air and are visible (65, 88b, 150, 153, 156, 161, 165, 174, 177).

3. A numberless, strong, irresistable force described as an army of beings before whom all is a garden, behind whom all is desert (14a, 32c, 41e). Also God comes to judge the wicked with thousands of his saints (31).

f. *Results of this event coupled with those of the war, persecution, and upheavals in nature:*

1. Apparently a three months' period is involved in a special way (152, 161). A famine or plague seems to follow the darkness (174, 182) and likewise exploits of the Great Monarch and his forces (q. v.).

2. Whereas the vengeance of God is directed against the army of evil (92), which completely defeated, flies to the Far East (162, 174); many men will lose their lives. In other words, the enemies of religion chiefly, but not exclusively, shall perish, yet even some of those enemies will be spared, become converted and be other St. Pauls (144, 147b, 150, 152, 154, 156, 174). But even so, the faithful shall have special protection, especially during the darkness (45a, 150, cf. g below).

3. The casualties shall be appalling: There will be few men left (8c, 161, 173b). Seven or even twelve women to every

man (84c, 92), this apparently because there are more faithful women than men (168, 185); innumerable deaths (41c, 60b, 65, 85b, 98, 104b, 112); the earth covered with the slain (9d, 32d, 154, 174; individuals, whole families, property, cities destroyed (150). One third, one half, three-fourths of mankind destroyed (32c, 157, 170, 174). Afterwards Europe will be too large for its people (184).

g. *Spiritual helps for the good during the evil times:* Stay where God has put you, hope in Him, pray and do penance (65, 88b, 137, 183). Communions of reparation, prayers for dying sinners offered through Our Lady to the Sacred Heart (147). For Spain, prayers to our Lady of the Pilar should be said (147). Our Lady has obtained a mitigation of the evils (168c) and she will protect the church (173b). Saints Peter and Paul will protect the faithful during the darkness; only blessed wax candles will then give light, one burns the three days; stay where you are, say the rosary, and don't look out or go out of the house through curiosity (147, 150, 156, 165, 174, 184). Devotion to the Precious Blood and Five Wounds is also recommended (178, 186).

B. *The Consoling Events or Event: Fire cleanses from below, love from above* (168b) :—

1. Immediately after the Darkness there will be a great light as the sun shining with a special brilliance (86b, 150, 173). This may be on a Feast of Our Lady (163).

2. The demons will be collected and bound through the agency of Saints Peter and Paul, and St. Peter may designate the person to be chosen as the new pope (150, 156).

3. It would seem that now begins the third period of time. Our Lady under the titles of Immaculate Conception, Queen of Men's Hearts, Queen of Heaven and Earth, but especially Queen of the Angels would have been responsible for saving France and Spain, and mitigating generally, God's Anger. She had been given especial power over hell for the latter times. She may appear in the heavens with angels and saints (130, 135, 158a, b, 168, 169, 173, 184, 185, 189, 193, 197b, 198) (cf. concerning the coming of the Son of Man 14a, 20b, 130).

4. The Kingship of Christ and the Sacred Heart are devotions which will flourish towards the end (102b, 128b, 147, 177).

5. In the times before Christ God the Father, as it were, ruled. In the second period God the Son. In the third period it shall be *God the Holy Ghost*, the Spirit of Love (114, 141, 168b, 177). This reign of the Holy Ghost begins with the defeat of Germany (104c, 117).

IV. GREAT PERSONAGES OF THE LATTER DAYS: These are the Great Pope and the Great Ruler. The two appear frequently in prophetic writings. Their respective qualities and accomplishments are not always kept distinct, and many results which in one place are attributed directly to heaven, in others are attributed to either of these figures or both. This does not necessitate contradictions, for both work together and each is but a divine agent.

A. *The Great Monarch*:

a. referred to as: The Orient or from the East (17b, 60c, 63, 78, 85b); from the West (83); from the North (68, 72b, 95, 106, 131); a prince, knight, Emperor, King (60c, 67, 68, 72b, 83, 86, 90, 97, 100, 117, 129); a Lion or an Eagle (63, 72, 81, 85, 93, 112, 124, 168); a Bourbon, Lily or white flower (64, 87, 94); a star (96); a duke (138); of Spanish origin (106); great Celt but not Irish (123m, 201); a scion of Charlemagne, Pepin, Clovis, etc., of the French Kings (67, 90, 91, 97, 102, 112, 114, 121, 129, 137, 139, 145); a great warrior (68, 70c); an exile or captive in his youth (67, 100, 102; his features noted (71, 127); he will be a Catholic (88, 157); not a German (129, 157b).

b. *Time:* near the end of time (77, 87, 91). In the third incursion of time (113, 168b), during (155), and after a terrible war (96), as a result of which the world in general, but especially France, and in France the provinces of the North and East are in terrible misery (67), and also as a result of which Germany is decisively defeated (or wholly converted) (104c, 117, 167). He will come into power at the moment that the Anti-Christian forces are on the point of Victory (40), and will succeed as ruler of Germany an elected ruler of humble birth

(140). All this will be after 1840 (121),
and item 123m could mean that he would
begin his rule in 1944 and reach the zenith
of his power in 1951.

c. *First achievements:* The great monarch is
helped into France by England (94, 175),
probably despite the unwillingness of America (175). The French are not expecting
him (72b). He comes from north to west
(106). There will be with him two aids
(78, 87). He will turn out to be a great
conqueror (92) and reformer (as noted
below) but this because he has the very
special aid of God (102, 106, 112, 117,
131, 141). It is he who puts down the revolt in France (168). He is in charge of
the army of the south in the Battle of Westphalia (89) where he defeats the Prussians
and Russians (76). He defeats the nation
that for three years ravages in the north and
the Emperor of the north who is the mystic
Anti-Christ (76, 81b, 139). Spain and
Poland aid him in some special way (86c,
96, 104c, 106). It seems to be after this
phase of the war that women must do the
farm work for one year (89b, 122a).

d. *His Army:* Whether this army is organized
before or after Westphalia is not clear. It is
composed of soldiers of various nations (64,
72b, 139). It is called "The Army of the
Church" (114, 139) or "of the Holy
Ghost" because in that period of time the
Holy Ghost dominates all things (114,
141), "of the Cross bearers" because in
that sign it conquers (106, 114, 189c).

It is rather a religious congregation whose members are the earth's greatest soldiers, scientists, and saints. They are divided into three orders: military knights, contemplative monks, and active religious. The angels fight on its side; it upholds disciple both temporal and spiritual universally after it has cleansed the world of evil. It lasts till the end of time. Every ruler is a member of this militia (114).

e. *His achievements, apparently after Westphalia:* He is made king of France (67, 72, 79, 84d, 87, 96, 97, 100, 112, 125, 144, 159, 162, 168) by the Pope (156) but eventually dominates Europe as its Emperor (90, 91, 145). Various countries, e. g. England (64, 72b, 73b, 85b, 96, 122a), Germany (76, 88, 106, 167, 157), Poland (86c, 104c), Italy (64, 83, 96), Greece (64), Ireland (68, 71), etc. He rules apparently through allied monarchs and after either conquering or relieving them of revolt. It would seem that he unites Germany, Spain, and France first, and only after much blood, the rest. His dominion eventually extends to the bounds of the Ancient Roman Empire (40, 66, 79, 129, 139). But apart from this he dominates the world (67, 100), and reforms it (111), that is, he restores order to Church, state, and family (133), and aids workmen (144). All other world forces he either destroys or enters into agreement with (63a, 64, 71, 78). In this process it is likely that Russia, China (168), several European governments

(131), Japan (100), other Eastern leaders (64, 72b, 122c, 144), the Arabs (78, 86), and for a certainty the Turkish Empire and other Mohammedan countries shall feel the force of his arms to bring them into line (64, 104c, 106, 114, 122c, 131, 132, 138, 167). At any rate he relieves every land (63, 111, 112, 139), destroys evil laws (63c, 94, 102, 144), destroys all tyrants (111, 114), makes it possible for all exiles, fugitives and captives to return home (140, 158b, 160), and ends war (63c, 94, 97, 101, 104d). It is no wonder then that the people gladly accept his rule (78, 160). His reform is apparently a gradual process (64, 134).

f. *His reign:* Under him Peace reigns in all the earth (40, 84d, 85b, 86b, 87, 89b, 100, 102, 104c, 106, 117, 125, 131, 141, 163, 165). Justice likewise (86b, 129), happiness (77, 140), and abundance (60c, 85b, 86b, 97, 104c, 106, 117, 151, 163). Iron is used only for tools (84a). New cities are founded (106). No taxes for twelve years! (78).

g. *Religion under the Great Monarch:* His place in the divine scheme is to crush the enemies of Christ (40, 114, 132, 140), and to promote, and in cooperation with the Pope, achieve not only Christian Unity but also the conversion of all Mohammedans (106, 132) or Pagans, as well as many, if not all, Jews (64, 106). His good example is his chief weapon (151). Since this accomplishment results from the miraculous events and the Great Pope, as well as the Great Monarch, more details are given below. Suffice it to remark here that he restores the true Pope and church property (72, 138) and changes many kingdoms to strengthen the faith (129).

h. *The length of his reign is quite uncertain but at some time during it,* probably after his defeat of the Turks and Arabs, *he establishes the Kingdom of Jerusalem* (72b, 91, 97, 106, 125). He abdicates his throne in Jerusalem (64, 77, 79, 83, 85b, 96). Thus ends the Roman Empire and apparently the kingdoms of France and of England (77, 79). At any rate He is said to be the last and greatest French King and Roman Emperor and the last King of England, but on the other hand it is said that France will exist till the end of time (66) and that there will be men of the stock of the Great Monarch also till the end of time (113).

B. *The Great Pope (or Popes):* This divine agent is usually referred to as the *Angelic Pastor* (e. g., 82, 113b, 136). He will be born before the end of the 19th century (112). He is said to come from the North (113b), to be French (125), Galician (168c), or a Sabine (124). Some think he will be a Franciscan (131, 142). All agree that he will be a holy man (81, 99, 104, 109, 129). The Paduan Prophecy calls him Gregory (136). He is to be protected by the angels and to be a Prophet, a miracle worker (83, 97).

He will come after Pius XI (136) when the world is wartorn and the Church persecuted (81b,

83, 96, 97, 112, 123, 125), also after the wicked
have been or while they are being chastised (83,
97, 112), at the same time as the Great Monarch
(101, etc.).

It seems that here there is the question of a
succession of popes who should rather be called the
Angelic Pastors (97). The number would probably be five (95) who would all together rule 17
years (123q). In another light, however, the number might be considered only four (81). Looked
at this way the pope who ruled when the Great
Monarch appeared would form one with his predecessor, i.e., his times, policies, and even name
might be identical, so that it could be said the
pope died and lived again (173c, 190). This
pope would be the one who dies in exile, during
the persecution. His successor (being the first of
a series of four great men) would be chosen by
divine intervention and probably by a method laid
down by the exile (100, 139, 150, 173). This
succession would last till the time of Anti-Christ
(129).

V.   THE AGE OF THE CHURCH'S TRIUMPH.

A. *Church and State:* When the Great Monarch has
   achieved total victory there shall be on earth only
   One Emperor and twelve monarchs. The Emperor
   shall be supreme in things temporal, the pope in
   things spiritual (67, 81, 97, 104d, 114, 129).

B. *Things spiritual:*

   1. When God has ended the confusion a new
      world begins similar to its first state (34,
      54, 65), a world dominated by the King-
      dom of God (12, 28). Satan is bound
      many years (54, 129, 141).

2. The Church is reorganized (91, 93b, 97, 99, 113, 114, 150), Apostolic discipline is restored (113), and religious orders are reestablished and flourish, as do vocations, chiefly among the workers and poor (113, 150, 167, 173b), penance and good works abound (67, 140, 151). At first the state helps finance worship but apparently the Pope puts the church on a freewill offering basis, for the most part (97, 139).

3. It then falls to the lot of the Holy See and the Church to rebuild society (64, 104, 112, 160). Accordingly the Pope will lead the bishops in a crusade of instruction (144, 173). Some speak of twelve apostles of the new age and other marvelous things connected with a campaign of this nature (139, 156, 168b, 172, 184). It will be realized that failure to preach God's word previously had resulted in the punishments (173). Thus the Gospel will be preached in all lands (97). This is the age of the triumph of the Church, happy those who live to see it. The people will be like the primitive Christians and unbelievers seeing the Church's glory will flock into her (100, 107, 137, 144, 145, 149, 150, 161, 163, 164, 172). Heresy will disappear at least in so far as it is organized, also schism; certainly they will lose government support. In some instances whole nations will become Catholic (67, 83, 84d, 102, 104c, 114, 117, 129, 130, 138, 156, 166, 169). Many heathen also will be converted (84d). (It would seem, however, that many, but

not all Jews — q. v. — would join the church).

4. Concerning specific nations then are the following items: Arabs or Asiatics or both make an attempt against Europe. Poland is in the fray. They fail and one army is driven into the far east while the other (Mohammedan) retires into North Africa. The Moslems become Christian, also the Chinese (Tartars) and other heathens (89, 99, 123d, e, 129, 130, 135, 156, 157, 184). The Greeks and the Russians return to the Church (99, 156). England loses her Eastern colonies and ceases to be a great power but she returns to the Church which again flourishes there. Ireland is in some way instrumental in this (70d, 72b, 80, 82b, 84c, 122, 128, 129, 156, 163). After Germany is defeated, disarmed, and dismembered, she returns to Christian unity and monarchy (103, 104b, 129). A four-nation Slav Federation with the Capitol at Warsaw and with St. Andrew Bobola as patron plays an important role against Asiatics and Moslems, and in the new Christian world (148, 157, 173c, 175, 182). Belgium, Spain, France (despite her sins), and other Catholic nations laid waste in war and persecution, regain their sovereignty and something more (66, 69b, 74, 76, 147a, 173c), but nations which have irreparably lost the true faith disappear (147c).

So, as the reign of the Great Monarch progresses Christian Unity is achieved, ap-

parently even to the point where it can be
said that there is but one Flock and one
Shepherd (8, 16b, 17b, 40c, 60b, c, 67,
72b, 81, 87, 90, 92, 93b, 97, 99, 100,
101, 104d, 109, 114, 125, 138, 139, 146,
168, 169).

VI. THE SIXTH EPOC OF TIME: After this period in which
all nations submit to the Church, especially after
the Turks submit (87, 156), the sixth epoc draws
to a close (129). Christians will not appreciate
the graces of the sixth epoc of time. Fervor grows
cold; darkness, crime, and revolt gradually increase
till evil is worse than before (40, 67, 78). God
releases Lucifer and Hell (40). The False Prophet, precursor of Anti-Christ, appears. The people
will have been especially lax concerning Confirmation (sacrament of the Holy Ghost who dominates
the sixth period of time) and it will be especially
the unconfirmed who fall into the snares of the
False Prophet (111). Then comes the Anti-Christ
(29, 38, 67, 79, 101, 111, 129).

VII. JEWS AND THE LATTER TIMES.

   A. *Causes:* By reason of God's promises to the fathers
   (1, 2, 22, 41g, 48, 56), and for a purpose worthy
   of God Himself (9g, 39, 183), the Jews shall not
   be entirely cast off or destroyed (1, 2, 22, 39).

   B. *Time:*

      a. Jerusalem shall be downtrodden (20f); and
      the Jews shall live under alien God-willed
      rule (9e, 11a, 49, 50), without King or
      priesthood, many days, indeed (13), so
      long that they will have forgotten their
      lands, tribes, and tongue (56).

      b. But in the fullness of the time of the Gentiles
      (22), also called the time of the nations

(20f, 22) and the latter days, times, or ages (2, 172), but more often the last days or end of the world (4, 13, 35, 43, 51), or more precisely when the following conditions are fulfilled:

1. When there is no peace on earth (3)
2. When Jews, having abandoned farms (43), do evil in general (43, 49, 54) or some very great and particular evil[1] (12b, 103)
3. and are being or have been severely punished as a result (9g, 12b, 47c)
4. When in Germany there are few (16c, 88a), if indeed any Jews (140), but apparently many in England (122c).
5. When the power of the Turk is broken (62, 72)
6. When there are many false Christs (53b)
7. And on the other hand, when the Jews have begun to return to God and to serve Him (2, 10, 13, 45, 46, 50, 52) and to cry again to Him for liberation from captivity or persecution in a strange land (46).

C. *Salvation:*

1. This time God will not turn a deaf ear (7, 18, 42, 102). A (large) remnant of the Jews (9g, 18, 22), meaning either all God-fearing Jews (6), or all surviving Jews (22, 42, 44c, 45), shall be gathered from the north country, the east and the west, many if not all lands, yes, even from the

[1]The studies of Belloc in "The Jews" might explain this, read Chapters III and VIII.

ends of the earth (9g, 11d, 17, 181), back into their own land, the land of Abraham, now called Palestine (6, 9g, 10, 11d, 15, 140, 142, 172, 181). This return is facilitated by the Great Monarch (q. v.) (55).

2. The Great Monarch or the Great Pope (q.v.) (72, 97) shall reestablish the Kingdom of Jerusalem (11d, 72) and give it to the Jews as the rightful owners (10, 42). They may again have a king as of old (11d, 13, 15, 157). Jerusalem will be rebuilt (42, 43); also the Temple or House of the Lord (6, 15, 46), but it will not be like the former one (42, 44c); yet the Ark, Tabernacle, and Altar of Insense will be found (18). This nation of the Jews will be mighty (16c).

3. God will make a new covenant with His people (10, 57). They will acknowledge the Messiah and His rule (13, 35, 62). Under the Great Pope they, enjoying tranquility (97), will become Christians[1] (8, 16b, 44c, 49, 100, 106, 168b, 172), but as Christians they will not lose the distinction of being Jews (122c). At this time Satan (the Chief Cause of Evil) will be bound in all the world (54) (This to occur after Anti-Christ).

4. Thereafter till the end of time the Jews will serve God very well (2, 6, 11d, 46, 53).

---

[1]Prophecy 139 says that the conversion of the Jews is reserved till the end of time. It is probable that, whereas many Jews will become Christians under the Great Monarch and Great Pope (prophecy 34d), the conversion of the Jewish nation will take place only after it has been fooled by Anti-Christ whom at first it will consider the Messiah. Prophecy 19a may mean that the Son of Man comes (q. v.) before all Jews are converted.

They will be happy and enjoy peace (9g, 14b, 52), and material prosperity (9g, 14b, 46). They will henceforth neither be persecuted in the nations (97, 122c), nor disturbed in the possession of their own land (10, 15, 16, 42).

VIII. NOTIONS SPECIFICALLY REFERRING TO THIS GENER-ATION:

1. People in our times (especially those who need them) pay no heed to divine warnings. There are few devout souls (183, 187). God's wrath is about to strike in the form of great suffering, including war, plague, flames, famine, and especially a "yellow fog" over Europe. Men and beasts will perish (183, 184, 186, 187, 191, 194, 195). Prayer will no longer delay divine Justice (186, 187, 195) but it will aid dying sinners (187), help individuals in their sufferings (186), and bring trouble to a quicker end (183, 189b, 197b). The devotions recommended for these things are: To the Precious Blood (186), Rosary (184), Queen of the Angels (185, 189), Immaculate Heart (179c), Perpetual Adoration (197a, b).

2. The war begins under Pius XI (179c). The war will involve persecution of the Church (179c). The persecution is connected with a hooked cross or hook and cross which can mean either the swastika of the Nazi or the hook (sickle) and cross (hammar shaped like the tau cross) of the Communists (184). The reigning pope dies in exile (195). The Immaculate Conception saves France and Italy from the worst (184). For other countries involved see 178b, 193, 198. The Time is designated as beginning already before

1936 (183, 184). Germany is marked for defeat by Russia in 1943 (193, 196). When the land of the great fleet enters the Mediterranean it is the time to expect great suffering in Europe (184) (1943). The war ends with a miracle (194, 197b, 198). As a result of all this Europe will be too large for the survivors (183). In fact there will be few men on earth (184).

3. The Pope will gather the remnant, among them many saints. The Dominicans and Franciscans will preach and turn the world back to Christ (184). There will be many Crusader volunteers of a new and Christian society. It will take about a generation to instruct in the new order (183, 184, 189c, 193). The era of the peace of Christ begins in the United States. It will be a time of Christianity and the heart. Men will be like the early Christians. Then will be a great return to the land. The powerful industrial organizations will collapse. Monastaries and convents will flourish as never before (183, 194b). Mary will triumph and peace will reign (179c).

PART III

THE PROPHETIC TEXTS

Old Testament _____nos.   1 to   18

New Testament _____ "   19 to   32

The Fathers of the Church _____ "   33 to   40

Apocrapha of the Old Testament_____ "   41 to   56

Apocrapha of the New Testament_____ "   57 to   61

The Talmud and the Sybil_____ "   62 and 63

Oracles from the Middle Ages_____ "   64 to 119

The Prophets of the 16th and 17th centuries "   120 to 132

Predictions in the 18th century_____ "   133 to 144

Early 19th Century Prophecies_____ "   145 to 161

Late 19th Century Seers_____ "   162 to 176

Published works from the 20th century_____ "   177 to 189

Two Prophetic Interpretations_____ "   190 and 191

Examples of Contemporary American Oracles
   (not previously published) _____ "   192 to 199

Two Unidentified Prophecies_____ "   200 and 201

Holy Ghost, with power divine,
Cleanse this guilty heart of mine;
In Thy mercy pity me,
From sin's bondage set me free.

Holy Ghost, with joy divine,
Cheer this saddened heart of mine:
Yield a sacred, settled peace;
Let it grow and still increase.

PROPHECIES FROM SACRED SCRIPTURES
OLD TESTAMENT

1. "And yet for all that when they (the Jews) were in the land of their enemies, I did not cast them off altogether, neither did I so despise them that they should be quite consumed, and I should make void my covenant with them. For I am the Lord their God" (Lev. 26:44).

2a. "After all the things aforesaid shall find thee, in the latter time thou shalt return to the Lord thy God, and shalt hear his voice. Because the Lord thy God is a merciful God: He will not leave thee, nor altogether destroy thee, nor forget the covenant, by which he swore to thy Fathers" (Deut. 4:30-31).

2b. "If there rise in the midst of thee a prophet or one that saith he hath dreamed a dream, and he foretell a sign and a wonder, and that come to pass which he spoke, and he say to thee: Let us go and follow strange gods, which thou knowest not, and let us serve them: Thou shalt not hear the words of that prophet or dreamer: for the Lord your God trieth you, that it may appear whether you love him with all your heart, and with all your soul, or not" (Deut. 13:1-3).

3. "At that time (return of Jews), there shall be no peace to him that goeth out cometh in, but terrors on every side among all the inhabitants of the earth. For nation shall fight against nation, and city against city, for the Lord will trouble them with all distress" (2 Par. 15:5-6).

4a. "Why have the Gentiles raged, and the people devised vain things? The kings of the earth stood up, and the princes met together, against the Lord, and against his Christ. Let us break their bonds asunder: and let us cast away their yoke from us. He that dwelleth in heaven shall laugh at them; and the Lord shall deride them. Then shall he speak to them in his anger, and trouble them in his rage" (Ps. 2:1-5).

4b. "O ye sons of men, how long will you be dull of heart? Why do you love vanity, and seek after lying?" (Ps. 4:3).

4c. "O God, why has thou cast us off unto the end: why is thy wrath enkindled against the sheep of thy pasture? Remember thy congregation, which thou hast possessed from the beginning. The sceptre of thy inheritance which thou hast redeemed: Mount Sion in which thou hast dwelt. Lift up thy hands against their pride unto the end; see what things the enemy hath done wickedly in the sanctuary. And they that hate thee have made their boasts, in the midst of thy solemnity. They have set up their ensigns for signs, and they knew not both in the going out and on the highest top. As with axes in a wood of trees, they have cut down at once the gates thereof, with axe and hatchet they have brought it down. They have set fire to thy sanctuary: they have defiled the dwelling place of thy name on the earth. They said in their heart, the whole kindred of them together: Let us abolish all the festival days of God from the land" (Ps. 73:1-8).

5. "It was not enough for them to err about the knowledge of God, but whereas they lived in a great war of ignorance, they call so many and so great evils peace. For either they sacrifice their own children, or use hidden sacrifices, or keep watches full of madness. So that now they neither keep life, nor marriage undefiled, but one killeth another through envy, or grieveth him by adultery. And all things are mingled together, blood, tumults and perjury, disquieting of the good, forgetfulness of God, defiling of souls, changing of nature, disorder in marriage, and the irregularity of adultery and uncleanness. For the worship of abominable idols is the cause, and the beginning and end of all evil. For either they are mad when they are merry: or they prophesy lies, or they live unjustly, or easily foreswear themselves. For whilst they trust in idols which are without life, though they swear amiss, they look not to be hurt. But for two things they shall be justly punished, because they have thought not well of God, giving heed to idols, and have sworn unjustly, in guile despising justice. For it is not the power of them, by whom they swear, but the just vengeance of sinners

always punisheth the transgression of the unjust" (Wis. 14: 22-31).

6. "And our brethren, that are scattered abroad from the land of Israel, shall return to it. And all the land thereof that is desert shall be filled with people, and the house of God which is burnt in it, shall again be rebuilt: and all that fear God shall return thither" (Tob. 14:6, 7).

7. "Who art registered in the judgments of times to appease the wrath of the Lord, to reconcile the heart of the father to the son, and to restore the tribes of Jacob" (Ecclus. 48:10).

8a. "In the last days the mountain of the house of the Lord shall be prepared, on the top of mountains, and it shall be exalted above the hills, and all nations shall flow unto it. And many people shall go, and say: Come and let us go up to the mountain of the Lord, and to the house of the God of Jacob, and he will teach us his ways, and we shall walk in his paths: for the law shall come from Sion, and the word of the Lord from Jerusalem. And he shall judge the Gentiles, and rebuke many people: and they shall turn their swords into plough-shares, and their spears into sickles: nation shall not lift up sword against nation, neither shall they be exercised any more to war" (Is. 2:2-4).

8b. "And the people shall rush one upon another, and every man against his neighbour: the child shall make a tumult against the ancient, and the base against the honourable" (Is. 3:5).

8c. "Behold the Lord shall lay waste the earth, and shall strip it, and shall afflict the face thereof, and scatter abroad the inhabitatns thereof. And it shall be as with the people, so with his master as with the handmaid, so with her mistress: as with the buyers, so with the seller: as with the lender, so with the borrower: as with him that calleth for his money, so with him that oweth. With desolation shall the earth be laid waste, and it shall be utterly spoiled: for the Lord hath spoken this word. The earth mourned, and faded away, and is weakened:

the world faded away, the height of the people of the earth is weakened. And the earth is infected by the inhabitants thereof: because they have transgressed the laws, they have changed the ordinance, they have broken the everlasting covenant. Therefore shall a curse devour the earth, and the inhabitants thereof shall sin: and therefore they that dwell therein shall be mad, and few men shall be left. The vintage hath mourned, the vine hath languished away, all the merryhearted have sighed. The mirth of timbrels hath ceased, the noise of them that rejoice is ended, the melody of the harp is silent.

"They shall not drink wine with a song: the drink shall be bitter to them that drink it. The city of vanity is broken down, every house is shut up, no man cometh in. There shall be a crying for wine in the streets: all mirth is forsaken: the joy of the earth is gone away. Desolation is left in the city, and calamity shall oppress the gates. For it shall be thus in the midst of the earth, in the midst of the people, as if a few olives, that remain, should be shaken out of the olive tree: or grapes, when the vintage is ended. Fear, and the pit, and the snare are upon thee, O thou inhabitant of the earth (Is. 24:1ff).

8d. "In the latter days . . . it is a people that provoketh to wrath, and lying children, children that will not hear the law of God. Who say to the seers: See not: and to them that behold: Behold not for us those things that are right: speak unto us pleasant things, see errors for us. Take away from me the way, turn away the path from me, let the Holy One of Israel cease from before us . . . You have rejected this word, and have trusted in oppression and tumult" (Is. 30:8 ff).

8e. "And now what have I here, saith the Lord: for my people is taken away gratis. They that rule over them treat them unjustly, saith the Lord, and my name is continually blasphemed all the day long" (Is. 52:5).

8f. "In sinning and lying against the Lord: and we have turned away so they went not after our God, but spoke calumny and transgression: we have conceived, and uttered from the heart, words of falsehood. And judgment is turned away backward and justice hath stood far off: because truth hath fallen down in the street, and equity could not come in. And truth hath been forgotten: and he that departed from evil, lay open to be a prey: and the Lord saw, and it appeared evil in his eyes, because there is no judgment" (Is. 59: 13-15).

9a. "From the least of them even to the greatest, all are given to covetousness: and from the prophet even to the priest, all are given to deceit. And they healed the breach of the daughter of my people disgracefully, saying: Peace, peace: and there was no peace" (Jer. 6:13-14).

9b. "And the Lord said to me: The prophets prophesy falsely in my name: I sent them not, neither have I commanded them, nor have I spoken to them: they prophesy unto you a lying vision, and divination and deceit, and the seduction of their own heart" (Jer. 14:14).

9c. "I have heard what the prophets said, that prophesy lies in my name, and say: I have dreamed, I have dreamed. How long shall this be in the heart of the prophets that prophesy lies, and that prophesy the delusions of their own heart? Who seek to make my people forget my name through their dreams, which they tell every man to his neighbour: as their fathers forgot my name for Baal" (Jer. 23:25-28).

9d. "Thus saith the Lord of hosts: Behold evil shall go forth from nation to nation: and a great whirlwind shall go forth from the ends of the earth. And the slain of the Lord shall be at that day from one end of the earth even to the other end thereof: they shall not be lamented, and they shall not be gathered up, nor buried: they shall lie as dung upon the face of the earth. Howl, ye shepherds, and cry: and sprinkle yourselves with ashes, ye leaders of the flock: for the days of your slaughter and your dispersion are accomplished, and you shall fall like precious vessels. And the shepherds shall have no way to flee, nor the leaders of the flock to save themselves. A voice of the cry of the shepherds, and a howling of the prin-

cipal of the flock: because the Lord hath wasted their pastures.
And the fields of peace have been silent because of the fierce
anger of the Lord. He hath forsaken his covert as the lion, for
the land is laid waste because of the wrath of the dove, and
because of the fierce anger of the Lord" (Jer. 25:32-38).

9e. "Harken not to the words of the prophets that say to
you: You shall not serve the King of Babylon: for they tell
you a lie. For I have not sent them, saith the Lord: and they
prophesy in my name falsely: to drive you out, and that you
may perish, both you, and the prophets that prophesy to you"
(Jer. 27:14-15).

9f. "For thus saith the Lord of hosts, the God of Israel:
Let not your prophets that are in the midst of you, and your
diviners deceive you: and give no heed to your dreams which
you dream: for they prophesy falsely to you in my name: and
I have not sent them, saith the Lord" (Jer. 29:8-9).

9g. "For there shall be a day, in which the watchmen on
mount Ephraim, shall cry: Arise, and let us go up to Sion to
the Lord our God, For thus saith the Lord: Rejoice ye in the
joy of Jacob, and neigh before the head of the Gentiles: shout
ye, and sing, and say: Save, O Lord, thy people, the remnant
of Israel. Behold I will bring them from the north country and
will gather them from the ends of the earth: and among them
shall be the blind, and the lame, the woman with child, and
she that is bringing forth, together, a great company of them
returning hither. They shall come with weeping: and I will
bring them back in mercy: and I will bring them through the
torrents of waters in a right way, and they shall not stumble
in it: for I am a father to Israel, and Ephraim is my first born.
Hear the word of the Lord, O ye nations, and declare it in the
islands that are afar off, and say: He that scattered Israel will
gather him: and he will keep him as the shepherd doth his
flock. For the Lord hath redeemed Jacob, and delivered him
out of the hand of one that was mightier than he. And they
shall come, and shall give praise in Mount Sion: and they shall

flow together to the good things of the Lord, for the corn, and wine, and oil, and the increase of cattle and herbs, and their soul shall be as a watered garden, and they shall be hungry no more. Then shall the virgin rejoice in the dance, the young men and old men together: and I will turn their mourning into joy, and will comfort them, and make them joyful after their sorrow. And I will fill the soul of the priests with fatness: and my people shall be filled with my good things, saith the Lord" (Jer. 31:6-14).

9h. "Every man is become foolish by his knowledge: (the so-called 'learned men' of our day are here artly portrayed) every founder is confounded by his idol, for what he hath cast is a lie, and there is no breath in them. They are vain works, and worthy to be laughed at, in the time of their visitation they shall perish" (Jer. 51:17-18).

9i. "Thou dashest together for me the weapons of war, and with thee I will dash nations together, and with thee I will destroy kingdoms: And with thee I will break in pieces the horse, and his rider, and with thee I will break in pieces the chariot, and him that getteth up into it: and with thee I will break in pieces man and woman and with thee I will break in pieces the old man and the child, and with thee I will break in pieces the young man and the virgin: And with thee I will break in pieces the shepherd and his flock, and with thee I will break in pieces the husbandman and his yoke of oxen, and with thee I will break in pieces captains and rulers. Behold I come against thee, thou destroying mountain, saith the Lord, which corruptest the whole earth; and I will stretch out my hand upon thee, and will roll thee down from the rocks, and will make thee a burnt mountain" (Jer. 51:20-23, 25).

10. "And they shall turn away themselves from their stiff neck, and from their wicked deeds: for they shall remember the way of their fathers, that sinned against me. And I will bring them back again into the land which I promised with an oath to their fathers, Abraham, Isaac, and Jacob, and they shall be

masters thereof: and I will multiply them, and they shall not be diminished. And I will make with them another covenant that shall be everlasting, to be their God, and they shall be my people: and I will no more remove my people, the Children of Israel, out of the land that I have given them" (Bar. 2: 33-35).

11a. "And I scattered them among the nations, and they are dispersed through the countries: I have judged them according to their ways, and their devices. And when they entered among the nations whither they went, they profaned My holy name, when it was said of them: This is the people of the Lord, and they are come forth out of his land (Ez. 36:19-20).

11b. "Thus saith the Lord God: Woe to the foolish prophets that follow their own spirit, and see nothing. They see vain things, and they foretell lies, saying: The Lord saith: whereas the Lord hath not sent them: and they have persisted to confirm what they have said. Because they have deceived my people (Jews), saying: Peace and there is no peace: and the people built up a wall, and they daubed it with dirt without straw. And they violated me among my people, for a handful of ley, and a piece of bread, to kill souls which should not die, and to save souls alive which should not live, telling lies to my people that believe lies. Because with lies you have made the heart of the just to mourn, whom I have not made sorrowful: and have strengthened the hands of the wicked, that he should not return from his evil way, and live" (Ez. 13:3, 6, 10, 19, 22).

11c. "Son of man, when a land shall sin against me, so as to transgress grievously, I will stretch forth my hand upon it and will break the staff of the bread thereof: and I will send famine upon it, and will destroy man and beast out of it. And if I shall bring mischievous beasts also upon the land to waste it, and it be desolate, so that there is none than can pass because of the beasts. . . . I bring the sword upon that land, and say to the sword: Pass through the land: and I destroy man and beast out of it . . . I also send the pestilence upon that land, and pour out my indignation upon it in blood, to cut off from it man and beast" (Ez. 14:13, 15, 17, 19).

11d. "And thou shalt say to them: Thus saith the Lord God: Behold I will take the children of Israel from the midst of the nations whither they are gone: and I will gather them on every side, and will bring them to their own land. And I will make them one nation in the land on the mountains of Israel, and one king shall be king over them all: and they shall no more be two nations, neither shall they be divided any more into two kingdoms. Nor shall they be defiled any more with their idols, nor with their abominations, nor with all their iniquities: and I will save them out of all the places in which they have sinned, and I will cleanse them: and they shall be my people, and I will be their God" (Ez. 37:21-23).

12a. "Thus thou sawest, till a stone was cut out of a mountain without hands: and it struck the statue upon the feet thereof that were of iron and of clay, and broke them in pieces. Then was the iron, the clay, the brass, the silver, and the gold broken to pieces together, and became like the chaff of a summer's thrashing floor, and they were carried away by the wind, and there was no place found for them: but the stone that struck the statue, became a great mountain, and filled the whole earth. . . . But in the days of those kingdoms the God of heaven will set up a kingdom that shall never be destroyed, and his kingdom shall not be delivered up to another people, and it shall break in pieces, and shall consume all these kingdoms, and itself shall stand forever. According as thou sawest that the stone was cut out of the mountain without hands, and broke in pieces, the clay, and the iron, and the brass, and the silver, and the gold, the great God hath shewn the king what shall come to pass hereafter, and the dream is true, and the interpretation thereof is faithful" (Dan. 2:34-35; 44-45).

12b. "The king of the south being provoked shall go forth, and shall fight against the king of the north, and shall prepare an exceeding great multitude, and a multitude shall be given into his hand. And he shall take a multitude, and his heart shall be lifted up, and he shall cast down many thousands: but he shall not prevail. For the king of the north shall return and shall prepare a multitude much greater than before; and in the end of times and years, he shall come in haste with a great army, and much riches. And in those times many shall rise up against the king of the south, and the children of prevaricators of thy people shall lift up themselves to fulfill the vision, and they shall fall. And the king of the north shall come, and shall cast up a mount, and shall take the best fenced cities: and the arms of the south shall not withstand, and his chosen ones shall rise up to resist, and they shall not have strength. And he shall come upon him and do, according to his pleasure, and there shall be none to stand against his face: and he shall stand in the glorious land, and it shall be consumed by his hand. And he shall set his face to come to possess all his kingdom, and he shall make upright conditions with him, and he shall give him a daughter of women, to overthrow it; and she shall not stand, neither shall she be for him. And he shall turn his face to the islands, and shall take many: and he shall cause the prince of his reproach to cease, and his reproach shall be turned upon him. And he shall turn his face to the empire of his own land and he shall stumble, and fall, and shall not be found" (Dan. 11:11-19).

13. "For the children of Israel shall sit many days without king, and without prince, and without sacrifice, and without altar, and without ephod, and without theraphim. And after this the children of Israel shall return, and shall seek the Lord their God, and David their king: and they shall fear the Lord, and his goodness in the last days" (Osee 3:4-5).

14a. "The day of the Lord cometh, because it is nigh at hand. A day of darkness, and of gloominess, a day of clouds and whirlwinds: a numerous and strong people as the morning spread upon the mountains: the like to it hath not been

from the beginning, nor shall be after it even to the years of
generation and generation. Before the face thereof a devouring
fire, and behind it a burning flame: the land is like a garden
of pleasure before it, and behind it a desolate wilderness, neither
is there any one that can escape it. The appearance of them
is as the appearance of horses, and they shall run like horsemen.
They shall leap like the noise of chariots upon the tops of mountains, like the noise of a flame of fire devouring the stubble,
as a strong people prepared to battle. At their presence the people
shall be in grievous pains: all faces shall be made like a kettle.
They shall run like valiant men: like men of war they shall
scale the wall: the men shall march every one on his way, and
they shall not turn aside from their ranks. No one shall press
upon his brother: they shall walk every one in his path: yea,
and they shall fall through the windows and shall take no
harm. They shall enter into the city: they shall run upon the
wall, they shall climb up the houses, they shall come in at the
windows as a thief. At their presence the earth hath trembled,
the heavens are moved: the sun and moon are darkened, and
the stars have withdrawn their shining. And the Lord hath
uttered his voice before the face of his army: for his armies are
exceeding great, for they are strong and execute his word: for
the day of the Lord is great and very terrible: and who can
stand it?" (Joel 2:1b-11).

14b. "And you O children of Sion rejoice, and be joyful
in the Lord your God: because he hath given you a teacher
of justice, and he will make the early and the latter rain to come
down to you as in the beginning. And the floors shall be filled
with wheat, and the presses shall overflow with wine and oil.
And I will restore to you the ears which the locust, and the
bruchus, and the mildew, and the palmerworm have eaten;
my great host which I sent upon you. And you shall eat in
plenty, and shall be filled: and you shall praise the name of
the Lord your God, who hath done wonders with you, and
my people shall not be confounded for ever" (Joel 2:23-26).

14c. "And I will show wonders in heaven; and in earth, blood, and fire, and vapor of smoke. The sun shall be turned into darkness, and the moon into blood: before the great and dreadful day of the Lord doth come. Proclaim ye this among the nations: prepare war, rouse up the strong: let them come, let all the men of war come up. Cut your ploughshares into swords, and your spades into spears. Let the weak say: I am strong" (Joel 2:30-31; 3:9-10).

15a. "Therefore because you robbed the poor, and took the choice prey from him: you shall build houses with square stone, and shall not dwell in them: you shall plant most delightful vineyards, and shall not drink the wine of them. Because I know your manifold crimes, and your grievous sins: enemies of the just, taking bribes, and oppressing the poor in the gate. Therefore the prudent shall keep silence at that time, for it is an evil time" (Amos 5:11-13).

15b. "Behold the days come, saith the Lord, and I will send forth a famine into the land: not a famine of bread, nor a thirst of water, but of hearing the word of the Lord. And they shall move from sea to sea, and from the north to the east: they shall go about seeking the word of the Lord, and shall not find it. In that day the fair virgins, and the young men shall faint for thirst" (Amos 8:11-13).

15c. "In that day I will raise up the tabernacle of David, that is fallen: and I will close up the breaches of the walls thereof, and repair what was fallen: and I will rebuild it as in the days of old. That they may possess the remnant of Edom, and all nations, because my name is invoked upon them: saith the Lord that doth these things. Behold the days come, saith the Lord, when the ploughman shall overtake the reaper, and the treader of grapes him that soweth seed: and the mountains shall drop sweetness, and every hill shall be tilled. And I will bring back the captivity of my people Israel: and they shall build the abandoned cities, and inhabit them: and they shall plant vineyards, and drink the wine of them: and shall make gardens, and eat the fruits of them. And I will plant them upon their own land: and I will no more pluck them out of their land which I have given them, saith the Lord thy God" (Amos 9:11-14).

16a. "Then shall they cry to the Lord, and he will not hear them: and he will hide his face from them at that time, as they have behaved wickedly in their devices. Thus saith the Lord concerning the prophets that make my people err: that bite with their teeth, and preach peace: and if a man give not something into their mouth, they prepare war against him. Therefore night shall be to you instead of vision, and darkness to you instead of divination: and the sun shall go down upon the prophets, and the day shall be darkened over them. And they shall be confounded that see visions, and the diviners shall be confounded: and they shall all cover their faces, because there is no answer of God" (Mich. 3:4-7).

16b. "And it shall come to pass in the last days, that the mountain of the house of the Lord shall be prepared in the top of the mountains, and high above the hills: and people shall flow to it" (Mich. 4:1).

16c. "In that day, saith the Lord, I will gather up her that halteth: and her that I had cast out, I will gather up; and her whom I had afflicted. And I will make her that halted a remnant: and her that hath been afflicted, a mighty nation: and the Lord will reign over them in mount Sion, from this time now and for ever" (Mich. 4:6-7).

17a. "Thus saith the Lord of hosts: Behold I will save my people from the land of the east, and from the land of the going down of the sun. And I will bring them, and they shall dwell in the midst of Jerusalem: and they shall be my people, and I will be their God in truth and in justice" (Zach. 8:7-8).

17b. "Behold a man, the Orient is his name: and under him shall he spring up, and shall build a temple to the Lord. Yea, he shall build a temple to the Lord: and he shall bear

the glory, and shall sit, and rule upon his throne: and he shall
be a priest upon his throne, and the counsel of peace shall be
between them both" (Zach. 6:12-13).

18. "And when Jeremias came hither he found a hollow
cave: and he carried in thither the tabernacle, and the ark, and
the altar of incense, and so stopped the door. Then some of
them that followed him, came up to mark the place: but they
could not find it. And when Jeremias perceived it, he blamed
them, saying: The place shall be unknown, till God gather
together the congregation of the people, and receive them to
mercy" (2 Mac. 2:5-7).

New Testament

19a. "And you shall be brought before governors, and
before kings for my sake, for a testimony to them and to the
Gentiles: But when they shall deliver you up, take no thought
how or what to speak, for it shall be given you in that hour
what to speak. For it is not you that speak, but the Spirit of
your Father that speaketh in you. The brother also shall deliver
up the brother to death, and the father the son, and the children
shall rise up against their parents, and shall put them to death.
And you shall be hated by all men for my name's sake: but
he that shall persevere unto the end, he shall be saved. And
when they shall persecute you in this city, flee into another.
Amen, I say to you, you shall not finish all the cities of Israel,
till the Son of man come" (Mat. 10:18-23).

19b. "(Christ) answering said to them: An evil and
adulterous generation seeketh a sign: and a sign shall not be
given it, but the sign of Jonas the prophet" (Mat. 12:39).

19c. "Amen, I say to you, all these things shall come upon
this generation" (Mat. 23:36).

19d. "Take care that no one misleads you. For many
will come in My Name, asserting, 'I am the Christ,' and will
lead many astray . . . Then if anyone should say to you, 'Look,
here is the Christ!' or, 'There!' do not believe it. For false
christs and false prophets shall rise and exhibit great signs and

portents, so as to mislead, if possible, even the elect. Lo, I
have forewarned you. If, therefore, they tell you, 'Look, he
is in the desert!' do not go out; 'Look, he is in the private
chamber!' do not believe it. (Mat. 24:4ff).

19e. "Then shall they deliver you up to be afflicted and
shall put you to death: and you shall be hated by all nations
for my name's sake. And then many shall fall away, and shall
betray one another: and shall hate one another. And many
false prophets shall rise, and shall lead many astray. And
because iniquity hath abounded, the charity of many shall grow
cold" (Mat. 24:9-12).

20a. "When the Son of Man comes, will He find, do you
think, faith on the earth?" (Lk. 18:8).

20b. "And they will say to you: See here, and see there.
Go ye not after, nor follow them: For as the lightning that
lighteneth from under heaven, shineth unto the parts that are
under heaven, so shall the Son of man be in His day" (Lk.
17:23-24).

20c. "And they asked Him, 'Master, when shall this be?
and what shall be the sign when this is about to occur?' 'Take
care not to be misled,' was His reply: 'For many will come
in My Name, asserting, 'I am the One,' and 'The time is at
hand;' do not go after them. And when you hear of wars and
insurrections do not be terrified; these events must occur, but
the end will not come immediately. Nation shall rise against
nation, and empire against empire, and there shall be great
earthquakes, and pestilences and famines in various places"
(Lk. 21:7-11).

20d. "Henceforth there will be five divided in one house,
three against two, and two against three. They shall be divided,
father against son, and son against father; mother against
daughter and daughter against mother; mother-in-law against
her daughter-in-law, and daughter-in-law against her mother-
in-law" (Lk. 12:52-53).

20e. "But before all these things they will lay their hands

on you, and persecute you, delivering you up to the synagogues and into prisons, dragging you before kings and governors, for my name's sake" (Lk. 21:12).

20f. "Jerusalem shall be trodden down by the Gentiles till the times of the nations be fulfilled" (Lk. 21:24b).

21. "They will put you out of the synagogues; yea, the hour cometh that whosoever killeth you, will think that he doth a service to God. And these things will they do to you; because they have not known the Father, nor me. But these things I have told you, that when the hour shall come, you remember that I told you of them" (John 16:2-4).

22. "I say then: Hath God cast away his people? God forbid. For I also am an Israelite of the seed of Abraham, of the tribe of Benjamin. God hath not cast away his people, which he foreknew. Know you not what the scripture saith of Elias; how he called on God against Israel, Lord, they have slain thy prophets, they have dug down thy altars; and I am left alone, and they seek my life. But what saith the divine answer to him? I have left me seven thousand men, that have not bowed their knees to Baal. Even so then at this present time also, there is a remnant saved according to the election of grace. And if by grace, it is not now by works: otherwise grace is no more grace. What then? That which Israel sought, he hath not obtained: but the election hath obtained it; and the rest have been blinded. As it is written: God hath given them the spirit of insensibility; eyes that they should not see; and ears that they should not hear, until this present day. And David saith: Let their table be made a snare, and a trap, and a stumbling-block, and a recompense unto them. Let their eyes be darkened, that they may not see: and bow down their back always. I say then, have they so stumbled, that they should fall? God forbid. But by their offence, salvation is come to the Gentiles, that they may be emulous of them. Now if the offence of them be the riches of the world, and the diminution of them, the riches of the Gentiles; how much more the

fullness of them? For I say to you, Gentiles: as long indeed as I am the apostle of the Gentiles, I will honor my ministry. If, by any means, I may provoke to emulation them who are my flesh, and may save some of them. For if the loss of them (Jews) be the reconciliation of the world, what shall the receiving of them be, but life from the dead? For if the first fruit be holy, so is the lump also: and if the root be holy, so are the branches. And if some of the branches be broken, and thou, being a wild olive, art ingrafted in them, and art made partaker of the root, and of the fatness of the olive tree, boast not against the branches. But if thou boast, thou bearest not the root, but the root thee. Thou wilt say then: The branches were broken off, that I might be grafted in. Well: because of unbelief they were broken off. But thou standest by faith: be not highminded, but fear. For if God hath not spared the natural branches, fear lest perhaps he also spare not thee. See then the goodness and the severity of God: towards them indeed that are fallen, the severity; but towards thee, the goodness of God, if thou abide in goodness, otherwise thou also shalt be cut off. And they also, if they abide not still in unbelief, shall be grafted in: for God is able to graft them in again. For if thou were cut out of the wild olive tree, which is natural to thee; and contrary to nature, were grafted into the good olive tree; how much more shall they that are the natural branches, be grafted into their own olive tree? For I would not have you ignorant, brethren, of this mystery (lest you should be wise in your own conceits), that blindness in part has happened in Israel, until the fulness of the Gentiles should come in. And so all Israel should be saved, as it is written: There shall come out of Sion, he that shall deliver, and shall turn away ungodliness from Jacob. And this is to them my covenant: when I shall take away their sins. As concerning the gospel, indeed, they are enemies for your sake, but as touching the election, they are most dear for the sake of the fathers. For the gifts and the calling of God are without repentance. For as you also in times past did not believe God, but now have obtained mercy, through their unbelief; so these also now have not believed, for your mercy, that they also may obtain mercy. For God hath concluded all in unbelief, that he may have mercy on all" (Rom. 11:1-32).

23. "Of the times and moments, brethren, you need not, that we should write to you; For yourselves know perfectly, that the day of the Lord shall so come, as a thief in the night. For when they shall say, peace and security: then shall sudden destruction come upon them, as the pains upon her that is with child and they shall not escape" (1 Thes. 5:1-3).

24. "For the mystery of iniquity already worketh; only that he who now holdeth, do hold, (St. Michael?) until he be taken out of the way. And then the wicked one shall be revealed . . . and his coming is according to the working of Satan with all power and signs and lying wonders, and with all wicked deception to those who are perishing. For they have not received the love of truth that they might be saved. Therefore God shall send them the operation of error, to believe lying: That all may be judged who have not believed the truth, but have consented to iniquity" (2 Thes. 2:7-12)

25. "Let no one deceive you with empty arguments; for on account of these things the wrath of God is coming upon the sons of disobedience" (Eph. 5:6).

26. "Let no man seduce you, willing in humility, and religion of angels, walking in the things which he hath not seen, in vain puffed up by the sense of his flesh" (Col. 2:18).

27a. "The Spirit expressly says that in the last times some will depart from the faith, giving assent to seducing spirits and to doctrines of demons through the hypocrisy of men who speak lies, whose consciences are seared, who forbid marriage, and command abstinence from foods which God created to be partaken of with thanksgiving (1 Tim. 4:1-4) . . . O Timothy! guard the deposit! Avoid the profane and fruitless discussions and disputations of knowledge falsely so styled. By professing it some have missed the mark as regards the faith (1 Tim. 6:20-21) . . . "There shall come a time when people will not endure the sound doctrine; but having itching ears they will, in accordance with their own desires, accumulate teachers for themselves, and will turn away their ears from the truth, and stray off after fictions (2 Tim. 4:3-4) . . . In the last days there shall come terrible times. For men shall be lovers of self, fond of money, pretentious, arrogant, railers, disobedient to parents, ungrateful, impious, without natural affection, implacable, slanderers; profligates, untamed, hostile to good, traitors, headstrong, befogged with conceit; lovers of pleasure instead of lovers of God, holding a semblance of religion after having denied its power (2 Tim. 3:1-5) . . . Among such are those who creep into families, and capture silly women crushed with sins and led by various impulses" (2 Tim. 3:6).

27b. "And all that will live godly in Christ Jesus, shall suffer persecution. But evil men and seducers shall grow worse and worse: erring, and driving into error" (2 Tim. 3:12-13).

28. "It is important that you should know this: that in the last days scoffers will come with mockery, men living in accordance with their own lusts" (2 Pet. 3:3).

29a. "Little children, it is the last hour and as you have heard that Anti-Christ cometh, even now there are become many Anti-Christs: whereby we know that it is the last hour" (1 Jn. 2:18).

29b. "Dearly beloved, believe not every spirit, but try the spirits if they be of God: because many false prophets are gone out into the world" (1 Jn. 4:1).

30. "For many seducers are gone out into the world, who confess not that Jesus Christ is come in the flesh: this is a seducer and an Anti-Christ" (2 Jn. 7).

31. "Now of these Enoch also, the seventh from Adam, prophesied, saying: Behold, the Lord cometh with thousands of his saints, to execute judgment upon all, and to prove all the ungodly for all the works of their ungodliness, whereby

they have done ungodly, and of all the hard things which
ungodly sinners have spoken against God. These are murmurers, full of complaints, walking according to their own desires,
and their mouth speaketh proud things, admiring persons for
gain's sake. But you, my dearly beloved, be mindful of the
words which have been spoken before the apostles of our Lord
Jesus Christ, Who told you, that in the last time there should
come mockers, walking according to their own desires in un-
godlinesses. These are they, who separate themselves, sensual
men, having not the spirit" (Ju. 14-19).

32a. "And when he had opened the fifth seal, I saw under
the altar the souls of them that were slain for the word of God,
and for the testimony which they held. And they cried with
a loud voice, saying: How long O Lord, holy and true, dost
thou not judge and revenge our blood on them that dwell on
earth? And white robes were given to every one of them one;
and it was said to them, that they should rest for a little time,
till their fellow servants, and their brethren, who are to be
slain, even as they, should be filled up"[1]

"I saw when He opened the sixth seal; for there was a great
earthquake, and the sun became black as haircloth, and the
whole moon became like blood; and the stars of the sky fell
upon the earth, as a fig tree casts its belated figs when it is shaken
by a strong wind"[2] (Apoc. 6:9-13).

32b. "They were commanded not to injure the grass of
the earth, nor any verdure, nor any tree; but only such men
as have not the seal of God upon their foreheads. And it was
granted them, not to kill, but to torment for five months (Communistic rule?); and their torture was like the torture of a scor-
pion when it stings a man. And during those days men will
seek death and shall by no means find it, and shall long to die,
and death shall fly from them. And the shapes of the locusts
were like horses prepared for war;" and on their heads they wore

---

[1]For Berry's Commentary see No. 180a.
[2]For Berry's Commentary see No. 180b.

as it were, crowns like gold; and their faces were like the faces of men; and they had tresses of women; while their teeth were like the teeth of lions. And they had breastplates of iron; and the roar of their wings was like the roar of chariots of many horses charging to battle. And they have tails such as scorpions have, and stings; and in their tails is their power to hurt mankind for five months. They have over them a king—the Angel of the Fathomless Pit. His name in Hebrew is Abaddon; and in the Greek he has the name Appollyon"

"The first Woe hath passed[2]; behold,—hereafter two Woes are still to come. And the sixth angel sounded his trumpet, and I heard a single voice from the four horns of the golden altar which is before God; and it said to the sixth angel who had the trumpet: 'Loose the four angels who are bound on the great river Euphrates.' Then were loosed the four angels who had been held ready for the hour and day and month and year, in order that you should kill the third part of men. And the number of the troops of the cavalry was twenty thousand times ten thousand; I heard the number thereof. And this is the manner after which the horses and they that sat upon them appeared in my vision: they wore breastplates the colour of fire, and of hyacinth and of sulphur; and the heads of the horses were as heads of lions, and out of their mouths issue fire and smoke and sulphur. By these three plagues were killed the third part of men, by the fire, by the smoke, and by sulphur issuing from their mouths. For the power of the horses is in their mouth and in their tails; for their tails are like serpents, with heads, and by means of them they do harm. And the other men, who were not killed by these plagues, did not repent of the works of their hands, and cease adoring the devils and idols of gold and silver and bronze and stone and wood, which can neither see nor hear nor walk; and they did not repent of their murders, nor of their enchantments, nor of their impurity, nor of their thefts" (Apoc. 9:4-21).

---

[1]For Berry's Commentary see No. 180c
[2]For Berry's Commentary see No. 180d

32c. "Then I saw another mighty Angel descending out of heaven robed in a cloud; and the rainbow was upon his head; and his countenance was like the sun, and his feet like pillars of fire; and he held in his hand a small open book. And he set his right foot upon the sea, and his left upon the land. And he cried with a great voice as a lion roars; and when he cried the seven thunders uttered their voices.[1] And when the seven thunders uttered their voices I was about to write; but I heard a voice from heaven saying to me, 'Seal up the things the seven thunders have uttered, and write them not.' Then the Angel whom I saw standing upon the sea and upon the land lifted up his right hand to heaven, and swore by Him who lives in the eternities of the eternities, who created the heaven and the things therein, that there shall be no more delay, but that in the days of the voice of the seventh Angel, when he is about to sound, then shall the mystery of God achieve its full perfection, as He declared to his servants the prophets.

"Then the voice which I had heard from heaven again spoke to me, saying, 'Go, take the little book which is open in the hand of the angel who stands on the sea and on the land.' So I went to the Angel, telling him to give me the Little Book. And he said to me, 'Take it and devour it; and it shall embitter thy stomach, but in thy mouth it shall be sweet as honey.' So I took the little book out of the Angel's hand and devoured it; and it was in my mouth as sweet as honey, but when I had eaten it my stomach was embittered" (Apoc. 10:1-10).

32d. "Then I looked, and saw a white cloud; and upon the cloud one like a Son of Man sitting, wearing a golden crown upon His head and holding a sharp sickle in His hand. And another Angel came out of the temple calling with a great voice to the One sitting upon the cloud, 'Thrust in thy sickle and reap; for the harvest-time to reap is come, for the harvest of

---

[1]For Berry's Commentary see No. 180e; for Holzhauser's, No. 129c.

the earth is overripe.' And the One sitting upon the cloud
swung His sickle over the earth; and the earth was reaped.

"Then another Angel came out of the temple which is in
heaven, and he too had a sharp sickle. And another Angel
came from the altar—he that has power over fire—and called
with a great voice to the one who had the sharp sickle, saying,
'Thrust in thy sharp sickle, and strip off the clusters of the
vine of the earth; for its grapes are ripe.' And the Angel swung
his sickle over the earth, and cast the vintage into the great wine
press of wrath of God. And the wine press was trodden outside
the city; and blood issued from the wine press up to the horses'
bridles as far as two hundred miles"[1]   (Apoc. 14:14-20).

PROPHECIES FROM FATHERS OF THE CHURCH

33. *Didache and Apostolic Constitutions* (90-100)

"In the last days false prophets shall be multiplied, and
such as corrupt the word, and the sheep shall be changed into
wolves, and love into hatred: for through the abounding of
iniquity the love of many shall wax cold. For men shall hate,
and persecute, and betray one another."

34. *Pastor Hermes* (2nd century)

"When these things thus come to pass then He who is
Lord, looking upon what is done and opposing His own will
to the disorder, He cleanses the wickedness, partly by inundating
the world with much water, and partly burning it with most
rapid fire, and sometimes pressing it with wars and pestilences,
He will bring His world to its ancient state."

34a. *Hyppolitus* (d. 235)

"The Great French Monarch, who shall subject all the
East, shall come around the end of the world."

35. *St. Augustine* (d 430)

"Jacob was also called Israel, which name his progeny
bore after him. This name the Angel that wrestled with him

---

[1]For Berry's Commentary See No. 180f; for Holzhauser's No. 129d.

as he returned from Mesopotamia gave, him being an evident
type of Christ; for whereas Jacob prevailed against him by his
own consent, to form the mystery, is signified the passion of
Christ wherein the Jews seemed to prevail against Him. And
yet Jacob obtained a blessing from him whom he had overcome; and the changing of his name was that blessing; for
Israel is as much as 'seeing God' which shall come to pass in
the end of the world."

36. *St. Chrysostom*

"The world will be faithless and degenerate after the birth
of Anti-Christ."

37. *St. Gregory the Great*

"After the birth of Anti-Christ most of mankind will be
such as corrupt the word; and the sheep shall be changed into
godless or fallen into heresy. Churches will be empty and
dilapidated, priests will have little zeal for souls and pious
people will be few. Most people will be given up to all imag-
inable vices."

38. *Lactantius*

"As the end of this world approaches, the condition of
human affairs must undergo a change, and through the prevalence of wickedness, become worse. After the birth of Anti-
Christ most people will possess something that they stole, they
will be greedy, godless, selfish, hard-hearted. Justice will have
disappeared from the earth, man will neither know law, order
nor discipline. Murderers and robbers will fill the whole world.
Priests will act like wolves, care little for spiritual things and live
with women. Impiousness, lust and lasciviousness will rule the
world. For righteousness will so decrease, and impiety, avarice,
desire, and lust will so greatly increase, that if there shall then
happen to be any good men, they will be a prey to the wicked,
and will be harassed on all sides by the unrighteous; while the
wicked alone will be in opulence, and the good will be afflicted
in all calumnies and want. All justice will be confounded and
the laws will be destroyed. No one will then have anything

except that which has been gained or defended by the hand: boldness and violence will possess all things. There will be no faith among men, nor peace, nor kindness, nor shame, nor truth; and thus also there will be neither security, nor government nor any rest from evils. For all the earth will be in a state of tumult. The time of 'nation fighting against nation' will occur after the birth of Anti-Christ, (and then) the world shall be despoiled of beauty through the destruction of men.

"When the close of the times draws nigh, a great prophet (Henoch or Elias?) shall be sent from God to turn men to the knowledge of God, and he shall receive the power of doing wonderful things. Wherever men shall not hear him, he will shut up the heaven and cause it to withhold its rains; he will turn their water into blood, and torment them with thirst and hunger; and if any one shall endeavor to injure him, fire shall come forth out of his mouth, and shall burn that man. By these prodigies and powers he shall turn many to the worship of God: and when his works shall be accomplished, another king shall arise out of Syria, born from an evil spirit, the overthrower and destroyer of the human race" (Anti-Christ).

39. St. Jerome

"The destruction of the Holy City, the ruin of the House of God, the dispersion of the chosen people into all the kingdoms of the earth, and their continued existence as a nation, notwithstanding every attempt to exterminate them, or to compel them to forsake those ordinances which distinguish them to this very day from all other nations is emphatically one of the strongest evidences we can have of the truth of the Bible and of our religion. Jerusalem was indeed once a great city, and the Temple magnificent; but the Jews themselves were greater than either; hence, while the two former have been given over to spoliation, the latter having been wonderfully (miraculously) preserved. The annals of the world do not contain anything so remarkable in human experience, so greatly surpassing human power and human prescience. Exiled and dispersed, reviled and persecuted, oppressed and suffering, often denied the commonest rights of humanity, and still more often made the victim of ruthless fanaticism and bigoted prejudice, the Jews are divinely preserved for a purpose worthy of a God."

40. *St. Methodius* (385)

"A time will come when the enemies of Christ will boast: 'We have subjected the earth and all its inhabitants, and the Christians cannot escape our hands.' Then a Roman emperor will rise in great fury against them . . . Drawing his sword, he will fall upon the foes of Christianity and crush them. Then peace and quiet will reign on earth, and the priests will be relieved of all their anxieties.

"In the last period Christians will not appreciate the great grace of God who provided a Great Monarch, a long duration of peace, a splendid fertility of the earth. They will be very ungrateful, lead a sinful life, in pride, vanity, unchastity, frivolity, hatred, avarice, gluttony and many other vices that the sins of men will stink more than a pestilence before God. Many men will doubt whether the Catholic faith is the true and only saving one and whether the Jews are perhaps correct when they still expect the Messias. Many will be the false teachings and resultant bewilderment. The just God will in consequence give Lucifer and all his devils power to come on earth and tempt his godless creatures."

PRIVATE PROPHECIES
Apocraphal Scriptures
Jewish Tradition

41a. "God answered and said unto me: 'Into twelve parts is the end divided, and each one of them is reserved for that which is appointed for it. In the first part there shall be the beginning of commotions. And in the second part there shall be slayings of the great ones. And in the third part the fall of many by death. And in the fourth part the sending of the sword. And in the fifth part famine and the withholding of rain. And in the sixth part earthquakes and terrors" (Bar. 27:1-7).

41b. "For that time shall arise which brings affliction; for it shall come and pass by with quick vehemence, and it shall be turbulent coming in the heat of indignation. And it shall come to pass in those days that all the inhabitants of the earth shall be moved one against another, because they know not that My judgment has drawn nigh.

41c. "For there shall not be found many wise at that time, and the intelligent shall be but a few: Moreover, even those who know shall most of all be silent. And there shall be many rumours and tidings not a few, and the doings of phantasmata shall be manifest, and promises not a few be recounted, some of them shall prove idle, and some of them shall be confirmed. And honour shall be turned into shame, and strength humiliated into contempt, and probity destroyed, and beauty shall become ugliness. And many shall say to many at that time: 'Where hath the multitude of intelligence hidden itself, and whither hath the multitude of wisdom removed itself?' And whilst they are meditating these things, then envy shall arise in those who had not thought aught of themselves and passion shall seize him that is peaceful, and many shall be stirred up in anger to injure many, and they shall rouse up armies in order to shed blood, and in the end they shall perish together with them. And it shall come to pass at the self-same time, that a change of times shall manifestly appear to every man, because in all those times they polluted themselves and they practiced oppression, and walked every man in his own works, and remembered not the law of the Mighty One. Therefore a fire shall consume their thoughts, and in flame shall the meditations of their reins be tried: for the Judge shall come and will not tarry. Because each of the inhabitants of the earth knew when he was transgressing. But My law they knew not by reason of their pride. But many shall then assuredly weep, Yea, over the living more than over the dead.' And I answered and said: 'O Adam, what hast thou done to all those who are born from thee?' And what will be said to the first Eve who hearkened to the serpent? For all this multitude are going to corruption, nor is there any numbering of those whom the fire devours." (Bar. 48:31-43).

41d. "Behold! the days come, and it shall be when the time of the age has ripened, and the harvest of its evil and good seeds has come, that the Mighty One will bring upon the earth and its inhabitants and upon its rulers perturbation of spirit and stupor of heart. And they shall hate one another, and provoke one another to fight" (Bar. 70:2-3).

41e. "And when those things which were predicted have come to pass, then shall confusion fall upon all men, and some of them shall fall in battle, and some of them shall perish in anguish, and some of them shall be destroyed by their own. Then the Most High will reveal those peoples whom He has prepared before, and they shall come and make war with the leaders that shall then be left. And it shall come to pass that whosoever gets safe out of the war shall die in the earthquake, and whosoever gets safe out of the earthquake shall be burned by the fire, and whosoever gets safe out of the fire shall be destroyed by famine" (Bar. 70:6-8).

41f. "For all the earth shall devour its inhabitants" (Bar. 70:10).

41g. "If ye so do these things, He will continually remember you, He who always promised on our behalf to those who were more excellent than we, that He will never forget or forsake us, but with much mercy will gather together again those who were dispersed" (Bar. 78:7).

42. "God will again have mercy on them (Jews) and God will bring them back into the land of Israel, and they will again build the house, but not like the first, until the time when the time of the seasons be fulfilled; and afterward they will return, all of them, from their captivity, and build up Jerusalem with honour, and the house of God shall be builded in her, even as the prophets of Israel spake concerning her. And they shall

bless the everlasting God in righteousness. All the children of
Israel that are delivered in those days, remembering God in
truth, shall be gathered together and come to Jerusalem and
shall dwell for ever in the land of Abraham with security, and
it shall be given over to them" (Tobit 14:5, 7).

43. "In the last times your sons will forsake singleness and
will cleave unto insatiable desires; and leaving guilelessness will
draw near to malice; and forsaking the commandments of the
Lord they will cleave unto beliar (Satan); and leaving hus-
bandry they will follow after their own wicked devices" (Test.
Is. 6:1 ss).

44a. "When sin and righteousness, blasphemy and violence
and all kinds of deeds increase, an apostasy in transgression and
uncleanness increase, a great chastisement shall come from
heaven" (Enoch 91: 7).

44b. "Sinners will alter and pervert the words of righteousness in many ways, and will speak wicked words, and lie,
and practice great deceits, and write books concerning their
words" (Enoch 104: 10).

44c. "I saw till the Lord of the sheep brought a new house
greater and loftier than that first, and set it up in the place of
the first which had been folded up: all its pillars were new,
and its ornaments were new and larger than those of the first,
the old one which He had taken away, and all the sheep were
within it" (Enoch 90:29).

45a. "The flame of fire and the wrath against the unrighteous shall not touch him, when it goeth forth from the face of
the Lord against sinners, to destroy all the substance of sinners,
for the mark of God is upon the righteous that they may be
saved. Famine and sword and pestilence shall be far from the
righteous, for they shall flee away from the pious as men pursued in war; but they shall pursue sinners and overtake them,
and they that do lawlessness shall not escape the judgment of
God; as by enemies experienced in war shall they be overtaken,
for the mark of destruction is upon their forehead. And the

inheritance of sinners is destruction and darkness. And their iniquities shall pursue them unto Sheol beneath. Their inheritance shall not be found of their children, for sins shall lay waste the houses of sinners, and sinners shall perish forever in the day of the Lord's judgment, when God visited the earth with His judgment" (Ps. Sol. 15:6-12).

45b. "May God cleanse Israel against the day of mercy and blessing, against the day of choice when He bringeth back His anointed. Blessed shall they be that shall be in those days, in that they shall see the goodness of the Lord which He shall perform for the generation that is to come, under the rod of chastening of the Lord's anointed in the fear of his God, in the spirit of wisdom and righteousness and strength; that he may direct every man in the works of righteousness by the fear of God, that he may establish them all before the Lord, a good generation living in the fear of God in the days of mercy" (Ps. Sol. 18:6-10).

46. "After this they will turn to Me from amongst the Gentiles with all their heart and with all their soul. I will disclose to them abounding peace with righteousness, and I will plant them in this land of uprightness, with all My heart and with all My soul, and they shall be for a blessing and not for a curse, and they shall be the head and not the tail. And I will build My sanctuary in their midst and I will dwell with them, and I will be their God and they shall be My people in truth and righteousness. And I will not forsake them nor fail them; for I am the Lord their God. I know their contrariness and their thoughts and their stiffneckedness, and they will not be obedient till they confess their own sin and the sin of their fathers. And after this they will turn to Me in all uprightness and with all their heart and with all their soul, and I will circumcise the foreskin of their heart and the foreskin of the heart of their seed, and I will create in them a holy spirit, and I will cleanse them so that they shall not turn away from Me from that day unto eternity. And their souls will cleave to Me and

to all My commandments, and they will fulfill My commandments, and I will be their Father and they shall be My children.
And they all shall be called children of the living God, and
every angel and every spirit shall know that I am their Father
in uprightness and righteousness, and that I love them. . . .
The Lord will appear to the eyes of all, and all shall know that
I am the God of Israel and the Father of all the children of
Jacob, and King on Mount Zion for all eternity. And Zion
and Jerusalem shall be holy.' And the angel of the presence
who went before the camp of Israel took the tables of the divisions of the years—from the time of the creation—of the law
and of the testimony of the weeks of the jubilees, according to
the individual years, according to all the number of the jubilees
from the day of the new creation when the heavens and the
earth shall be renewed and all their creation according to the
powers of heaven, and according to all the creation of the earth,
until the sanctuary of the Lord shall be made in Jerusalem on
Mount Zion, and all the luminaries be renewed for healing and
for peace and for blessing for all the elect of Israel, and that
thus it may be from that day and unto all the days of the earth"
(Jubilees 1:15-29).

47a. "Behold, the days come when the inhabitants of earth
shall be seized with great panic, and the way of truth shall be
hidden, and the land be barren of faith. And iniquity shall be
increased above that which thou thyself now seest or that thou
hast heard of long ago" (Ez. 5:1-3).

47b. "Then shall the sun suddenly shine forth by night
and the moon by day; and blood shall trickle forth from wood,
and the stone utter its voice: The people shall be in commotion,
the outgoings of the stars shall change. And one whom the
dwellers of earth do not look for shall wield sovereignty, and
the birds shall take to general flight, and the sea shall cast forth
its fish. And one whom the many do not know will make his
voice heard by night; and all shall hear his voice. And the
earth o'er wide regions shall open, and fire burst forth for a

long period: The wild beasts shall desert their haunts" (Ez. 5:4-6).

47c. "Behold the days come, and it shall be, when I am about to draw nigh to visit the dwellers upon earth, and when I require from the doers of iniquity the penalty of their iniquity, and when the humiliation of Sion shall be complete, and when the Age which is about to pass away shall be sealed, then will I show these signs: the books shall be opened before the face of the firmament, and all see together. And one-year-old children shall speak with their voices; pregnant women shall bring forth untimely births at three or four months, and these shall live and dance. And suddenly shall the sown places appear unsown, and the full storehouses shall suddenly be found empty; and the trumpet shall sound aloud, at which all men, when they hear it, shall be struck with sudden fear. And at that time friends shall war against friends like enemies, the earth shall be stricken with fear together with the dwellers thereon, and the springs of the fountains shall stand still so that for three hours they shall not run" (Ez. 6:18-24).

47d. "For with many afflictions shall they be afflicted that inhabit the world in the last times, because they have walked in great pride" (Ez. 8:50).

47e. "When in the world there shall appear quakings of places, tumult of peoples, schemings of nations, confusion of leaders, disquietude of princes, then shalt thou understand that it is of these things the Most High has spoken since the days that were aforetime from the beginning (Ez. 9:3-4).

47f. "In the last days thereof the Most High will raise up three kings and they shall renew (change) many things therein, and shall exercise lordship over the earth and over the dwellers therein with much oppression, above all those that were before them. Therefore are they called the heads of the eagle: for these are they that shall bring to a head his wickedness, and consummate his end. And whereas thou didst see that the great head disappeared—one of them shall die upon his bed, but yet with pain; but as for the two who remain, the sword shall devour them. For the sword of the one shall devour him that was with him; nevertheless this one also shall fall by the sword in the last days" (Ez. 12:23-28).

47g. "Behold, the days come when the Most High is about to deliver them that are upon the earth. And there shall come astonishment of mind upon the dwellers on earth: and they shall plan to war one against another, city against city, place against place, people against people, and kingdom against kingdom" (Ez. 13:29-31).

48a. "With Abraham thou didst make an everlasting covenant, and didst promise him that thou wouldst never forsake his seed. And thou gavest him Isaac, and to Isaac thou gavest Jacob and Esau. And thou didst set apart Jacob for thyself, but Esau thou didst hate; and Jacob became a great host" (4 Ezra 3:15-16).

48b. "The weaker the world grows through age, so much the more shall evils increase upon the dwellers of the earth. Truth shall withdraw further and falsehood be near at hand" (4 Ezra 4:16-17).

49. "Ye shall have no place that is clean; but ye shall be among the Gentiles a curse and a dispersion until He shall again visit you, and in pity shall receive you through faith and water" (Levi 16:5).

50. "Until the Lord visit you, when with perfect heart ye repent and walk in all His commandments, and He bring you up from captivity among the Gentiles" (Judah 23:5).

51. "Again, through the wickedness of your works, shall ye provoke Him to anger, and ye shall be cast away by Him unto the time of consummation" (Zabulin 9:9).

52. "So when ye return to the Lord ye shall obtain mercy, and He shall bring you into His sanctuary, and He shall give you peace" (Dan. 5:9).

53. "The saints shall rest in Eden, and in the New Jerusalem shall the righteous rejoice, and it shall be unto the glory

of God for ever. And no longer shall Jerusalem endure desolation, nor Israel be led captive; for the Lord shall be in the midst of it living amongst men and the Holy One of Israel shall reign over it" (Dan. 5:12-13).

54. "For he (Satan) knoweth that upon the day on which Israel shall repent the kingdom of the enemy shall be brought to an end. For the very angel of peace shall strengthen Israel, that it fall not into the extremity of evil. And it shall be in the time of the lawlessness of Israel, that the Lord will not depart from them, but will transform them into a nation that doeth His will for none of the angels will be equal unto him. And His name shall be in every place in Israel, and among the Gentiles" (Dan 6:4-7).

55. "The Lord shall scatter them upon the face of the earth, until the compassion of the Lord shall come, a man working righteousness and working mercy unto all them that are afar off, and to them that are near" (Napthali 4:5).

56. "Therefore do ye also, my children, tell these things to your children, that they disobey Him not. For I have known that ye shall assuredly be disobedient, and assuredly act ungodly, not giving heed to the law of God, but to the commandments of men, being corrupted through wickedness. And therefore shall ye be scattered as Gad and Dan my brethren, and ye shall know not your lands, tribe and tongue. But the Lord will gather you together in faith through His tender mercy, and for the sake of Abraham, Isaac, and Jacob" (Asher 7:4-7).

CHRISTIAN APOCRAPHA

57a. "God said: 'First I will make an earthquake for the fall of four-footed beasts and of men; and when you see that brother gives up brother to death, and that children shall rise up against their parents, and that a woman forsakes her own husband, and when nation shall rise up against nation in war, then you will know that the end is near. For then neither brother pities brother, nor man wife, nor children parents, nor friends friends, nor a slave his master, for he who is the adver-

sary of men shall come up from Tartarus (Hell), and shall
show men many things" (Revelation of Esdras).

57b. "Take heed that no man deceive you, and that ye
be not doubters and serve other gods. Many shall come in My
name, saying: I am the Christ. Believe them not, neither draw
near unto them. . . . Verily I say unto thee, when the twigs
of the fig tree have sprouted forth in the last days (the fig tree
is the House of Israel) then shall feigned Christs awake expect-
ations, saying: I am the Christ that am now come into the
world" (Ethiopic Text of Ep. of Apos.)

58. "In the last days the kinsman shall show no favor to
his kinsman, nor any man to his neighbor. And they that were
overthrown shall rise up and behold them that overthrew them;
and men shall take from one and give to another. . . . But
they that are deceivers in the world and enemies of righteousness, upon them shall come the fulfillment of the prophecy of
David, who said: Their feet are swift to shed blood, their
tongue uttereth slander, adders' poison is under their lips. I
behold thee companying with thieves, and partaking with adul-
terers, thou continuest speaking against thy brother and puttest
stumbling-blocks before thine own mother's son. . . . And there
shall be many that believe on my name and yet follow after evil
and spread vain doctrine. And men shall follow after them
and their riches, and be subject unto their pride, and lust for
drink, and bribery, and there shall be respect of persons among
them. . . . There shall come forth another doctrine, and because
they shall strive after their own advancement, they shall bring
forth an unprofitable doctrine. And therein shall be a deadly
corruption (of uncleanness), and they shall teach it, and shall
turn away them from eternal life. But woe unto them that
falsify this my word and commandment, and draw away them
that hearken to the commandment of life; for together with
them they shall come into everlasting judgment" (Epistle of
the Apostles).

59a. "There shall be wonders and strange appearances in

heaven and on earth before the end of the world come. 'Tell us now, how shall we perceive it?' And he answered us: 'I will teach it to you; and not that which believe, as well as them who shall hear that man and believe in me. In those years and days shall it come to pass.'

"The sun and the moon fighting one with the other, a continual rolling and noise of thunders and lightnings, thunder and earthquake; cities falling and men perishing in their over-throw, a continual dearth for lack of rain, a terrible pestilence and great mortality, mighty and untimely, so they that die lack burial: and the bearing forth of brethren and sisters and kins-folk shall be upon one bier. The kinsman shall show no favour to his kinsman, nor any man to his neighbour. And they that were overthrown shall rise up and behold them that overthrew them, that they lack burial, for the pestilence shall be full of hatred and pain and envy: and man shall take from one and give to another, and thereafter shall it wax yet worse than before. Then shall my Father be wroth at the wickedness of men, for many are their transgressions and the abominations of their uncleanness weigheth heavy upon them in the corrup-tion of their life"

59b. "Lord will not then the nations say: 'Where is their God?' And he answered and said unto us: 'Thereby shall the elect be known, that they, being plagued with such afflictions, come forth.' We said: 'Will then their departure out of the world be by a pestilence which giveth them pain?' He answered us: 'Nay, but if they suffer such affliction, it will be a proving of them.'

"In those years and days shall war be kindled upon war, the four ends of the earth shall be in commotion and fight against each other. Thereafter shall be quakings of clouds, darkness, and dearth, and persecutions of them that believe in me and against the elect. Thereupon shall come doubt and strife and transgressions against one another" (Ep. of James).

60a. "Hear thou, Thomas, the things which must come to

pass in the last times: there shall be famine and war and earth-quakes in divers' places snow and ice and great drought shall there be, and many dissensions among the peoples."

60b. "At that time shall be very great rising of the sea, (common people?) so that no man shall tell news to any man. The kings of the earth and the princes and the captains shall be troubled, and no man shall speak freely. Grey hairs shall be seen upon boys, and the young shall not give place unto the aged. After that shall arise another king, a crafty man, who shall hold rule for a short space: in those days there shall be all manner of evils, even the death of the race of men from the east even unto Babylon. And thereafter death and famine and sword in the land of Channaan even unto Rome. Then shall all the fountains of waters and wells boil over and be turned into dust and blood. The heaven shall be moved, the stars shall fall upon the earth, the sun shall be cut in half like the moon, and the moon shall not give her light.

"On the fourth day at the first hour, the earth of the east shall speak, the abyss shall roar: then shall all the earth be moved by the strength of an earthquake. In that day shall all the idols of the heathen fall, and all the buildings of the earth. These are the signs of the fourth day. And on the fifth day, at the sixth hour, there shall be great thunderings suddenly in the heaven, and the powers of light and the wheel of the sun shall be caught away, and there shall be great darkness over the world until evening, and the stars shall be turned away from their ministry. In that day all nations shall hate the world and despise the life of this world. These are the signs of the fifth day."

60c. "After a little space there shall arise a king out of the east, a lover of the law, who shall cause all good things and necessary to abound in the house of the Lord: he shall show mercy unto the widows and to the needy, and command a royal gift to be given unto the priests: in his days shall be abundance of all things" (Apoc. of Thomas).

60d. "In the last times there shall be . . . many dissentions among the. peoples, blasphemy, iniquity, envy, and villainy, indolence, pride and intemperance, so that every man shall speak that which pleaseth him. And my priests shall not have peace among themselves, but shall sacrifice unto me with deceitful minds: therefore will I not look upon them. Then shall the priest behold the people parting from the House of the Lord and turning unto the world, as well as transgressing in the House of God . . . The House of the Lord shall be desolate and her altars be abhorred . . . The place of holiness shall be corrupted, the priesthood polluted, distress shall increase, virtues shall be overcome (i.e., vices made to appear as virtues?), joy perish, and gladness depart (i.e., without holiness there can be no peace—without peace no real happiness) . . . . In those days evils shall abound: there shall be respectors of persons, hymns shall cease out of the House of the Lord, truth shall be no more, covetousness shall abound among the priests; an upright man shall not be found" (Apoc. of Thomas).

61. "Many of them shall be false prophets, and shall teach ways and diverse doctrines of perdition. And they shall become sons of perdition. And then shall God come unto my faithful ones that hunger and thirst and are afflicted and prove their souls in this life, and shall judge the sons of iniquity. Take heed that no man deceive you, and you be not doubters and servers of other gods. Many shall come in My name, saying: I am the Christ: believe them not, neither draw near unto them . . . In the last days shall feigned Christs come and awake expectation, saying: I am the Christ, now come into the world" (Apoc. of Peter).

OTHER ANCIENT ORACLES

62. *Sephr Haggadah of the Talmud*
A kid my father bought for two pieces of money.
Then came the cat and ate the kid.
Then came the dog and ate the cat that ate the kid.
Then came the staff that beat the dog, etc.

Then came the fire that burned the staff, etc.

Then came the water that quenched the fire, etc.

Then came the ox and drank the water, etc.

Then came the butcher and slew the ox, etc.

Then came the Angel of Death and killed the butcher, etc.

Then came the Holy One, blessed be He, and killed the Angel of Death who killed the butcher, who slew the ox, that drank the water, that quenched the fire, that burned the staff, that beat the dog, that bit the cat, that ate the kid, that my father bought for two pieces of money.

It is interpreted (as of 1731) as a summary of Israel's history, past, present, and future, thus:

1. The kid, as a ceremonially clean animal, represents the Hebrew race. The Father is God. The two pieces of money are Moses and Aaron.

2. The cat represents the Assyrians who led Israel into captivity.

3. The dog is the Babylonians who conquered the Assyrians and the Jews, and took the Jews captive.

4. The staff is the Medes and Persians who conquered Babylon.

5. The fire is the Grecian Empire that conquered Persia under Alexander the Great.

6. The water is the Romans who conquered the Grecian Empire, including Palestine.

7. The ox is the Saracens who subdued Palestine and drove out both Jews and Romans.

8. The butcher is the Crusaders who fought the Saracens.

9. The angel of death is the Turkish power.

10. The Holy One is Christ who will take vengeance on the Turks, after whose overthrow the Jews will be restored and will shortly live under the government of the Messiah.

63a. *Sibyline Oracle*

"The destruction of the world will occur when faith in

godliness shall perish from men, and justice is hidden away in the world, and men become renegades and, living on unholy enterprises, commit deeds of shame, and acts, dastardly and evil; and no man takes account of the godly, but even in their senselessness, fond fools, they destroy themselves, rejoicing in acts of violence, turning their hands to deeds of bloodshed."

63b. "Now I will tell thee a very evident sign, that thou mayst understand when the end of all things is coming on the earth. When swords in the starlit heaven appear by night towards dusk and towards dawn, and straightway dust is carried from heaven to earth, and all the brightness of the sun fails at midday from the heavens, and the moon's rays shine forth and come back to earth, and a sign comes from the rock with dripping streams of blood; and in a cloud ye shall see a battle of foot and horse, as a hunt of wild beasts, like unto misty clouds, this is the consummation of war which God, whose dwelling is in heaven, is bringing to pass. From the sunrise God shall send a king who shall give every land relief from the bane of war: some he shall slay and to others he shall consecrate faithful vows. Nor shall he do all these things by his own will, but in obedience to the good ordinances of the mighty God. And again the people of the mighty God shall be laden with excellent wealth, with gold and silver and purple adornment. The land shall bear her increase, and the sea shall be full of good things. And kings shall begin to be weary of repelling evil one against another with wrath. Envy is no good thing for miserable mortals."

63c. "The Lion Monarch shall be made famous unto all and shall subvert kingdoms, peoples and nations. Then God shall send a King from the sun, who shall cause all the earth to cease from disastrous war. He will take away the intolerable yoke of slavery which is placed on our neck, and he will do away with impious laws and violent chains. When He shall come there shall be fire and darkness in the midst of the black night."

THE WORDS OF SAINTS AND SAGES

PROPHECIES FROM THE MIDDLE AGES:

64. *St. Cataldus of Tarentino* (cir. 500)

"The Great Monarch will be in war till he is 40 years of age; a King of the House of Lily, he will assemble great armies and expel tyrants from his empire. He will conquer England and other island empires. Greece he will invade and be made king thereof. Clochis, Cyprus, the Turks and barbarians he will subdue and have all men to worship the Crucified One. He will at length lay down his crown in Jerusalem."

65. *Prophecy of Premol* (496)

"Is such a sacrifice not enough to appease your wrath, O Lord? But no, what then is this noise of arms? these cries of war and fear? What do the four winds bring? Ah! the dragon has appeared in all countries and has brought terrible confusion everywhere. There is war everywhere. Men and people have risen up one against the other. War, war, war—civil war and foreign war. What frightening onsets. Everything is mourning and death; famine reigns in the fields.

"The general revolution has followed. In these future happenings will Paris be destroyed? Jerusalem! Jerusalem! (Paris) save yourself from the fire of Sodom and Gomorrah, and from the sack of Babylon. Why Lord, do you not stop all this with Your Arm? Is the fury of men not enough without flaming ruins? Must the elements still serve Your wrath? Stop, Lord, stop! Towns are ruined. The elements are let loose. Cities are destroyed by earthquakes. Mercy and grace for Zion (Rome?); but You are deaf to our cries, and the Mount of Zion tumbles down with a crash. And here it is that the King of Zion (Pope?) along with his cross, with his sceptre and his triple crown, shaking off, on the ruins, the dust of his shoes, hastens to flee towards other shores. And is it not so, O Lord, that Your Church is rent asunder by her own children?

"The sons of Zion are divided into two camps—one faithful to the fugitive Pontiff, and the other inclined or disposed to the government of Zion respecting the Sceptre, but breaking in pieces the triple crown.

"But my spirit wanders and my eyes become obscured at the sight of this terrible cataclysm. But the Spirit said to me, that the man who hopes in God does penence, because the all powerful and merciful God will draw the world out of confusion and a new world will commence. Then the Spirit said to me: 'Here is the beginning of the end of Time which begins!' And I awoke terrified."

66. *St. Remigius* (d. 535)

"The kingdom of France is predestined by God for the defense of the Roman Church, which is the only true Church of Christ. This kingdom shall one day be great among the kingdoms of the earth, and shall embrace all the limits of the Roman Empire, and shall submit all other kingdoms to its own sceptre. It shall last until the end of time. It shall be victorious and prosperous as long as it will remain faithful to the Holy Roman See, and will not be guilty of any of those crimes which ruin nations; but it shall be rudely punished every time that it will become unfaithful to its vocation."

67a. *St. Caesar of Arles* (469-543)

"When the entire world, and in a special manner France, and in France more particularly the provinces of the North, of the east, and above all, that of Lorraine and Champagne, shall have been a prey to the greatest miseries and trials, then the provinces shall be succored by a prince who had been exiled in his youth, and who shall recover the crown of the lilies.

"This prince shall extend his dominion over the entire universe. At the same time there will be a great Pope, who will be most eminent in sanctity and most perfect in every quality. This Pope shall have with him, the Great Monarch, a most virtuous man, who shall be a scion of the holy race of the French kings. This Great Monarch will assist the Pope in the reformation of the whole earth. Many princes and nations that are living in error and impiety shall be converted, and an admirable peace shall reign among men during many years, because the wrath of God shall be appeased through their repentence, penance, and good works. There will be one common law, one only faith, one baptism, one religion. All nations shall recognize the Holy See of Rome, and shall pay homage to the Pope. But after some considerable time fervor shall cool, iniquity shall abound, and moral corruption shall become worse than ever, which shall bring upon mankind the last and worse persecution of Anti-Christ, and the end of the world."

67b. "There shall be a great carnage and as great an effusion of blood as in the time of the Gentiles: the Universal Church and the whole world shall deplore the ruin and capture of that most celebrated city, the capital and mistress of France: the altars and temples shall be destroyed; the holy virgins after experiences many outrages, shall fly from their monasteries: the pastors of the Church shall abandon their pulpits and the Church itself be despoiled of all temporalities."

68. *St. Bearcan* (d. 544)

"After the man whose cognomen will be Ruadh (Red), a spirit of fire will come from the north; he will march towards Dublin;—there will be but one Lord over all Ireland. It is he that will bring affliction on the Galls (non celts), by which their savage hordes shall suffer; until he will sail across the azure sea to Rome he will be a great king renowned for feats of arms."

69. *St. Senanus* (d. 560)

"Impart to me, O Senanus, information concerning the latter ages of the world; what shall be the condition of the race of people who will not observe rectitude in their judgments, who will entertain false and treacherous intentions; shall any individual of them be admitted into the regal mansions of heaven? Falsehood will characterize that class of men who will sit in judgment to pass sentence according to law:—between the father and his own son, litigations will subsist. The clergy of the holy church will be addicted to pride and injustice; the advantages they will aim at shall be the possession of worldly substance. Women will abandon feelings of delicacy, and co-habit with men out of wedlock; they will follow those prac-tices without secrecy, and such habits will become almost un-suppressable. All will rush into iniquity against the will of the Son of the Blessed Virgin Mary. The earth will not produce its fruits for the race of people to whom I allude; full mansions will be deserted, and unpleasant will be the tidings concerning them. Dreadful plagues will come upon all the race of Adam.

69b. "They (English) themselves will betray each other; in consequence of which their sovereignty will be broken; they will stain their swords and battle-axes with blood;—they will be a selfish race devoid of benignity. The son of the King of Saxon will come to join them across the sea; he will part with the sovereignty of the English in the country whence he will come. The English and the Irish of Ireland will unite in one confederation against the forces of the Saxons, their confed-eracy cannot be dissolved. The king of the Saxon's son will come at the head of his forces; in consequence of the protection he will extend to them, Ireland shall be freed from her fears. One monarch will rule in Ireland, over the English and the pure Irish; from the reign of that man, the people shall suffer no destitution."

70a. *St. Columbkille* (d. 597)

"Hearken, thou, Until I relate things that shall come to pass in the latter ages of the world. Great carnage shall be made, justice shall be outraged, multitudinous evils, great suffering shall prevail, and many unjust laws will be administered. The time shall come when they will not perform charitable acts, and truth shall not remain in them. They will plunder the prop-erty of the church, they will be continually sneering at each other, they will employ themselves at reading and writing. They will scoff at acts of humanity, and at irreproachable humil-ity; there shall come times of dark affliction, of scarcity, of sorrow, and of wailing; in the latter ages of the world's exist-ence, and monarchs will be addicted to falsehood. Neither jus-

tice nor covenant will be observed by any one people of the
race of Adam; they will become hard-hearted and penurious,
and will be devoid of piety. The clergy will become fosterers,
in consequence of the tidings of wretchedness, (that will reach
them); churches shall be held in bondage, (i.e., become private
property), by the all-powerful men of the day. Judges will
administer injustice, under the sanction of powerful, outrageous
kings; the common people will adopt false principles, oh, how
lamentable shall be their position! Doctors of science shall have
cause to murmur, they will become niggardly in spirit; the aged
will mourn in deep sorrow, on account of the woeful times
that shall prevail. Cemeteries shall become all red (dug up),
in consequence of the wrath that will follow sinners; wars and
contentions shall rage in the bosom of every family. Excellent
men shall be steeped in poverty, the people will become inhospitable to their guests, the voice of the parasite will be more
agreeable to them than the melody of the harp touched by the
sage's finger. In consequence of the general prevalence of sinful
practices, humility shall produce no fruit. The professors of
science shall not be rewarded, amiability shall not characterize
the people; prosperity and hospitality shall not exist, but nig-
gardliness and destitution will assume their place. The changes
of seasons shall produce only half their verdure, the regular
festivals of the Church will not be observed; all classes of men
shall be filled with hatred and enmity towards each other. The
people will not associate affectionately with each other during
the great festivals of the seasons; they will live devoid of justice and rectitude, up from the youth of tender age to the aged.
The clergy shall be led into error by the misinterpretation of
their reading; the relics of the saints will be considered powerless, every race of mankind will become wicked! Young women
will become unblushing, and aged people will be of irascible
temper; the kine will seldom be productive, as of old; lords
will become muderers. Young people will decline in vigour,
they will despise those who shall have hoary hair; there shall

be no standard by which morals may be regulated, and marriages will be solemnized without witnesses. Troublous shall be the latter ages of the world, the dispositions of the generality of men I will point out, from the time they shall abandon hospitable habits—with the view of winning honour for themselves, they will hold each other as objects for ridicule. The possessors of abundance shall fall through the multiplicity of their falsehoods; covetousness shall take possession of every glutton, and when satiated their arrogance will know no bounds. Between the mother and daughter anger and bitter sarcasms shall continually exist; neighbors will become treacherous, cold, and false-hearted towards each other. The gentry will become grudgeful, with respect to their trifling donations; and blood relations will become cool towards each other; Church livings shall become lay property. Such is the description of the people who shall live in the ages to come; more unjust and iniquitous shall be every succeeding race of men. The trees shall not bear the usual quantity of fruit, fisheries shall become unproductive and the earth shall not yield its usual abundance. Inclement weather and famine shall come and fishes shall forsake the rivers. The people oppressed for want of food, shall pine to death. Dreadful storms and hurricanes shall afflict them. Numberless diseases shall then prevail. Fortifications shall be built narrow during those times of dreadful danger."

70b. "Then a great event shall happen. I fail not to notice it: rectitude shall be its specious motive, and if ye be not truly holy, a more sorrowful event could not possibly happen."

70c. "I cannot observe after the death of Conn, aught but a sameness among his kindred clans—until the son of Ruadh from the glen appear, the span of the kingly reign shall be but brief. After the blameless son of Ruadh, Cathbarr from Cruachin shall assume the sovereign power, though many fraudulent acts will be committed during his reign, he will be upon the whole a friend to the church."

70d. "After the conclusion of a long and bloody rule of

Ireland by England 'the garment of death will descend and
the rowing wheels will arrive. Ten hundred compartments
shall be in the fleet, and each compartment shall contain ten
hundred men. The armament will spread its forces over sea and
land and rear up mounds with mangled bones. They will
inflict on their enemies a severe, flesh-hew-ing course of warfare
to such a degree that scarce a man of them shall escape. The
fleet of rowing wheels will remain two short years and a half.'

"This fleet that will come across the sea shall consist of ten
ships, ten hundred fairy barks (planes?), ten hundred boats,
ten hundred cock-boats and ten hundred spacious skiffs. The
principal seaport belonging to the country abroad shall look to
the west. Such a large assemblage of men never before met in
the east or west; and never again shall such a muster congre-
gate while Ireland is a seagirt island.

"The nobility shall sink into humble life before the great
war; that war that will be proclaimed against them from beyond the seas, by means of which the frantically-proud race
shall be subdued. The enemies of the English shall be aroused
into activity—they who reside in the eastern and western parts
of the world—so that they will engage in a battle on the circum-
scribed sea (Mediterranean?), in consequence of which the
English shall be defeated.

"A fleet belonging to a foreign country will come hither,
manned by the descendants of Golimh of the gold-embroidered
garments, they shall lay prostrate the Galls of the ships, and
liberate the people who have been held in bondage. This fleet
that will arrive here from the east, cannot be impeded on the
mighty ocean; through the impetuosity of its noisy breathing,
its strange appearance shall be marked by flaming mouths.[1]
They will engage in a furious conflict, it shall be a wonder
that it will not be a mutual slaughter, the conflict of those who
will come hither to sever the intricate knot.

---

[1]This description of a battleship may be based on Job 40: 20ff, where
the "Leviathan" is spoken of. See Ressehc: The Leviathan.

"After the English shall be defeated in this battle, they shall be harassed from every quarter; like a fawn surrounded by a pack of voracious hounds, shall be the position of the English amidst their enemies. The English afterwards shall dwindle down into a disreputable people, and every obstacle shall be opposed to their future prosperity: Because they did not (rather: so long as they do not) observe justice and rectitude, they shall be forever after deprived of power! Three warnings will be given them before their final fall, the burning of the Tower of the great kings; the conflagration of the dockyard of the English, and the burning of the Treasury where gold is deposited."

71. *St. Ultan* (d. 656)

"Then the Ruadh will proceed to the south, he will offer much opposition to the English; my confidence is in the Redhead for valour—he will free Eire from her difficulties. In a month after that hard-fought battle, another king will come from the north; I assure you, without the least deception, that three battles will be broken in one day. The battle shall continue during a whole week, it will be fought by the sons of a sovereign prince; it is at the termination of a week; after that, the aliens shall be dispersed. Wednesday will be the day of the battle, by which the aliens shall be driven from their strongholds; none of them shall remain after that but what birds would be able to carry off in their claws!"

72a. *Merlin* (7th century)

"There will come a German Anti-Pope. Italy and Germany will be sorely troubled. A French King will restore the true Pope."

72b. After destruction of England by seven kings there "shall come a dreadful dead man, and with him a Royal Great Monarch of the best blood in the world and he shall set England on the right way and put out all heresies. He shall be the last King over England.

"When the tail of Virgo shall enter Leo, and Scorpio shall ascend the back of Saggitarius, the northern kingdoms shall be wasted by reapers; the southern principalities shall end in lust; and the powers of the Island Monarchies shall be harnessed.

"Cruel wars shall be scattered by the wind—whose beginning were by a staff; their growth and continuance by bastards—and gulled by a revengeful hail.

"The sun itself shall play on the tinterell, clad with a vermillion coat, and the moon with dun-buskins (brown—symbol of tragedy) shall amble to the fair.

"Those on whom these things shall come, for grief and sorrow shall pine away. A prince of royal stock shall come forth, crowned from the northern parts—to his own people unexpected, but desired by foreigners—who, because he shall bear a 'rampant lion' shall therefore be called a Lion. He shall advance his conquering armies against his enemies and by woeful successes shall harass the territories of neighbor Princes. He shall exceed Alexander the Great in virtue and Cyrus in success. He shall cross the sea and be saluted Emperor by many kings. A certain ancient city he shall lay level with the ground.

"In the meanwhile a powerful Prince out of the East shall provoke him to battle. Against whom the Lion shall march with all his forces and pitching his camp on this side (west) of the Euphrates, shall await him. If the Prince shall come over the river the Lion shall be overcome; but he (Lion) shall cross the river with his army and give his enemy a bloody defeat and be master of all the East.

"Whilst these things are happening, divers petty kings from India shall break into Syria with mighty armies. Provided for battle, they shall wait for the Lion about the Valley of Jehosaphat, where they shall, by him, be all wholly cut off. Not long afterwards the Lion himself will die in eminent piety, after having established the Kingdom of the Fugitives ('transfugarum'—Jews?).

73a. *Old Welsh Prophecy*

"Ovens shall be esteemed as much as churches; as one sows, another shall reap. Death shall be better than wretched life; charity shall be with few men."

73b. "After that time (of irreligion) there shall come through the south with the Sun, on horse of tree, and upon all waves of the sea, the chicken of the Eagle (soldiers of the Great Monarch?) sailing into Britain."

74. *St. Maeltamhlacht* (7th century)

"In the latter ages destitution will fall upon many people, and whenever the English willl commit great evils against the children of Eire, then the English will be expelled and Eire become the property of her rightful owners."

75. *Old Irish*

"A peace shall be dissembled, that peace may well be trembled; that peace shall false be proved, all peace shall be removed; Why? A most grievous fight shall rise upright."

76. *St. Odile* (d. 740)

"Listen, listen oh my brother, for I have seen the terror of the forests and of the mountains. Fear has seized the people because never in any region of the universe has one given testimony of such trouble. The time has come when Germany will be called the most belligerent nation of the world. The period has arrived when out of her bosom will come the terrible warrior who will undertake to spread war in the world. The men in arms will call him the Anti-Christ. He will be cursed by mothers by thousands who will lament like Rachel over the fate of their children, and who will refuse consolation because they will no longer be of this world and all will be devastated in their homes.

"The conqueror will come from the banks of the Danube. He will be a remarkable chief among men. The war that he will make will be the most terrifying that men have ever undertaken. His arm will be flamboyant and the helmets of his soldiers will bear points darting flashlights, while their hands will carry lighted torches. It will be impossible to calculate the number of cruelties committed. He will be victorious on land, sea, and even in the air because one will see winged warriors, in these unbelievable attacks, mounting to the heavens to seize the stars and throw them on the cities from one end of the universe to the other in order to start gigantic fires. The nations will be astonished and will say: 'whence comes this force?' 'How is he able to undertake such a war?' The earth will tremble at the shock of the fighting. The rivers will run red with blood and sea monsters will disperse with terror to the top of the oceans, while black storms will spread desolation everywhere. Future generations will be astonished to see that his powerful and numerous enemies will not have been capable of stopping the march of his victories.

"And the war will be long. The conqueror will have attained the apogee of his triumphs towards the middle of the sixth month of the second year of hostilities. This will be the end of the first period of bloody victories. He will say 'accept the yoke of my domination,' while continuing his victories. But his enemies will not submit and the war will continue and he will cry out: 'Misfortune will make them fall because I am the conqueror.'

"The second part of the war will be equal in length to half of the first part. They will call it the period of 'diminuition.' It will be full of surprises which will make the earth tremble when twenty belligerent nations will clash. Towards the middle of this period the little nations submissive to the conqueror will cry out: 'Give us peace.' But there will not be peace for these nations. This will not be the end of these wars but the beginning of the end and the combats of body against body will take place in the citadel of citadels. Then will see a revolt among the women of his own country who will wish to stone him. But one will also see prodigies in the Orient.

"The third period will be the shortest of all and the con-

queror will have lost confidence in his warriors. This period
will be called the 'period of invasion' because by just retribution
the soil of the conqueror by reason of his injustice and his
atheism, will be invaded in all parts and pillaged. Around the
mountains torrents of blood will flow. This will be then the
last battle.

"The nations will sing hymns of gratitude in the temples
of God and will thank the Most High for their deliverance
because then will have appeared the warrior (Great Monarch?)
who will disperse the troops of the conqueror, the armies of
which will be annihilated by an unknown and frightful illness. This evil will discourage his soldiers, while the nations
will say: 'The finger of God is there. It is a just chastisement.'

"Because God is just—while sometimes allowing cruelty
and depredations—all the spoliated people, who will have
believed Him, will recover what they have lost and something
additional as a reward on earth."

77. Bl. Rabanus Maurus (d. 856)

"Our principal doctors agree in announcing to us, that
towards the end of time one of the descendants of the kings
of France shall reign over all the Roman Empire; and that he
shall be the greatest of the Empire; and that he shall be the
greatest of the French monarchs, and the last of his race.

"After having most happily governed his kingdom, he
will go to Jerusalem, and depose on Mount Olivet his sceptre
and crown. This shall be the end and conclusion of the Roman
and Christian Empire."

78. Leo the Philosopher (d. 911)

"There will arise an imperial deliverer—an oriental Fred-
erick—who will save the kingdom and the people. He will
come from the Mohammedans over whom he will rule—
adorned with all virtue—poor but needing nothing—two
angels in the form of eunuchs will accompany him—mankind
will accept him as their ruler. He will conquer the Arabs—no

taxes after twelve years. Immediately after, there will set in a period of darkness, crime and revolution."

79. *Monk Adso* (d. 992)

"Some of our teachers say that a King of the Franks will possess the entire Roman Empire. This King will be the greatest and last of all monarchs, and after having prosperously governed his kingdom, he will come in the end to Jerusalem and he will lay down his sceptre and his crown upon the Mount of Olives. This will be the end and consummation of the Empire of Rome, and immediately afterwards Anti-Christ will come."

80. *Saint Edward* (d. 1066)

"The extreme corruption and wickedness of the English nation has provoked the just anger of God. When malice shall have reached the fullness of its measure, God will, in His wrath, send to the English people wicked spirits, who will punish and afflict them with great severity, by separating the green tree from its parent stem the length of three furlongs. But at last this same tree, through the compassionate mercy of God, and without any national assistance, shall return to its original root, reflourish, and bear abundant fruit." (Concerns the English departure from and return to Christian unity.)

81a. *Monk Hilarion* (d. 1476)

"Before the Christian churches are renovated and united, God will send the Eagle (Great Monarch) who will travel to Rome and bring much happiness and good. The Holy Man (Angelic Pastor?) will bring peace between the clergy and the Eagle and his reign will last for four years. Then after his death God will send three men who are rich in wisdom and virtue. These men will administer the laws of the Holy Man and spread Christianity everywhere. Then there will be one flock, one shepherd, one faith, one law, one life and one baptism throughout the world."

81b. "The people of the Peninsula of Europe (Italy?) will suffer by unnecessary wars until the Holy Man comes. The

people of Pannonia (Austria: Hitler?) will be the cause of
a great war, overcome a neighbor and become an independent
nation. Then will a Scourge of God come and chastise them,
a Lion, which will reign a long time over the nation. That Lion
will come from a high mountain in the enlightened nation.
Then will the people of the Half-Moon of the Tribe of Agar
overrun many nations toward midnight (North) and commit
many depredations. Three years will they reign destroying all.
Yet in the third year will one of the unconquerable Eagles,
who reign over the Enlightened Nation between the Rhine and
the North Sea, with a great army meet them by the mouth of
the River Rhine and in a fearful battle almost entirely annihilate
them." (see also no. 115 below).

82a. *St. Malachy* (d. 1148)

"Religio Depopulata" (Religion without people: Benedict XV, 1914-1922—was designated by this verse).

"Fides Intrepida" (Fearless faith: Pius XI, 1922-1939
—is aptly described by these words).

"Pastor Angelicus (Angelic shepherd: This would be
Pius XII, 1939- —but probably his two successors also).

"Pastor et Nauta" (Shepherd and sailor).

"Flos Florum" (Flower of flowers).

"De Labore Solis" (from, by or of the work of the sun).

"De Gloria Olivae" (from, by or of the glory of the olive
tree).

"During the last persecution of the Holy Roman Church,
there will sit upon the throne, Peter the Roman, who will feed
the sheep amid great tribulations, and when these are passed,
the City of the Seven Hills (Rome) will be utterly destroyed,
and the awful Judge will then judge the people." (see no.
113b and 136).

82b. "Ireland will undergo English oppression for a week
of centuries but will preserve her fidelity to God and His Church.
At the end of this time Ireland will be delivered and the English
in turn must suffer severe chastisements. Ireland, however, will

be instrumental in bringing back the English to the unity of faith."

83. *Thos. á Becket* (d. 1170)

"A knight shall come from the West—he shall capture Milan, Lombardy, and the three crowns, and then sail to Famagoste and Cyprus and land at Jaffa and reach Christ's grave, where he will fight. War and wonders later shall befall till the people believe in Christ—toward the end of the world."

84a. *St. Hildegard* (d. 1179)

"The time is coming when princes and people will renounce the authority of the Pope. Individual countries will prefer their own Church rulers to the Pope. The German Empire will be divided. Church property will be secularized. Priests will be persecuted. After the birth of Anti-Christ heretics will preach their false doctrines undisturbed, resulting in 'Christians having doubts about their holy Catholic faith.'" (See 82a "Religio Depopulata".)

84b. "Toward the end of the world, mankind will be purified through sufferings. This will be true especially of the clergy, who will be robbed of all property. . . . When the clergy has adopted a simple manner of living, conditions will improve."

84c. "A powerful wind will rise in the North carrying heavy fog and the densest dust (darkness?) by divine command and it will fill their throats and eyes so they will cease their savagery and be stricken with a great fear. So after that there will be so few men left that seven women will fight for one man, that they will say to the man: 'marry me to take the disgrace from me,' for in those days it will be a disgrace for a woman to be without child, as it was by the Jews in the Old Testament."

"Before the Comet comes, many nations, the good excepted, will be scoured with want and famine. The great nation in the ocean that is inhabited by people of different tribes and descent by an earthquake, storm and tidal waves will be devastated. It will be divided, and in great part be sub-merged. That nation will also have many misfortunes at sea, and lose its colonies in the East through a Tiger and a Lion (two other nations?). The Comet by its tremendous pressure, will force much out of the ocean and flood many countries, causing much want and many plagues. All sea coast cities will be fearful and many of them will be destroyed by tidal waves, and most living creatures will be killed and even those who escape will die from a horrible disease. For in none of those cities does a person live according to the laws of God."

84d. "Peace will return to Europe when the white flower (Bourbon: Great Monarch) again takes possession of the throne of France. During this time of peace the people will be forbidden to carry weapons and iron will be used only for making agricultural implements and tools. Also during this period the soil will be very productive and many Jews, heathens and heretics will join the Church."

85a. *Old English Prophecies*

"When pictures look alive, with movements free; when ships like fishes swim beneath the sea; when men, outstripping birds, can soar the sky; then half the world, deep drenched in blood, shall die." (From a tombstone at Kirby Cemetery, Essex, England).

"Nation shall rise with nation, and make confederation. That 'all English' situation shall be taught by operation, to read upon the Passion."

"In Germany begins a dance, which passeth through Italy, Spain and France, but England shall pay the piper."

"When Our Lord shall lie in Our Lady's lap, then England will meet with a strange mishap." (Good Friday on Mar. 25?).

"The Lily (France) shall be moved against the feet of the Lion (England) and he shall stand on one side amongst the thorns (revolt?) of his own Kingdom and country."

85b. "There shall come a time when a George, the son of George shall come to the throne of England. And then, at that time, an eagle shall drink the blood of princes from a headless cross. And at that time death shall fall from the sky and an army of sleeping horsemen (fifth columnists?) from beneath the earth, shall come forth and drive the enemy from the land."

85c. "In the last year (of war) there shall come an Eagle (Great Monarch), out of the East, and his wings spread with the beams of the Son of Man. And that year shall be destroyed castles upon the Thames, and there shall be great fear over the whole world, and in a part of the land there shall be great battles amongst many kingdoms: that day shall see the "bloody field" and the Lily shall lose his crown, and therewith shall be crowned the Son of Man."

"In the fourth year many battles shall be fought for the faith and most of the world shall be stoopen: but the Son of Man with the Eagle shall be preferred—and there shall be universal peace over the whole world. Then shall the Son of Man receive a marvelous token, and there shall be great plenty of all manner of fruit and then shall he go to the Land of the Cross (Palestine)."

86a. *Old Scotch*

"Falsehood shall rule five years, a peace shall be tried out but not last and punishment shall soon come."

86b. "The untrue shall tremble—but when venom is banished and right rules, we shall have peace and plenty. The sun and moon shall no longer be dark (implies a period of darkness). The dead shall rise and live to comfort a knight (Great Monarch?) whom fortune chooses. He shall fight in Syria and win the Holy Cross. The Lion and the Lioness shall reign as Bannister, Ambrose, Merlin, Wigythington and Thomas say."

86c. "When the Cock of the north (Russia?) bids birds to fly (planes?), the Lion (England?) shall be loose and a

Dragon (United States?) shall help him. A Leonard (Great Monarch?) shall rise in the South.

"A battle shall be fought on a broad moor (Westphalia?). The Wolf (Poland?) shall be true to the Lion, and from Bamborough shall the Leopard with the Fleur-De-Lis sail.

"That winter shall many lords perish, when Tarburt Crags fall into the sea—Bede and Banister say so."

87. *Old Saxon*

"The seven-headed city, now more brave than Jerusalem, shall be a place more desolate than Jerusalem. This Dog (that entered Germany at a loss) shall afterwards forsake his Master and choose him a New Man, whereby the Scriptures shall be fulfilled. This dog shall signify the Turk, which shall forsake his Mahomet and choose unto him the name Christian, which is a sign the day of Doom is at hand, when all the earth is subject unto God, or that all people acknowledge one only God.

"England and France shall live long at variance, but at length agree.

"The bowels of Spain shall be split asunder, and divided for want of Government.

"The 'Fleur-de-Lis' (Bourbon emblem) and France shall live long at variance, but at length agree. Then shall the clear Word spring forth and flourish through the world, which never shall be taken away.

"After this shall a milk white Dove be lifted up to honor with two Golden Lions and receive a Crown of Gold; but after all these things the end of the world shall approach, and there shall be heavy and pitiful days, with much wars and other altercations in the world and not long after universal peace."

88a. *Old German* (12th century)

"A great war will come, after which the Kaiser will leave the country. Troubled times will follow, although the land is at peace. Then a man of lowly birth will come into power and win many successes so that Germany will become 'Great

Germany.' There will be few Jews in the country. When at the height of his power this man will do something to cause another world war, resulting in Germany's downfall. Germany will become small again, but, under a Catholic monarch, will regain power and prestige. At that time a Pope will reign who has not long occupied the throne of Peter and who, through pressure of circumstances, will leave Rome."

88b. "Munster will be destroyed from the air. The atmosphere will become so pestiferous that no one will dare open a window. Then a Catholic Kaiser will enter the city on horseback, have his steed shod by a one-eyed smith, remount on the wrong side and then cease to reign. Despite this, prayer will avert much misery. In these years many people will wear red shoes."

89a. *Birch-Tree Prophecy* (Old German)

"When the world becomes Godless: revolutions will break out against kings; fathers will be against sons and sons against fathers; dogma will be perverted; men will try to overthrow the Catholic Church; mankind will be lovers of pleasure. A terrible war will find the north fighting the south. The south will be led by a Prince wearing a white coat with a cross on the front; he will be lame afoot. He will gather his forces at Bremen for Mass. Then he will lead them into battle beyond Werl near the birch-tree country (Westphalia). After a terrible battle at a brook running west to east near Berdberg and Sondern the south will be victorious."

89b. *Another Version of the "Birch-Tree Prophecy"*— Peter Schlinkert)

"Near the birch-tree (Westphalia) the army of the West will fight a terrible battle against the army of the East, and after many bloody sacrifices be victorious. The soldiers of the East will retreat over the Haar, and when the villagers see Rune on the Werler and Haar on fire, they must quickly flee into Armsberger Wood. Another battle will be fought near the Ruhr Bridge by Obeneimer, but here only with artillery.

A few days later will be fought the last great battle on German soil and that by the village Schmerleck on the so-called Lusebrinke. The army of the East will be almost entirely annihilated and only a very few will be left to bring the news home. After these days of mishap and misery happiness and peace will return to Germany, though in the first year the women will have to do the farm work."

90. *Chronicle of Madgeburg*

"Of the blood of the Emperor Charles the Great and of the King of France shall arise an Emperor named Charles, who shall rule imperially in Europe, by whom the decayed estate of the Church shall be reformed and the ancient glory of the Empire again restored."

91. *Aystinger the German*

"There shall arise in the last times, a Prince, sprung from the Emperor Charles who shall recover the land of promise and reform the Church. He shall be Emperor of Europe."

92. *Anonymous*

Last periods before the peace of Christ

"January—Blood will rain one hour in the land of Europe that shall be destroyed first.

February—Wars and rumors—everywhere preparing for war—land and sea traffic restricted—countries forced to live on their own products.

March—Great waves and floods—island of the double cross government (England?) submerged because of sins of rulers.

April—Terrible naval battle—waters turn red—England in the fight.

May—War and bloodshed everywhere: twelve women to each man.

June—In the East a whole nation will fight for an evil man—God will rain fire on his army of wealth and treasures.

July—Great drought over the world.

August—Plagues, pestilences (from East) famines—worse than Jerusalem.

September—Seasons unnatural—the soil will not be tillable —cattle will rot and vermin poison the earth.

October—Famine (corn) over Europe.

November—'Great Conqueror' will give peace to the Earth.

December—Religion spread universally—peace trumpet sounds."

93a. *Old Italian*

"When the White Pope and the Black Pope (Head of Jesuits or an Anti-Pope) shall die during the same night, then there will dawn upon the Christian nations the Great White Day."

93b. "Woe unto the City of Philosophers, woe unto Lombardy for thy towers of joy shall be broken down; all the tyrants shall be put out of God's church, and there shall occur a general conversion to the faith of Christ under the Great Lion."

94. *Old Latin* (Bishop Ageda?)

"In these times (world in terrible distress) a mercurial hero, a son of the Lion, shall inherit the crown of the Fleur-de-Lis (Bourbons) by means of the kingdom of England. He shall be a lover of peace and justice, not swerve from the same, and by his means the nation's religion and laws shall have an admirable change. When these things come to pass there shall be a firm alliance between the Lion and the Eagle and they shall live in peace between themselves for a long time. In these times mortals wearied with wars shall desire peace."

95. *Old Roman*

"In the first age the nobility will flourish; in the second age the Church will rule; in the third age the law will tyrannize, and thereafter war will destroy everything."

96. *Sibylla Tiburtina*

"A star shall arise in Europe over the Iberians (Great Monarch), toward the great house of the North (Hapsburg?), whose beams shall unexpectedly enlighten the whole world.

This shall be in a most desired time, when mortal men, being weary of armies, with joint consent embrace peace. Almost at the same time of this star, a light as ancient as the former (Pope), of the same age (young), burning with far more eager flames, shall extend his government to the coasts of the Antipodes. France shall first be yoked by this King or Prince. Britain shall humbly cast herself at his knees. Italy, pausing with great deliberation upon high enterprises, will contribute to him her languishing right hand. But this very light shall hide itself in the clouds of the gods long before his time (die young—comparatively short reign) with the mighty desire of mortal men."

97. Abbot "Merlin" Joachim (d. 1202)

"After many prolonged sufferings endured by Christians, and after a too great effusion of innocent blood, the Lord shall give peace and happiness to the desolated nations. A remarkable Pope will be seated on the pontifical throne, under the special protection of the angels (Angelic Pastor?). Holy and full of gentleness, he shall undo all wrong, he shall recover the states of the Church, and reunite the exiled temporal powers. He shall be revered by all people, and shall recover the kingdom of Jerusalem. As the only Pastor he shall reunite the Eastern to the Western Church, and thus one only faith will be in vigor. The sanctity of this beneficent Pontiff will be so great that the highest potentates shall bow down before his presence. This holy man shall crush the arrogance of religious schism and heresy. All men will return to the primitive Church, and there shall be one only pastor, one law, one master—humble, modest, and fearing God (Pope). The true God of the Jews, our Lord Jesus Christ, will make everything prosper beyond all human hope, because God alone can and will pour down on the wounds of humanity the oily balm of sweetness.

"The heavens proclaim the glory of God, and the faithful are in joy and happiness, because the Lord has vouchsafed to be merciful to them. He shall invite his elect to the banquet

of the Lamb, where melodious canticles and harmonious con-
certs will be heard.

"The power of this Pontiff's holiness will be so great as
to be able to check the fury and impetuosity of threatening
waves. Mountains shall be lowered before him, the sea shall
be dried up, the dead shall be raised, the churches shall be re-
opened and altars erected.

"It should be known that there will be two heads, one
in the East, and the other in the West. This Pope shall break
the weapons and scatter the fighting hordes. He will be the
joy of God's elect. This angelic Pope will preach the gospel in
every country. Through his zeal and solicitude the Greek
Church shall be forever reunited to the Catholic Church.

"Before, however, being firmly and solidly established in
the Holy See, there will be innumerable wars and violent conflicts during which the sacred throne shall be shaken. But
through the favor of Divine clemency, moved by the prayers
of the faithful, everything will succeed so well that they shall
be able to sing hymns of thanksgiving to the glory of the Lord.

"This holy Pope shall be both pastor and reformer.
Through him the East and West shall be in everlasting concord. The city of Babylon shall then be the head and guide
of the world. Rome, weakened in temporal power, shall forever preserve her spiritual dominion, and shall enjoy great peace.
During these happy days the Angelic Pope shall be able to address to Heaven prayers full of sweetness. The dispersed nation
(Jews) shall also enjoy tranquility. Six and a half years after
this time the Pope will render his soul to God. The end of his
days shall arrive in an arid province, situated between a river and
a lake near the mountains. . . .

"At the beginning, in order to obtain these happy results,
having need of a powerful temporal assistance, this holy Pontiff
will ask the cooperation of the generous monarch of France
(Great Monarch). At that time a handsome monarch, a scion
of King Pepin, will come as a pilgrim to witness the splendor

of this glorious pontiff, whose name shall begin with R . . . A temporal throne becoming vacant, the Pope shall place on it this king whose assistance he shall ask.

"When a monster shall appear to thee in the sky, thou shalt find a ready escape towards the east, and after nine years thou shalt render thy soul to God.

"A man of remarkable sanctity will be his successor in the Pontifical chair. Through him God will work so many prodigies that all men shall revere him, and no person will dare to oppose his precepts. He shall not allow the clergy to have many benefices. He will induce them to live by the tithes and offerings of the faithful. He shall interdict pomp in dress, and all immorality in dances and songs. He will preach the gospel in person, and exhort all honest ladies to appear in public without any ornament of gold or precious stones. After having occupied the Holy See for a long period of time he shall happily return to the Lord.

"His three immediate successors shall be men of exemplary holiness. One after the other will be models of virtue, and shall work miracles, confirming the teaching of their predecessors. Under their government the Church shall spread, and these Popes shall be called the Angelic Pastors."

98. Bishop Christianos Ageda (d. 1204)

"In the twentieth century France's union with England will prove to be her utter destruction: for there will be great shedding of blood by the people of the Kingdom. There will be wars and fury which will last long: provinces divested of their people and kingdoms in confusion; many strongholds and noble houses shall be destroyed and their cities and towns shall be forsaken of their inhabitants; in divers places the ground shall be untilled and there shall be great slaughter of the nobility; their sun shall be darkened and never shine again, for France shall be desolate and her leader destroyed. There shall be great mutations and changes of kings and rulers, for the right hand

of the world shall fear the left and the north prevail over the
south."

99. *Roger Bacon* (d. 1294)

There shall arise a "righteous true and holy priest to reform
the Church. The Greeks will return (to the Church), the Tartars will be converted, the Saracens destroyed, there will be one
fold and one shepherd."

100. *John of Vatiguerro* (13th cent.)

"Spoliation, devastation and pillage of that most famous
city, which is the capitol and mistress of the whole kingdom
of France," will take place when the Church and world will be
grievously troubled: "The Pope will change his residence; the
Church will not be defended for the duration of twenty-five
months, and more, because during all this time there will be
no Pope, no Emperor of Rome and no ruler in France. Afterwards a young captive prince shall recover the crown of the
Lilies and shall extend his dominion over all the universe.
Once established he shall destroy the Sons of Brutus[1] and their
Isle so that their memory shall pass into everlasting forgetfulness.

"After many tribulations a Pope will be elected out of those
who escaped persecution. He, by his sanctity, will reform the
clergy and the whole world will venerate them for their virtue
and perfection. He will travel barefoot and be devoid of fear.
Almost all unbelievers and the Jews will be converted and there
will be one law, one faith, one baptism, one life. All people
will love one another and peace will last a long time.

101. *Werdin d'Otrante* (13th cent.)

"The Great Monarch and the Great Pope will precede Anti-
Christ."

"The nations will be in wars for four years and a great
part of the world will be destroyed. All the sects will vanish.
The capital of the world will fall. The Pope will go over the

---

[1]Whether this phrase which occurs also in prophecy 102a means Englishman (because of the Robert "Bruce") or traitorous rulers is not evident.

sea carrying the sign of redemption on his forehead, and after the victory of the Pope and the Great Monarch peace will reign on earth."

"The Pope will cross the sea in a year when the Feast of St. George (April 23rd) falls on Good Friday, and St. Mark's feast (April 25th) falls on Easter Sunday, and the feast of St. Anthony (June 13th) falls on Pentecost and the feast of St. John the Baptist (June 24th) falls on Corpus Christi" (all these concurrances will take place in the year 1943, not again until 2038).

"The Great Monarch will come to restore peace and the Pope will share in the victory."

102a. *Prophecy of Orval* (13 cent.)

"Howl, ye sons of Brutus.[1] Call upon you the wild beasts, which are ready to devour you. God alone is great! What booming of arms! There is not yet a full number of moons, and, behold, many warriors are coming. What fire goes together with his (God's?) arrows! Ten times six moons, and again six times ten moons have nourished his wrath. Woes to thee, populous city (Paris)! Behold kings armed by the Lord! . . . But fire hath already burned thee to the ground. . . . Thy just ones, however, shall not perish; God has heard them; the place of wickedness is purged by fire; the ample river (Seine?) has carried to the sea its waters all red with blood."

"It is finished. The mountain of God desolated (the Church) has cried to God, the children of Juda have invoked God from a strange land, and behold, God is no longer deaf. France, that appeared disintegrated, is on the point of being united. God loves peace. Come, young Prince, leave the Island of Captivity. Join the lion to the white flower. Come. God wills what has been foreseen. The ancient blood of centuries will also put an end to long divisions. Then shall be seen in France one shepherd only.

"The powerful man, assisted by God, will establish him-

---

[1]See note on prophecy 100.

self well. Many wise laws shall restore peace. The scion of Capet will be so prudent and wise that all men will believe God to be with him. Thanks to the Father of mercies, the Holy Sion (Catholic Church) sings again in the temples, One only God. Many poor wandering sheep shall come to drink of the living spring of truth and grace. Three princes and kings shall throw off the garb of error, and will see clearly in the faith of God. At this time two-thirds of a great nation of the sea (England?) shall return to the true faith."

102b. *St. Gertrude* (13th cent.)

"The love of the Incarnate Word as exemplified by His Divine Heart is reserved for the last ages to be made known; so that the world, carried away by follies, may regain a little of the warmth of early Christian Charity by learning of the love of the Sacred Heart."

103a. *Abbot Herman of Lehnin* (d. 1300)

Towards the end of the world "Israel will commit a terrible crime for which it will suffer death."

103b. "(In Germany) the Shepherd (pope) recovers his flock and the people their King. An era of prosperity follows."

104a. *Brother John of the Cleft Rock* (1340)

"Toward the end of the world the tyrants and the hostile people will suddenly rob the prelates and clergy of the Church of all their possessions and grievously afflict and martyr them. The ones who heap the most abuse upon them will be held in high esteem. The clergy cannot escape these persecutions, but because of them all servants of the Church will be forced to lead an apostolic life. At that time the Pope, with the Cardinals, will have to flee Rome under trying circumstances to a place where he will be unknown. He will die a cruel death in this exile. The sufferings of the Church will be much greater than at any previous time in her history."

104b. "All kingdoms will have to unite in the fight since the Cock (France?), the Leopard (England?), and the White Eagle (Russia?) will not be able to overcome the Black Eagle

(Germany), unless aided by the prayers and vows of all man-kind. The Black Eagle will attack the Cock which will lose many of his feathers, but will strike heroically with its spurs —it would soon be exhausted were it not for the help of the Leopard and its claws. The Black Eagle from the land of Luther will surprise the Cock from another side and will invade half of the land of the Cock. The White Eagle coming from the North will attack the Black Eagle; and the other Eagle will invade his land from one end to the other.

"The Black Eagle will find himself compelled to let the Cock go in order to fight the White Eagle, but the White Eagle and the Cock will pursue the Black Eagle into his own land, thus helping the White Eagle. The battles waged until then will be trifling to those that will take place in he land of Luther because the seven angels simultaneously pour fire from their censors on the impious land of Luther.

"When the Beast sees that he is lost he will become furious —it is ordained that for several months the beak of the White Eagle, the claws of the Leopard, and the spurs of the Cock must tear his vitals. Rivers will be forded over masses of dead bodies: in some places this will change the course of waters— only the great will receive burial for the carnage caused by fire-arms will but be added to the numberless dead due to famine and plague.

"The Black Eagle will ask for peace again and again, but the seven angels who preceded the three animals (defenders of the Lamb) have declared that victory must involve the absolute crushing of the Black Eagle. As a consequence, the executors of the justice of the Lamb (the three animals) cannot stop the fighting as long as the Black Eagle has a soldier left to defend him. This ruthless sentence of the Lamb against the Black Eagle is because he has claimed to be a Christian and to be acting in the name of God—hence if he did not perish the fruit of the Redemption would be lost and the gates of Hell prevail against the Savior.

"It is obvious that this combat, which will be fought where the Black Eagle forges his arms is no human contest . . .

"The three animals (defenders of the Lamb) will exterminate the Black Eagle's last army, but the battlefield (Westphalia?) will become a funeral pyre larger than the greatest cities with the corpses changing the very landscape. The Black Eagle will lose his crown and will die abandoned and insane—his Empire will be divided into twenty-two states with neither fortifications, army nor navy."

104c. "The White Eagle (Great Monarch), by order of the Archangel Michael, will drive the crescent from Europe where none but Christians will remain—he himself will rule from Constantinople. An era of peace and prosperity will begin for the world. There will no longer be Protestants or Schismatics; the Lamb will reign and the bliss of the human race will begin. Happy will they be who have escaped the perils of that terrible time, for they can taste of its fruit through the reign of the Holy Ghost and the sanctification of mankind, which can be accomlished only after the defeat of the Black Eagle.

104d. "God will raise up a holy Pope over whom the angels will rejoice. Enlightened by God, this man will reconstruct almost the entire world through his holiness and lead all to the true faith, and everywhere fear of God, virtue, and good morals will be dominant. He will lead all erring sheep back to the fold, and there shall be only one faith, one law, one rule of life, one baptism on earth. All men will love each other and do good, and all quarrels and war will disappear."

105. *Richard Rolle of Hampole* (d. 1349)

"There will be a general defection from the Church near the end of the world, especially regarding obedience to Her."

106a. *St. Bridget of Sweden* (d. 1373)

"The son of man, the parvenu of the sea, shall be most invincible in war and shall subdue all Germany. The great house (German Empire?) shall almost be pulled down. At last the Eagle will come from the North to the West, and shall, together with her children, be surrounded by the towers of Spain and they will raise Germany up again. The Eagle will also invade Mohometan countries and will carry the admirable sign in the land of promise (Palestine). Peace and abundance shall return to the world.

"This most unhappy war shall end when an emperor of Spanish origin will be elected, who will, in a wonderful manner, be victorious through the sign of the Cross. He shall destroy the Jewish and the Mahometan sects: he will restore the church of Santa Sophia (in Constantinople), and all the earth shall enjoy peace and prosperity; and new cities will be erected in many places."

106b. "Let the Greeks know that their empire, their kingdoms, or dominions, shall never be secure or in settled peace, but will always be held in subjection by their enemies, from whom they shall have to suffer most grievous hardships and constant distresses: until, with true humility and good will, they shall have devoutly submitted themselves to the Church of Rome and to her faith, conforming themselves entirely to the holy ordinances and rites of that Church.

"When the Feast of St. Mark (April 25) shall fall on Easter, the Feast of St. Anthony (June 13) on Pentecost, and that of St. John (June 24th) on Corpus Christi, the whole world shall cry, Woe!" (These feasts concur in 1943 but not again till 2038).

106c. "The time of Anti-Christ will be near when the measure of injustice will overflow and when wickedness has grown to immense proportions, when the Christians love heresies and the unjust trample underfoot the servants of God."

107. *St. Cathrine of Siena* (d. 1380)

"The bride (Church) now all deformed and clothed in rags, will then gleam with beauty and jewels and crowned with the diadem of all virtue. All believing nations will rejoice and have such excellent and holy shepherds, and the unbelieving world, attracted by the glory of the Church, will be converted to her."

108. *Cyril the Hermit* (14th cent.)

"A German ruler will persecute priests and monks and do much harm to the Church."

109. *Dolciano* (14th cent.)

"Under a Holy Pope there will be universal conversion."

110. *Cardinal d'Ally* (d. 1414)

"If the world last until those times, which God alone knows, there will occur many great and wonderful renovations and changes in the world, especially regarding laws."

111. *St. Vincent Ferrer* (d. 1418)

"Armies from West, East and North will fight together in Italy and the Eagle (Great Monarch?) shall capture the counterfeit king, and all things shall be made obedient unto him, and there shall be a new reformation in the world. Woe then to the shaven orders whose crowns are shaved. (Religious who cannot disguise themselves?)

"In the days of peace that are to come after the desolation of revolutions and wars, before the end of the world, the Christians will become so lax in their religion that they will refuse to receive the Sacrament of Confirmation, saying 'it is an unnecessary Sacrament'; and when the false prophet, the precursor of Anti-Christ comes, all who are not confirmed will apostatise, while those who are confirmed will stand firm in the faith, and only a few will renounce Christ."

112. *Fr. Jerome Votin* (d. 1420)

"Woe! yes, thousand times woe, to the people who rebelled against all authority, and abolished the laws; they pulled up from the root the source of their prosperity; they tore to pieces the Lily but the Eagle shall seize upon them; it shall catch and destroy its prey, said the Spirit. The earth shall be deluged with the blood of its inhabitants. Her children, armed with iron, shall perish by the sword. Her innumerable calamities, says the Lord, shall not appease my wrath. My right hand shall be lifted up against the people; the power that will oppress them shall be my instrument of indignation against them, and against other nations. This is what the Spirit says.

"Some time after four centuries the altars of Beelzebub shall be destroyed. The workers of iniquity shall be punished and shall perish; the heavenly dew shall fall upon the desolated earth, and over the Church afflicted. A son of royal blood shall be born from the race of Artois. He shall govern France with prudence and with honor; the spirit of God will be with him; the Spirit said so.

"Before the end of the nineteenth century, another Pastor (a pope) shall rise (be born?) who will lead the people in equity, and the kings in justice. He shall be honored by princes and by the people; but before his empire is established, let those who have not bowed down before Baal fly from Babylon.

"Let everybody think how to save his life; for behold the time wherein the Lord will have, with the severity of His punishments, to demonstrate the multitude and enormity of the crimes with which she (Babylon) is defiled. The Lord will cause to revert upon that city all the evils with which she has tyrannized over others. This impious city, the ravager of nations, the executioner of her own priests, of her kings, and of her own children, has been used by the Lord as the hand for presenting the cup of his vengeance to all the nations of the earth. All nations have drunk the wine of her frenzy; they shall suffer the anguish of her captivity and of her barbarity.

"But on a sudden this Babylon is fallen and in her fall she is broken to pieces, said the Spirit. All this shall come to pass for the purification of the just, and for the destruction of the wicked; in order to make men honor the Church of God, and fear and serve the Lord.

"Such are the words which the Spirit revealed to his servant Jerome, who wrote these things by his orders, the truth of which shall, in due time, be acknowledged."

113a. *St. John Capestran* (d. 1456)

"There shall arise a certain grave and constant man near Aquisgrave of the Rhine; who being chosen, shall restore the

Apostolic Discipline: and in the third incursion of time, shall prevail and do great things; and there shall be of his race to the day of judgment."

113b. *(On the Last Eight Popes)*

The ox shall again be full of life and his trumpets shall resound with sweet lowing. (Pius XI.)

A great city beast (Industrialism?) shall succeed and devour the pastures of little ones. (Pius XII.)

He shall come from the North Wind (Aquilone), enter into the Sanctuary and the Church will renew her seed. (Angelic Pastor.)

He shall explain the ten heads of the Dragon (water serpent) and he shall destroy in the Holy Land the Author of Wickedness. (Pastor and Sailor.)

The people will be dying with hunger when he is created (Cardinal?) who will divide and give to the poor. (Flower of Flowers.)

The Tree shall give forth its fruits, but the destroying beast shall devour them. (From the Half Moon.)

The brightness of the exposed countenance shall be lifted, and the faces of the proud shall fall before the face of the oppressor. (The Glory of the Olive Tree.)

There shall be signs of the sun and moon when there shall be created a man stronger than any prince, and he shall renew the face of the Church. At this time Anti-Christ shall have been trodden under foot and all the world shall enjoy the faith and peace of the Most High. (Peter the Roman.) (See no. 82, 136).

114a. *St. Francis de Paul (1470)*

"From your lordship, (Simeon de Limena, Lord of Montalto), shall be born the great leader of the holy militia of the Holy Spirit, which shall overcome the world, and shall possess the earth so completely that no king or lord shall be able to exist, except he belongs to the sacred host of the Holy Ghost.

These devout men shall wear on their breasts, and much more within their hearts, the sign of the living God, namely, the cross.

"The first members of this holy order shall be natives of the city of . . . where iniquity, vice, and sin abound. However, they shall be converted from evil to good; from rebels against God they shall become most fervent and most faithful in His divine service. That city shall be cherished by God and by the Great Monarch, the elect and the beloved of the Most High Lord. For the sake of that place all holy souls who have done penance in it shall pray in the sight of God for that city and for its inhabitants. When the time shall come of the immense and most right justice of the Holy Spirit, His Divine Majesty wills that such city become converted to God, and that many of its citizens follow the great prince of the holy army. The first person that will openly wear the sign of the living God shall belong to that city, because he will through a letter be commanded by a holy hermit to have it impressed in his heart and to wear it externally on his breast.

"That man will begin to meditate on the secrets of God, about the long visitation which the Holy Spirit will make and the dominion that he will exercise over the world through the holy militia. O! happy man, who shall receive from the Most High the greatest privileges! He will interpret the hidden secrets of the Holy Ghost, and he shall often excite the admiration of men by his revealed knowledge of the internal secrets of their hearts. Rejoice, my Lord, because that Prince above other princes, and King over other kings, will hold you in the greatest veneration, and after having been crowned with three most admirable crowns, will exalt that city, will declare it free, and the seat of the Empire, and it shall become one of the first cities in the world."

114b. "You and your consort desire to have children; you shall have them. Your holy offspring shall be admired upon earth. Among your descendants there will be one who shall be like the sun amidst the stars, he shall be a first-born son;

in his childhood he will be like a saint; in his youth, a great sinner; then he will be converted entirely to God and will do great penance; his sins will be forgiven him, and he shall become a great saint.

"He shall be a great captain and prince of holy men, who shall be called 'the holy Cross-bearers of Jesus Christ,' with whom he shall destroy the Mahometan sect and the rest of the infidels. He shall annihilate all the heresies and tyrannies of the world. He shall reform the Church of God by means of his followers, who shall be the best men upon earth in holiness, in arms, in science, and in every virtue, because such is the will of the Most High. They shall obtain the dominion of the whole world, both temporal and spiritual, and they shall spuport the Church of God until the end of time."

114c. "God Almighty will exalt a very poor man of the blood of the Emperor Constantine, son of St. Helena. and of the seed of Pepin, who shall on his breast wear the sign which you have seen at the beginning of this letter (a red Cross). Through the power of the Most High he shall confound the tyrants, the heretics, and infidels. He will gather a grand army, and the angels shall fight for them; they shall kill all God's enemies."

114d. "From the beginning of the world, after the creation of man, and to the end of human generation, there have been and there shall be seen wonderful events upon the earth. Four hundred years shall not pass when his Divine Majesty shall visit the world with a new religious order much needed, which shall effect more good among men than all other religious institutions combined. This religious order shall be the last and the best in the Church; it shall proceed with arms, with prayer, and with hospitality. Woe to tyrants, to heretics, and to infidels, to whom no pity shall be shown, because such is the will of the Most High! An infinite number of wicked men shall perish through the hands of the Cross-bearers, the true servants of Jesus Christ. They shall act like good husbandmen when they extirpate noxious weeds and prickly thistles from the wheatfield. These holy servants of God shall purify the earth with the deaths of innumerable wicked men."

114e. "How spiritually blind are those persons who, having no thought about the things of God, fix their end in earthly objects. Wretched men! by far worse than the very beasts which are guided by their senses, because they cannot have reason; but when men abandon the use of their reason, they become brutalized. Hence they shall ever be in confusion. Let, therefore, the princes of this world be prepared for the greatest scourges to fall upon them. But from whom? First from heretics and infidels, then from the holy and most faithful Crossbearers elected by the Most High, who, not succeeding in converting heretics with science, shall have to make a vigorous use of their arms. Many cities and villages shall be in ruins, with the deaths of an innumerable quantity of bad and good men. The infidels also will fight against Christians and heretics, sacking, destroying, and killing the largest portion of Christians. Lastly, the army, styled 'of the Church,' namely, the holy Cross-bearers, shall move, not against Christians or Christianity, but against the infidels in pagan countries, and they shall conquer all those kingdoms with the death of a very great number of infidels. After this they shall turn their victorious arms against bad Christians, and shall destroy all the rebels against Jesus Christ. These holy Cross-bearers shall reign and dominate holily over the world until the end of time. The founder of these holy men shall, my lord, be one of your posterity. But when shall this take place? When crosses with the stigmas shall be seen, and the crucifix shall be carried as the standard.

"The time is coming when his Divine Majesty will visit the world with a new religious order of holy Cross-bearers, who will carry a crucifix, or the image of our crucified Lord, lifted up upon the principal standard in view of all. This standard will be admired by all good Catholics; but at the beginning it will be derided by bad Christians and by infidels. Their sneers shall, however, be changed into mourning when they shall witness the wonderful victories achieved through it against tyrant, heretics, and infidels. Many wicked men and obstinate rebels against God shall perish: their souls will be plunged into hell. This punishment shall fall upon all those transgressors of the Divine commandments who with new and false doctrines will attempt to corrupt mankind and turn men against the ministers of God's worship. The same chastisement is due to all obstinate sinners, but not to those who sin through weakness, because these being converted, doing penance, and amending the conduct of their life, shall find the divine mercy of the Most High full of kindness towards them. O holy Cross-bearers of the Most High Lord, how very pleasing you will be to the great God much more than the children of Israel! God will, through your instrumentality, work more wonderful prodigies than he has ever done before with any nation. You shall destroy the sect of Mahomet, and all infidels of every kind and of every sect. You shall put an end to all the heresies of the world by extinguishing all tyrants. You will remove every cause of complaint by establishing a universal peace, which shall last until the end of time. You will work the sanctification of mankind. O holy men: People blessed of the Most Holy Trinity! Your victorious founder shall triumph over the world, the flesh, and the Devil.

"One of your posterity shall achieve greater deeds and work greater wonders than your lordship. That man will be a great sinner in his youth, but like St. Paul he shall be drawn and converted to God. He shall be the great founder of a new religious order different from all the others. He shall divide it into three classes, namely: 1. Military knights; 2. Solitary priests; 3. Most pious hospitallers. This shall be the last religious order in the Church, and it will do more good for our holy religion than all other religious institutes. By force of arms he shall take possession of a great kingdom. He shall destroy the sect of Mahomet, extirpate all tyrants and heresies. He shall bring the world to a holy mode of life. There will be one fold and one Shepherd. He shall reign until the end of time. On the whole earth there shall be only twelve kings, one emperor, and one pope. Rich gentlement shall be very few, but all saints. May Jesus Christ be praised and blessed; for He has vouched to grant to me, a poor unworthy sinner, the spirit of prophecy, not in an obscure way as to His other servants, but has enabled me to write and to speak in a most clear manner. I know that unbelieving and reprobate persons will scoff at my letters and will reject them; but they will be received by those faithful Catholic souls who aspire to the possession of heaven. These letters shall infuse such sweetness of divine love in their hearts, that they will be delighted in perusing them often, and in taking copies of them, because such is the will of the Most High. In these letters it will be found out who belongs to our blessed Lord Jesus Christ and who does not, who is a predestinate or a reprobate. Much better will this be known through the holy sign of the living God. He shall be a saint of God who will take it, love it, and wear it."

115. *Monk Hilarion* (see no. 81)

"After the World War they will make peace but not a lasting peace. They will immediately begin again preparing to strike at one another."

116. *Bl. Johannes Amadeus de Sylva* (d. 1482)

"In the latter days there shall be great wars and bloodshed. The fury of the wars shall last a long time. Whole provinces shall be left naked, and uninhabited, many cities forsaken of people, the nobility slaughtered, principal persons ruined, great changes of kings, commonwealths and rulers."

117. "Germany and Spain will unite under a great prince designated by God. After much slaughtering, the other nations will be forced to come into this union. There is no hope for the unbelievers until all Germany becomes converted; then all will happen quickly. Because of Germany's unfaithfulness, the time will be prolonged until all countries unite under the Great Ruler. After this union mass conversions will take place

by the command of God, and peace and prosperity will follow."

118a. *Nicholas of Fluh* (d. 1487)

"The Church will sink still deeper until she will at last seem to be extinguished, and the succession of Peter and the other Apostles to have expired. After that she will be victoriously exalted in the sight of all doubters."

118b. *Nicholas of Fluh and Dionysius Ryckel*

"The Church will be punished because the majority of Her members—high and low—will become so perverted."

119. *Bernard de Busto* (d. 1490)

"At the time when Anti-Christ is about twenty years old, most of the world will have lost the faith."

PROPHETS OF THE XVI AND XVII CENTURIES

120. *One of the Founders of the Jesuits* (1534)

"The time will come when the Jesuits will be driven out like dogs—And again, other times will come when they will return like nobles."

121. *Blessed Catherine of Racconigi* (1547)

"After three centuries, a descendant of Frances I of France will rule Eurpoe like Charlemagne."

122a. *Mother Shipton* (d. 1551)

"The time will come when England shall tremble and quake for fear of a dead man that shall be heard to speak. 'Unhappy he that lives to see those days, but happy are the dead' Shipton's wife says." "Then will the Dragon give the Bull a great snap, and when the one is down they will go to London Towne. . . . Then will the ravens sit on the Cross and drink as much blood of the nobles as the commons—then woe is me—for London shall be destroyed forever after. . . . and then York shall be London and the Kingdom governed by three Lords appointed by a Royal Great monarch of the best blood in the world, who will set England aright and drive out heresy, and after this shall be a white harvest of corn gotten in by women."

122b. "Carriages without horses shall go,

And accidents fill the world with woe.
Around the earth thoughts shall fly
In the twinkling of an eye;
The world upside dow nshall be,
And gold be found at the foot of a tree.
Through hills man shall ride,
And no horse be at his side.
Under water men shall walk,
Shall ride, shall sleep, shall talk.
In the air men shall be seen
In white, in black, in green;
Iron in the water shall float,
As easily as a wooden boat.
Gold shall be found and shown
In a land that's not now known,
Fire and water shall wonders do,
England shall at last admit a foe."

122c. All England's sons that plow the land
Shall oft be seen with book in hand.
The poor shall then most learning know,
And water wind where corn doth grow;
Great houses stand in farflung vale,
All covered o'er with snow and hail.
Taxes for blood and war
Shall come to every door.
And state and state in fierce strife
Will seek after each other's life.
But when the North shall divide the South
An Eagle shall build in the Lion's mouth.
In London Primrose Hill shall be,
Its center hold a Bishop's See.
Three times shall lovely France
Be led to play a bloody dance;
Before the people shall be free,
Three tyrant rulers shall she see:

Three times the people's hope is gone,
Three rulers, in succession, be—
Each sprung from diff'rent dynasty.
Then, when the fiercest fight is done,
England and France shall be as one.
The British olive next shall twine
In marriage with the German vine.
England shall at last admit a Jew.
The Jew that once was held in scorn
Shall of a Christian then be born,
A house of glass shall come to pass
In England—but alas, alas!
A war will follow with the work
Where dwells the Pagan and the Turk."

122d. "A great man shall come and go,
Men walk beneath and over streams.[1]

123a. *Nostradamus* (d. 1566)

After Germany is prostrate "then a leader ("fuehrer" in German) shall arise from the barren state." (Austria was left barren of the fruit of conquest after World War I.) "He is quite different from former rulers and will come to guide the great empire. Far from joy and goodness will he be and base his parentage. Kingdoms will fall. Great unhappiness."

"Although nations talk peace, trouble brews everywhere. Militaristic parties rise in Germany and pagan cults revive. Opinions are not free and the people not enriched. The heir to the London government is over thrown for having made too many peace protests."

123b "The German fuehrer will deliver the people from meek and voluntary slavery (of the Versailles Treaty?). They will deprive Jupiter (literally God, the Father) of his dignity and honor and place themselves under Mars (i.e., stake all on war). This for the sake of the free city (of Danzig?) in

---

[1] The second and fourth lines of this verse are missing. The order of the prophecies apparently have been tampered with.

another little Mesopotamia (corridor between two rivers)."

"Germany shall initiate the war by unjustified alarms (war of nerves?). Near the city which the Wolf (Poland) shall have entered (Poland occupied Danzig after World War I), the hostilities shall begin. A foreign army will despoil a great country. Its citizens will not be forgiven for their determination (to resist), which will not be let long last, and thereby shall many be confounded."

"Many aids from people afar off desiring to oppose. Suddenly all will be hurried but for the time being they cannot resist." (Poland was prostrate in four weeks and her allies could not help her).

123c. "A deep gate made by the queen will make the place strong and inaccessable (cutting the dykes) but the army of the three lions (shield of Holland) will be defeated because of a terrible thing done inside (German spies beyond the flood frustrated Holland's resistance)."

"On the night when all feel secure because of a feigned oath, it (Belgium) shall be betrayed to the enemy. The people of Leige shall rush upon Brabant" (those fleeing from the east before the Germans blocked the roads to allied troops).

123d. "Horrible war develops in the west. The next year (1940) a plague of fire and blood will visit old and young, even animals shall not escape. The gods (pagan ideals) will make man see that they are the authors of the conflict."

123e. "In the year when figures turned, shall be the same, then bloody France look to't, beware thy fame, for all thy cruelties done, then shall pay, and now approaches fast the reckoning day." (e.g., 1881; 1961; MCM; MCM plus XXXX).

123f. "Peace is coming on one side and war on the other; there was never so great a pursuing man; women shall bewail the innocent blood that shall be spilt—it shall be in France and on all sides. Foot and horse upon the second watch shall come in, destroying all by sea; they shall come into the harbor of

Marseilles: tears, cries and blood—never was so bitter a time. Brooks and rivers shall be a stopping to evil. The old flame of anger being not yet ceased, shall run through France. Take this as an oracle: houses, manors, palaces, sects shall be razed. He that the principality shall keep by cruelty, at last shall see a great army, by fire, blow most dangerously."

"A captain of Great Germany shall come to yield himself through pretended aid to the king of kings so that his revolt will cause great shedding of blood" (not necessarily Hess).

"The Purveyor shall put all in disorder. When Mars (war) shall be in the sign of Aries joined with Saturn and Saturnith, the moon then shall be the greatest misfortune, the sun being then in its exaltation. O great Rome, thy ruin draweth near— not of thy walls; of thy blood and substance."

"France will be divided into two parts: one ruled by an old man for a while, but later the conqueror will deprive him of power."

123g. "A year after the Italian war, the Germans and French and the Spanish will fight for power—the 'schoolhouse of the Republics' will collapse in ruin— on the spot where it stood most people will die suffocated.

"King of Italy, flee. Flee Roman leader who is nearest to you. In the Appenines near Fiesule, a battle will take place; after it will follow a massacre, in which the leaders of the government will be seized—people of the Church, of both sexes will not be spared.

"Before the attack a speech will be made in Milan and will be a deceptives move; by the Eagle's trap the oldest outpost of civilization will be beaten down by cannons—very few people will escape the fire and carnage.

"There will be tears, cries, and complaints and terrors— the government will be marked by bestial cruelty. This will take place in Switzerland, England, and Italy. Blood will flow and no one will be spared.

123h. "Because of the power of three realms the Holy See

will be moved elsewhere. The blood of priests will flow in the streets and temples, as flows water after a furious rain. The Holy of Holies will be destroyed by Paganism and the Old and New Testament will be banished and burned.

"Armies shall fight in the air a great while, the Tree shall fall in the middle of the city; vermin, scabs, swords, firebrands in the face when the Monarch of Adria (Italy and Greece are on the Adriatic) shall fall."

123i. "Naples, Palermo and all of Sicily will be depopulated by order of a foreigner. In Corsica, Sardinia and Salerno the end of evils will follow famine, pest and war.

"The people of the isles (British?) long under siege will eventually gather a force sufficient to oppose and overcome their enemies. Those outside The Isles will be more famished afterwards than before the battle.

"Weep Milan, Lucca and Florence when your great leader ("Duce" in Italian) enters the war.

"The tyrant (of Italy?) will be slain at Port Selin, but the new ruler, being warlike in his vengeance, will not bring freedom to the people."

123j. "From Aquilo a great effort on the part of Hommasse (bad man) will cause Europe and the world to be fearful, but two eclipses (severe defeats?) will bring about his sudden overthrow, resulting in life and death to his people.

"The 'law of More' (Christian Utopia) will decay into another and more seductive teaching (Communism?)."

123k. "When St. George's day falls on Good Friday; when St. Mark's falls on Easter; when St. John's falls on Corpus Christi; then the end of the war will arrive." (1943 is one such year, the next will be 2038.) (See 106b.)

123l. "Arabian power will be installed in Europe—destruction by fire and sword will come with it. Meanwhile the great Asiatic Empire will spread across the sea and continents to destroy the Christian world. It will pass through Italy into

France over the eternal snows (Alps?) and will strike all with its stick."

123m. "A German heart with Trojan blood shall be born. He will rise to great power. He will wipe out the foreign Arabic race and return the Church to her old supremacy.

"In a cycle of the lily (Bourbon) a great prince is born. He comes late (into the fray?), yet early (in age?) into his dominion. Saturn will be in Libra, its exaltation. (1951 is the next year for this occurrance. This dates the zenith of his power. If true the Anti-Christ can be expected shortly thereafter.)

"The Great Pastor shall enter Rome at the head of a large band of exiles, while the great celt shall execute all those who united in the Alps for the Cock (France?).

"In a year when Saturn is in Aquarius together with the sun (e.g., June, 1944), the strong King will be crowned at Rheims and anointed at Aix."

123n. "Many shall come and talk of peace between Monarch and Lords very powerful: but it shall not be agreed to so soon if they do not show themselves more humble than their predecessors.

"While the Great Monarch is fighting victoriously over the Germans, the Italians and Arabs from Northern Africa will attack the South of France, but the Great Monarch will repulse them—many land and sea battles will occur on the south coast of France in the Mediterranean."

123o. "The New Pope will be elected at this time—related to the Great Monarch. He will begin his rule at Avignon, the new capitol of France, and later be restored to Rome by the Great Monarch."

123p. "He will crusade against the Arabs—and capture Constantinople and Jerusalem. He will be especially aided by Spain, then ruled by a King Charles.

"Orders issued at Avignon will be obeyed as far as the Gulf of Persia.

"At the end of King Henry's reign the Orient will attack the Occident. With the death of Henry, peace will cease in Europe —a great cataclysm will follow (reign of Anti-Christ?).

"The force of arms will be united with the sceptre—at a time of misery and calamitous war—shortly thereafter a new king will be anointed, who will reestablish peace."

123q. "After the seat is held seventeen years (Pius XI., Feb. 1922-Feb. 1939), five shall change in the same length of years. (That would be five popes between 1939 and 1956.)

124. *Gameleo*

"The Great Lion will arise when the Holy See has been moved to Mentz, and a Sabinian elected Pope. There will have been much dissension among the cardinals."

125. *Telesphorus of Cozensa* (d. 1388)

"A powerful French monarch and French Pope will regain the holy land after terrible wars in Europe, convert the world and bring universal peace. They will overcome the German Ruler.

"Terrible wars among nations of Europe will follow the secularization of Church property."

126. *Japanese prophecy* (probably Christian)

"When men fly like birds, ten great kings will go to war against each other, and the universe will be under arms."

127. *David Poreaus* (d. 1622)

"The Great Monarch will be of French descent, large forehead, large dark eyes, light brown wavy hair and an eagle nose. He will crush the enemies of the Pope and will conquer the East."

128a. *Fr. Balthassar Mas* (1630)

"I saw a land swallowed by the sea and covered with water, but afterwards I saw that little by little, the sea retreated and left the land visible, and the upper parts of the towers and turrets of the cities rose and appeared more beautiful than before being swallowed by the sea, and it was told me that was England."

128b. *St. Margaret Mary* (1674)

"I understand that devotion to the Sacred Heart is a last effort of His love towards Christians of these latter times, by proposing to them an object and means so calculated to persuade them to love Him."

129a. *Holzhauser* (d. 1658)

"When everything has been ruined by war; when Catholics are hard pressed by traitorous co-religionists and heretics; when the Church and her servants are denied their rights, the monarchies have been abolished and their rulers murdered . . . then the Hand of Almighty God will work a marvelous change, something apparently impossible according to human understanding. There will rise a valiant monarch anointed by God. He will be a Catholic, a descendant of Louis IX, (yet) a descendant of an ancient imperial German family, born in exile. He will rule supreme in temporal matters. The Pope will rule supreme in spiritual matters at the same time. Persecution will cease and justice shall reign. Religion seems to be oppressed, but by the changes of entire kingdoms it will be made more firm.

"He will root out false doctrines and destroy the rule of Moslemism. His dominion will extend from the East to the West. All nations will adore God their Lord according to Catholic teaching. There will be many wise and just men. The people will love justice, and peace will reign over the whole earth, for divine power will bind Satan for many years until the coming of the Son of Perdition (Anti-Christ).

"The reign of the Great Ruler may be compared with that of Caesar Augustus who became Emperor after his victory over his enemies, thereby giving peace to the world, also with the reign of Emperor Constantine the Great, who was sent by God, after severe persecutions, to deliver both the Church and State. By his victories on water and land he brought the Roman Empire under subjection, which he then ruled in peace."

129b. "On account of a terrible war Germany will wail, France will be the cause of all the woe, Germany will be miserably wounded, all will be impoverished. England shall suffer much. The King shall be killed.

"After desolation has reached its peak in England peace will be restored and England will return to the Catholic faith with greater fervor than ever before.

"The Great Monarch will have the special help of God and be unconquerable.

"The Fifth Epoch of time dates from the reign of Charles V until the reign of the Great Monarch.

"The Sixth Epoch from the Great Monarch until Anti-Christ. This Sixth Epoch of the Church—'the time of consolation'—begins with the Holy Pope and the Powerful Emperor, and terminates with the reign of Anti-Christ. This will be an age of solace, wherein God will console His Church after the many mortifications and afflictions she had endured in the Fifth period, for all nations will be brought to the unity of the True Catholic Faith."

129c. The "Angel" is the Great Monarch; "From Heaven" means he will be a Catholic; "Clothed in clouds" implies he will be humble and modest; "Rainbow" he will bring peace to the world; "Sunshine" refers to his wisdom, talents and title; "Feet" refers to his power and zeal; "Open Book" he will rule with justice; "Right and Left Foot," he will exercise power over all the wrold; "Lion Voice," he will put fear into the wicked. (See above, no. 32c.)

129d. "Golden Crown" refers to his Holy Roman (German) Empire; "Cutlass" means his victorious army; the other "angel" refers to the Pope, (Angelic Pastor), "Other angels" are the other helpers of the Great Monarch who will help him crush the Turks. (It may be that these "other angels" refer to other Popes who will reign at the same time as the Great Monarch but after the Angelic Pastor). (See above, no. 32d.)

130. *Sister Mary of Agreda* (d. 1665)

"It was revealed to me that through the intercession of the Mother of God that all heresies will disappear. This victory over heresies has been reserved by Christ for His Blessed Mother. In the last times the Lord will especially spread the renown of His Mother: Mary began salvation and by her intercession it will be concluded. Before the second coming of Christ Mary must, more than ever, shine in mercy, might and grace in order to bring unbelievers into the Catholic Faith. The powers of Mary in the last times over the demons will be very conspicuous. Mary will extend the reign of Christ over the heathens and Mohammedans and it will be a time of great joy when Mary, as Mistress and Queen of Hearts, is enthroned.

"An unusual chastisement of the human race will take place towards the end of the world."

131. *Rudolph Gekner* (d. 1675)

"A great prince of the North with a most powerful army will traverse all Europe, uproot all republics, and exterminate all rebels. His sword, moved by Divine power, will most valiantly defend the Church of Jesus Christ. He will combat in behalf of the true orthodox faith, and shall subdue to his dominion the Mahometan Empire. A new pastor of the universal Church (Pastor Funalis, Franciscan?) will come from the shore (of Dalmatia) through a celestial prodigy, and in simplicity of heart adorned with the doctrines of Jesus Christ. Peace will be restored to the world."

132. *Dionysius of Luxemberg* (1682)

"After the birth of Anti-Christ the people of the world will be very wicked and Godless. People of real virtue will be very scarce. Pastors in many places will neglect the service of God, and will live with women. Even the religious will crave for worldly things. The churches will be dreary and empty like deserted barns . . . at the time when Anti-Christ is about twenty years of age about the whole world will be without faith, subjects will be oppressed by rulers and others in authority. In every period of tribulation God aided His Church, and He will do it in the time before the coming of Anti-Christ. From the midst of His Church He will raise up a Christian ruler who will perform most remarkable deeds. With divine assistance, this ruler will not only lead erring souls back to the true faith but also deal a heavy blow to the foes of the empire, the Turks, take away their empire and restore it to Christianity."

PREDICTIONS FROM THE 18TH CENTURY

133. *Monk of Werl* (published 1701)

"The whole north of Europe will wage war against the whole south led by a strong monarch. This man will restore divine order in the Church, state and family, thus giving true peace to the nations."

134. *Father Lavinsky* (d. 1708)

"The world will be harrassed by civil wars and greater destruction than ever before. Germany will be partitioned and have many enemies. Religion will be greatly oppressed and monks will be banished. During their banishment, the Cross, to the astonishment of all, will shine in double splendor through many lands because of the great ruler."

135. *Blessed Louis de Montfort* (d. 1716)

"The power of Mary over all devils will be particularly outstanding in the last period of time. She will extend the Kingdom of Christ over the idolators and Moslems, and there will come a glorious era in which Mary will be the ruler and queen of human hearts." (See 130 and 179c.)

136. *Monk of Padua* (1740; last eight of his twenty entries)

1. "Here is the faith intrepid and a terrible immolation —King in Italy—Pius XI."

2. "Thou art the Angelic Pastor of Rome, O benevolent doctor, O most indulgent father—Hail, Gregory XVII, most Holy Father, necessary shepherd." (Pius XII now reigning did not take the name Gregory—next Pope?).

3. "Hail, O wise shepherd and pilot, most prudent of the Roman people. Our Very Holy Father, Paul VII (Paul VI; Benedict XV did not assume the name Paul as foretold by the Monk of Padua). Behold, perfect peace returned."

4. "Behold the flower of flowers, behold the lily crowning the virtues of his native land and the most holy acts predicted by the Lord. Our Most Holy Father, Clement XV. Thou, Rome, his daughter, venerate this King of Peace."

5. "From the half moon proceeds this pope sent to Rome by the Divine Doctor. Hail, O our well-beloved Father, Pius XII most Holy Mediator, Future Victim."

6. "Thanks to an excellent work of the sun, the earth has nourished the devoted flock of a most holy shepherd— our very Holy Father Gregory XVIII, a priest altogether admirable."

7. "Oh, what a messenger of peace of the glory of the olive tree, of the Lord, oh, what a protector, all filled with goodness!—the Pope, Leo XIV, energetic monarch, a glorious reign."

8. "In the last great desolation of the world the last High Priest of the true God will reign. Criminal Rome will be destroyed and the terrible Judge, in glory, will judge all nations." (See no. 82 and 113).

137a. *Father Nectou, S.J.* (d. 1772)

"When those things come to pass which will bring on the triumph of the Church, then will such confusion reign on earth that people will think God has permitted them to have their own contrary will and that the providence of God is not concerned about the world. The confusion will be so general that mankind will not be able to think aright, as if God had entirely withheld his providence from mankind, and that, during the worst crisis, the best that can be done would be to remain where God has placed us, and persevere in fervent prayer.

"Two parties will be formed in France which shall fight unto death. The party of evil will at first be stronger; the good side shall be weaker. At that time there shall be such a terrible crisis that people, frightened by events, shall believe that the end of the world is come. Blood shall flow in several large cities. The very elements shall be convulsed. It will be like a little general judgment. A great multitude of persons shall perish in these calamitous times. But the wicked shall never prevail. They indeed shall conspire for the destruction of the Church; but time shall not be allowed them, because this frightful crisis shall be of a short duration. When all will be considered lost, all shall be found safe.

"During this revolution (Communist?), which shall very likely be general, and not confined to France, Paris shall be destroyed so completely that, twenty years afterwards, fathers walking over its ruins with their children, these will inquire what place that was. To whom they will answer: My child, this was formerly a great city, which God has destroyed on account of her crimes. Paris shall certainly be destroyed, but before this occurs, such signs and portents shall be observed, that all good people will be induced to fly away from it. After this most terrible event, everything shall return to order; justice shall reign in the world, and the counter-revolution shall be accomplished. The triumph of the Church will then be so complete that nothing like it shall ever be seen, for this will be the last victory of the Church upon earth. Those persons who shall behold this last revolution will thank God for having preserved them to witness this glorious triumph of the Church."

137b. "A man disliked by France will be placed on the throne; a man of the house of Orleans will be made king. It is only after this event that the counter revolution shall begin.

"As when the fig tree begins to sprout and produce leaves, it is a certain sign that summer is near, so when England shall begin to wane in power, the destruction of Paris shall be near at hand. This shall be a sign. England shall, in her turn, experience a more frightful revolution than that of France. It shall continue long enough to give time to France to recover her strength, then she will help England return to order and peace."

138. *Fr. Laurence Ricci, S.J.* (d. 1775)

"After the rule of Napoleon a time will come when the people will become poor and the world will be punished in three ways: wars, famines, and pestilences. At a time when the whole world seems doomed, God will intervene. With His aid, a valiant duke will arise, from the ancient German house which was humiliated by the French monarch. This great ruler will restore stolen Church property. Protestantism will cease and the Turkish empire will end. This duke will be the most powerful monarch on earth. At a gathering of men noted for piety and wisdom, he will, with the aid of the Pope, introduce new rules, and ban the spirit of confusion. Everywhere there will be one fold and one shepherd."

139. *Capuchin Friar* (1776)

"All the ecclesiastics, both secular and regular, shall be stripped of all their possessions, and of every kind of property, and obliged to beg from lay persons their food and everything necessary for their support, and for the worship of God. All religious orders will be abolished, except one having the rules of the most rigid and most severe institute of the ancient monks. During these calamities the Pope shall die. Through the death of the Supreme Pontiff the Church will be reduced to the most painful anarchy, because from three hostile powers three popes will be contemporaneously elected: one Italian, another German, the third Greek, by force of arms, shall be placed on the throne. During this time much human blood shall be shed in Italy, and many cities, country towns, and castles shall be brought to ruin, with the death of many thousands of persons.

"By the Catholic clergy and people the true and lawful Pope will be elected, who shall be a man of great holiness and goodness of life, selected from the surviving monastic Order mentioned above.

"A scion of the Carlovingian race, by all considered extinct, will come to Rome to behold and admire the piety and clemency of this Pontiff, who will crown him, and declare him to

be the legitimate Emperor of the Romans, and from the Chair
of St. Peter, the Pope will lift up the standard, the crucifix, and
will give it to the new emperor.

"This new emperor, with the robust Italian and French
people, and with those of other nations, will form a most
powerful host, called the Church Army (see 114), through
which he shall destroy the Ottoman Empire, all heresies, and
shall also totally defeat the Emperor of the North, who is called
Mystic Anti-Christ.

"The above mentioned new emperor, with the assistnce of
God and of the Pope, will cooperate to the reformation of
abuses; will assume (with the free consent of the Pope) the
management of the temporal government; will assign a decent
pension to the Supreme Pontiff, and also the bishops and clergy;
and they all, being detached from earthly covetousness, will
live in peace, which shall last till the end of time.

"Finally, the Pope will selcet twelve subjects of his religion,
whom he will send through the world to preach missions. They
shall have the power of converting the nations to the faith of
our Lord Jesus Christ, excepting the Hebrews, who are reserved
for the end of the world."

140a. *Bernhardt Rembordt* (d. 1783)

"Cologne will be the scene of a terrible battle. Many foreigners will be slaughtered there: both men and women will
fight for their faith. It will be impossible to prevent this horrible devastation. People will wade up to their ankles in blood.
At last a foreign king (Great Monarch?) will appear and win
a victory for the cause of the righteous. The remaining enemy
will retreat to the birchtree (Westphalia?—see no. 89). There
the last battle will be fought for the just cause.

"At that time France will be divided. The German Empire
will select a simple man as the emperor, who will rule for a
short time. His successor will be the man for whom the world
has longed. He will be called a Roman emperor and give peace
to the world. He will restore Siegburg and Heisterbach. He is

the great monarch foretold by Holzhauser (See no. 129). At that time there will be no Jews in Germany and the heretics will admit their error. A good and happy era will follow. God will be praised on earth and war will be no more. . . . Then the fugitive brothers and their children's children will return and continue to live in peace in their native land."

140b. "When the Emperor of Germany flees for his life a man who carries his crown for him will be the man the world has long expected. He will be called 'Roman Emperor' and will give peace to the world."

141a. *Jane Le Royer* (d. 1798)

"My Father, God has manifested to me the malice of Lucifer, and the perverse and diabolical intentions of his emissaries (secret societies) against the Holy Church of Jesus Christ. At the command of their master these wicked men have traversed the earth like furies, with the intention of preparing the way and the place for Anti-Christ whose reign is approaching. Through the corrupted breath of this proud spirit they have poisoned the minds of men. Like persons infected with pestilence, they have reciprocally communicated the evil to each other, and the contagion has become general. What convulsions! what scandals! The thick vapors which I have seen rising from the earth, and obscuring the light of the sun, are the false maxims of irreligion and of license (falsely called liberty), which in part originated in France, and in part came to us from abroad. These have succeeded in confounding all sound principles, and in spreading everywhere such darkness as to obscure the light both of faith and of reason. The storm began in France, which shall be the first theatre of its ravages, after having been its forge."

141b. "The Church in council assembled shall one day strike with anathemas, pull down and destroy the evil principles of that criminal constitution. I saw in God's essence a numerous assembly of ministers of the Church, who, like an army in battle array, and like a firm and unflinching column, shall sustain the

rights of the Church, and of their Head, and shall reestablish its
ancient discipline . . . What consolation, what joy, for all the
truly faithful! . . . I saw in the Divinity a great power, guided
by the Holy Spirit, which shall destroy all the abuses of the
Revolution; religions shall be abolished (Protestantism); the
altars shall be reestablished, and religion shall more than ever
flourish."

141c. "When the persecution against the Church has spread
like a wild raging fire, even to places where it was thought there
was no danger, then the Lord, who knows how to draw glory
out of everything, will suddenly command the mighty fire
stream (war?) and Satan to halt. Then will a universal peace
be proclaimed."

142. *Venerable Bartholomew de Saluzzo* (18th century)

"Blessed friar of the Minorities, the Lord, after freeing thee
from thy afflictions, will give thee great honor and glory (Angelic Pastor). Fear not; thou shalt be endowed with very
great courage, and pusillianimity shall fly from thee. Bear all
thy trials with humble resignation, for the sake of the Lord.
Reflect that He suffered more than thou, and He will communicate His power and strength to thee."

143. *Helen Wallraff* (d. 1801)

"Some day a Pope will flee from Rome in company of only
four cardinals and come to Cologne." (Cologne was her home;
probably wishful thinking.)

144. *Sister Marianne* (d. 1804)

"So long as public prayers will be made, nothing shall happen; but a time will come when public prayers shall cease.
People will say, 'things will remain as they are.' It is then that
the great calamity shall occur. This great calamity shall consist: 1, in a great flight; 2, great tribulations in many large
cities of France; 3, a horrible massacre in the capitol, namely,
Paris. During the battle, people shall hear the noise of the
cannon nine leagues distant (27 miles).

"Before the great combat the wicked shall be masters. They will perpetrate all the evils in their power, but not as much as they desire, because they shall not have the time. Good and faithful Catholics, less in number, shall be on the point of being annihilated, but a stroke from Heaven will save them (three days darkness?)

"O power of God! O power of God! All the wicked shall perish, and also many good men. O, how frightful shall these calamities be! The churches shall be closed, but only for the space of twenty-four hours. Religious women, being terrified, shall be on the point of abandoning the convent, but they shall remain. At this time such extraordinary events shall take place that the most incredulous will be forced to say, 'the finger of God is there.' O power of God! There shall be a terrible night, during which no one shall be able to sleep. These trials shall not last long, because no person could endure them. When all shall appear lost, all will be saved. It is then that dispatches shall arrive, announcing good news, when the Te Deum shall be sung, in a manner in which it has never been heard before. It is then that the Prince shall reign, whom people will seek, that before did not esteem him. At that time the triumph of religion will be so great that no one has ever seen the equal. All injustices will be repaired, civil laws will be formed in harmony with the laws of God and of the Church. The instruction given to children will be most Christian;! pious guilds for workmen shall be reestablished; the triumph of the Church and of France shall be most glorious."

EARLY NINETEENTH CENTURY WORKS

145. *Josefa von Bourg* (d. 1807)

"God will choose a descendant of Constantine, Pepin and St. Louis, who has been tried by a long period of disappointment to come from exile to rule over Europe. He will have the sign of the cross on his breast and besides being a religious man, will be kind, wise, just and powerful. Under him the Catholic religion will spread as never before."

146. *Jean Paul Richter* (d. 1809)

"Through a terrible purgatory Europe will return to the faith."

147a. *Mother Maria Rafols* (Dated 1815; found, 1931)

"God begs me so insistently to write these things so that He might enable me to realize that poor sinners, no matter how obstinate, might, by reading these writings in the times to come, awake from their profound sleep and blindness and have recourse to His paternal and merciful Heart. Since they will be in need of His mercy, because of their ungratefulness they will forget Him and will even be anxious to obliterate His memory and His Blessed Name from this world.

"In the very difficult times to come the Sacred Heart of Jesus shall perform such wonders in this place (the Mother House of the Sacred Heart at Saragoza, Spain), so as to win sinners away from their corrupted lives.

"In the times to come such shall be the corruption of morality in every social class that My Eternal Father shall be forced to destroy entire cities should they not reform after His merciful call. So great shall be the putrefaction that they shall scandalize and pervert even the innocent little children so dear to My Sacred Heart. When these documents shall be found (1931) these enormities will be taking place not only in Spain but throughout the entire world.

"It is also my wish, My daughter, that in My beloved Spain every province, city, town and individual be consecrated to My Sacred Heart. Spain shall be the first nation to be consecrated to My Sacred Heart (It was, by King Alfonso), but I will not be satisfied with general consecration. I wish to preside over homes, families, professor's chairs, schools, offices, shops, and the cupolas of the churches. In every place I want My beloved sons to see and venerate My image. Even in the mountains My image shall be exposed. No family shall be established where My Heart does not preside. I am ready to pour down My graces but I want to be asked for them with unlimited trust.

"I wish many communions of Reparation. Also there is the Feast of Christ the King that shall be instituted by My will, and at the proper time by My beloved son, Pius XI. I wish that it be surrounded with the greatest possible solemnity and splendor. I want My kingdom to be spread throughout the entire world. But in My beloved Spain this Divine fire is to burn with greater intensity, and from there they will carry it throughout the whole world.

"In the times to come there will be many souls who will propagate the devotion to My Divine Heart, and this shall be very agreeable to Me, but those that must do this the most are the sons of My company, for I have chosen them principally for this work so pleasing to Me.

"It is My wish that all men visit the Image of My Most Merciful Heart, and to those who devoutly carry it on their person, I promise great graces for eternal salvation.

"All those who wear My medal devoutly shall receive My special protection at the hour of their death.

"Those who wish to obtain the conversion of sinners shall obtain it from My Merciful Heart, by asking it through the mediation of My Most Holy Mother. To all those who seek Me with a lively faith and spirit of prayer, through the intercession of My Most Holy Mother, My Merciful Heart will give itself. I shall never refuse any graces which are asked Me through the intercession of My Most Holy Mother.

"It is My desire also that the Feast of My Sacred Heart be celebrated throughout the entire Catholic Church with the greatest solemnity, that it be made a holy day of obligation and that all the faithful receive Holy Communion on that day.

"Men offend Me also by the lack of love that they have for one another; the rich seek to exploit the poor and the poor rebel against the rich. It is My wish that there be peace and union and that they have great love one for the other. There

are also many who do not desire to obey the commands of
Holy Mother Church and My Vicar on earth. There are also
many who persecute the Church and seek to destroy Her.
Neither priests nor religious are respected, yet I desire that all
be converted and perform acts of satisfaction to placate the
wrath of the Divine Justice of My Eternal Father.

"I desire that priests be a living model of My image, and
that all propagate devotion to My Divine Heart.

"There is, however, a thing which hurts My Heart still
more, and that is to be offended, forgotten and despised by
souls consecrated to Me. Oh how much do I love my priests
and how meager is their cooperation with My love. I have
called each one of them and I want My priests to be the salt
of the earth, to be holy, and to come to My tabernacle which
is forgotten by so many of them. They forget that I love them
with all My heart, that I want to be present in all their actions.
Tell them to visit My tabernacle where I am waiting to teach
and inspire them and to communicate My Spirit to them, so
that they may bring life to many souls. I want them to be very
humble, poor, and chaste. Let them never forget that it is
My greatest desire that they love one another as I have loved
them from the beginning and that lack of charity hurts My
Sacred Heart. Let them cover their defects with the cloak of
charity and thus avoid scandalizing the people.

"The Sacred Heart of Jesus was very sad on account of
the offenses which He continually receives from men by reason
of the sacrileges which they commit, and which they are going
to commit during the years when this writing will be found,
and also by reason of the coldness with which those who call
themselves Christians are going to serve Him."

147b. "He, (the Sacred Heart), makes me feel that, in
the times to come, there shall be in Spain and all over the world,
many persecutors of the religion and of the country, who will
be anxious to destroy all good things; and my sweet Jesus
orders me to write these examples of his protection in order that

they may keep up their spirit however big the wars and persecutions might be, having God with them they have nothing to fear. He will confuse the enemies of the Church, and many of them shall become zealous apostles, followers of St. Paul, who will conquer many souls for Him. I do not speak to you for your benefit, but for other sons of Mine, who one day shall be persecuted, and who shall be very uncertain and helpless in the combats prepared by the enemy, who shall try to wipe out not only religion, but even My name from the face of the earth. This period will begin openly in the year 1931.

"I am ready to pour out many graces upon My beloved Spain, which shall be persecuted so severely by Freemasonry. I will not let My faithful sons be overcome. Spain the beloved of My Blessed Mother, is My first beloved, and I would destroy all the nations of the world rather than let the Faith disappear from Spain.

"Many are they who persecute her (the Church) and seek to destroy her. Neither priests nor religious are respected, yet they are the select portion of My Church, and it is I Who receive all these offenses because it is to Me that they are done. Pray that fortitude be given to the Vicar of Christ (who shall be greatly persecuted). For My Name, and for My Sake, at all times and in all places, they (the Jesuits) will be greatly persecuted, as I was, in My mortal life, and the enemy, jealous of the great good that they do for souls, will work to make them disappear, but I make it known to you, My daughter, and through you to all men, that they will prevail until the end of time despite their enemies, and I will bless greatly the nations and towns who welcome them with loving good will, and one of these nations I desire to be My Beloved Spain. I (Mother Rafols) feel that there will be a great religious persecution, very much like the one we now suffer. Let them have confidence that all will pass, and when it appears to them that the Lord sleeps He stands, ever on watch, and when He says 'Enough,' all His enemies shall be confounded."

147c. "My Sweet Jesus gave me to understand that many of His sons all over the world (when these writings shall be found), guided by the infernal spirit, profaning and destroying temples, demolishing images, and above all, anxious to destroy His Blessed Name from the face of the earth. At hearing these things I was terribly impressed, and more yet when the Heart of Jesus and the Blessed Virgin made me see and feel more clearly, that the evil spirit would be firmly bent upon Spain, even more than upon any other nation, working incessantly to destroy the Christian Faith from all its inhabitants, and, in a special way, they will be anxious to take away, and they will succeed, from the eyes of their little children so beloved by His Sacred Heart, His Image, and they will forbid that his Divine doctrine might be taught to them, all with the infernal purpose that He might be ignored. My Sweet Jesus answered—'Do not be afraid: whatever means and machinations My unfortunate sons might invent to destroy the faith of Spain, they will not succeed, and I assure you, for your consolation and tranquility, that for the love of the just, pure and chaste souls that will always live in Spain, I will reign until the end of time in it, in a singular manner, and My Image will be venerated even in the streets and public squares.'

"The greatness and nobility of a nation shall depend on the faith and Catholic religion which exists there. If they lose their religion it shall be destroyed. I give them warning, through you, so that no one may deceive himself, and so that all may know the way that they must follow if they desire to please Me. They live apart from Him (His Heavenly Father) from My Catholic Church, from the orders of My Vicar on earth, and from My commandments. Oh, that I would find well disposed at least the souls which are consecrated to Me. But, my daughter, many have abandoned Me, and prefer their desires, their self-love, their own glory, because of which they live a very worldly life, and their heart is taken up with these vile things, and for Me they have no room.

"The offenses that I have received, and those that I shall yet receive are many, especially woman, with her immodest dress, her nakedness, her frivolity and her evil intentions. Because of all this she shall accomplish the demoralization of the family, and of mankind. Such shall be the corruption of morality in every social class, and so great unchastity, that My Eternal Father shall be forced to destroy entire cities should they not reform after this merciful call.

"Ordinarily the corruption of the family always has been the origin of the public calamities, and of the destruction of the Christian Faith; for the first purpose of our common enemy is the destruction of the Christian family; once he attains this, the infernal enemy is sure of victory. Therefore the great evil of these times, and of the even worse than these that shall come, always has been and always shall be to lose the memory and taste of the supernatural life, living only for earthly and sinful things."

147d. "When those turbulent and calamitous times will come, the mostpowerful means to give satisfaction to His Eternal Father, will be to invoke His Most Holy Mother under the invocation of El Pilar, who is the Patroness and Protectrix of our beloved Spain, and that the mental and vocal prayer, meditating on the Five Sorrowful Mysteries of the most holy rosary will be the most substantial devotion, and most pleasing to the Virgin of El Pilar, in times of wars, pestilence and persecutions against our most holy religion."

148. *Father Korzeniecki, O.P.* (1819)

St. Andrew Bobola appeared to him and caused him to see this vision which also he interpreted:

The priest saw an immense plain. Then the blessed martyr said to him: 'you behold now the fields of Pinsk, (Northern Poland) where I had the glory of suffering martyrdom for the faith of Jesus Christ.' He then beheld that vast field covered with Russian, Turkish, French, English, Austrian and Prussian armies, and others which he could not well discern, all of them fighting in a most furious manner one against the other. Not being able to comprehend the meaning of this vision, St. Andrew explained it to him in the following words: 'when the war which you see shall end, then the kingdom of Poland shall be re-established, and I shall be acknowledged its principal patron.' (Part of this was realized in 1918.) (Andrew Bobola was canonized by Pope Pius XI and would therefore now be in a position to be made Patron of Poland.)

149. *Mathew Lang* (d. 1820)

"After the Great war (World War I) there will be no peace. The people will rise and all will fight against each other. . . . The rich and nobles will be killed. The world war will not make people better but much worse. . . . Tell your children that their children will live to see the time when the earth will be cleared. God will do away with people because there will be no charity among men. Religious faith will decline; priests will not be respected; people will be intent only on eating and drinking; there will be many immensely rich people and large numbers of paupers; great wealth will not endure long, for the red caps (Communists?) will come. People will hide in the forests and many will go into exile. After this civil conflict and general clearing up people will love each other as much as previously they hated one another."

150. *Elizabeth Canori-Mora* (d. 1825)

"It seemed to me to behold the heavens opening, and St. Peter, Prince of the Apostles, coming down, surrounded with great glory and by a numerous escort of heavenly spirits, singing canticles. St. Peter was dressed in his pontifical robes, and held in his right hand the pastoral staff, with which he was drawing upon the earth an immense cross; at the same time the angels sang these words of the Psalmist, 'You will constitute them princes over the whole earth.'

"After this the holy Apostle touched with his staff the four extremities of the cross, from which instantly sprung up four beautiful trees loaded with blossoms and fruits. These mysterious trees had the form of a cross, and were surrounded by a splendid light. Then I comprehended in the depth of my soul that St. Peter had produced these four symbolic trees to the end that they may serve as a place of refuge to the little flocks of the faithful friends of Jesus Christ, and in order to preserve them from the fearful punishment which shall convulse the whole earth. All good Christians shall then be protected under these trees, together with all those religious persons who shall have faithfully preserved in their hearts the spirit of their order. I say the same thing in relation to the secular clergy and to all other persons of every class who shall have kept in their heart the Catholic faith—they shall all be protected. But woe, to those religious who do not observe their rule! thrice unhappy they! for they shall all be struck by that terrible punishment. I say the same to all secular clergy, and to all classes of people in the world who give themselves to a life of pleasure, and who follow the false maxims of modern ideas, which are opposed to the holy precepts of the gospel. These wretched people, who through their scandalous conduct deny the faith of Jesus Christ, shall perish under the weight of the indignant arm of God's justice. Not one of them shall be able to escape the punishment.

"I beheld these good Christians, who had sought a refuge under those mysterious trees, in the form of beautiful lambs confided to the care and vigilance of St. Peter, their good shepherd, testifying to him the most humble and most respectful obedience. As soon as St. Peter, the prince of the Apostles, had gathered the flock of Jesus in a place of safety, he reascended into heaven, accompanied by legions of angels. Scarcely had they disappeared, when the sky was covered with clouds so dense and dismal that it was impossible to look at them without dismay. On a sudden there burst out such a terrible and violent wind, that its noise seemed like the roars of furious lions. The sound of the dreadful hurricane was heard over the whole earth. Fear and terror struck not only men, but the very beasts.

"All men shall rise one against the other, and they shall kill one another without pity. During this sanguinary conflict the avenging arm of God will strike the wicked, and in his mighty power he will punish their pride and presumption. God will employ the powers of hell for the extermination of these impious and heretical persons who desire to overthrow the Church and destroy it to its very foundation. These presumptuous men in their mad impiety believe that they can overthrow God from His throne; but the Lord will despise their artifices, and through an effect of His Mighty Hand He will punish these impious blasphemers by giving permission to the infernal spirits to come out from hell. Innumerable legions of demons shall overrun the earth, and shall execute the orders of Divine Justice by causing terrible calamities and disasters; they shall attack everything; they shall injure individual persons and entire families; they shall devastate property and alimentary productions, cities and villages. Nothing on earth shall be spared. God will allow the demons to strike with death those impious men, because they gave themselves up to the infernal powers, and had formed with them a compact against the Catholic Church.

"Being desirous of more fully penetrating my spirit with a deeper sentiment of His Divine Justice, God showed to me the awful abyss; I saw in the bowels of the earth a dark and frightful cavern, whence an infinite number of demons were issuing forth, who under the form of men and beasts came to ravage the earth, leaving everywhere ruins and blood. Happy will be all true and good Catholics! They shall experience the powerful protection of the holy Apostles, St. Peter and St. Paul, who will watch over them lest they may be injured either in their persons or their property. Those evil spirits shall plunder every place where God has been outraged, despised, and blasphemed; the edifices they profaned will be pulled down and destroyed, and nothing but ruins shall remain of them.

"After this frightful punishment I saw the heavens opening, and St. Peter coming down again upon earth; he was vested in his pontifical robes, and surrounded by a great number of angels, who were chanting hymns in his honor, and they proclaimed him as sovereign of the earth. I saw also St. Paul descending upon the earth. By God's command, he traversed the earth and chained the demons, whom he brought before St. Peter, who commanded them to return into hell, whence they had come.

"Then a great light appeared upon the earth which was the sign of the reconciliation of God with man. The angels conducted before the throne of the prince of the Apostles the small flock that had remained faithful to Jesus Christ. These good and zealous Christians testified to him the most profound respect, praising God and thanking the Apostles for having delivered them from the common destruction, and for having protected the Church of Jesus Christ by not permitting her to be infected with the false maxims of the world. St. Peter then chose the new pope. The Church was again organized; religious orders were reestablished; the private families of ordinary Christians, through their great fervor and zeal for the glory of God, became like the most exemplary religious communities. Such is the glorious triumph reserved for the Catholic Church; she shall be praised, honored, and esteemed by all men. All men shall become Catholics, and shall acknowledge the Pope as Vicar of Jesus Christ." (Some of the above may refer to the time of Anti-Christ.)

151. *Abbe Souffrand* (d. 1828)

"The Great Ruler will perform such great and noble deeds that the infidels will be forced to admit the working of God's Providence. Under his reign the greatest righteousness will be practiced and the earth will bear in overabundance."

"Between the cries, 'Everything is lost,' and 'Everything is saved,' there will be scarcely any interval."

152. *Nursing Nun of Belez* (d. 1830)

"There will be a great slaughtering whereby the wicked will try to eradicate the religion of Jesus Christ. After they have killed a great number they will raise a cry of victory, but suddenly the good will receive help from above. This great crisis, in which eventually the good triumph, will be of short duration, namely, about three months. The majority of the wicked will perish and the living will be very much afraid over the chastisement of the others. They cannot but recognize the finger of God and adore His omnipotence. Many will then be converted and order and justice restored."

153. *Bishop George Michael Wittman* (d. 1833)

"Woe is me! Sad days are at hand for the Holy Church of Jesus Christ. The Passion of Jesus will be renewed in the most dolorous manner in the Church and in her Supreme Head. In all parts of the world there will be wars and revolutions, and much blood will be spilled. Distress, disasters, and poverty will everywhere be great, since pestilential maladies, scarcity, and other misfortunes will follow one another.

"Violent hands will be laid on the Supreme Head of the Catholic Church; bishops and priests will be persecuted, and schisms will be provoked, and confusion reign amid all classes. Times will come, so pre-eminently bad, that it will seem as if the enemies of Christ and of His Holy Church, which He founded with His blood, were about to triumph over her. But the priesthood will remain firm and resolute, and good people will adhere faithfully to that body. A general separation will be made. The wheat shall be winnowed, and the floor swept. Secret societies will work great ruin, and exercise a marvelous monetary power, and through that many will be blinded, and infected with most horrible errors; however, all this shall avail naught. Christ says, He who is not with Me is against Me, and he who gathereth not with Me, scattereth. Scandals will be but too rife, and woe to those by whom they come! Although the tempests will be terrible, and will turn many in their pas-

sage, nevertheless they cannot shake the rock whereon Christ
has founded His Church: "Portae inferi non prevalebunt."

"The faithful sheep will gather together, and in unions
of prayer will offer potent resistance to the enemies of the Catholic Church. Yes, yes, the flock will become small. Many of
you will see those sad times and days which will bring such
evil in their train; but I shall not behold them. A marvelous
thing will occur, but then hell will rise in opposition against
it, and terrible agitation will ensue. Great confusion will reign
amid princes and nations. The incredulity of the present day
is preparing those horrid evils."

154. *Bl. Casper del Bufalo* (d. 1837)

He foretold "the destruction of impenitent persecutors of
the Church during the three days darkness. He who outlives
the darkness and fear of the three days—it will seem to him
as if he were alone on earth because of the fact that the world
will be covered everywhere with carcasses."

155. *Cardinal La Roque*

"A regeneration of Faith will appear in Asia through a
descendant of Mohammed."

"Three nations will appear on the ocean with mighty fleets.
In that time the Great Monarch will be in Europe. Devastating
storms and earthquakes will frighten the inhabitants of Switzerland and remind them of their fraility. Plagues amonst
humans and beasts will accompany the earthquakes. The
sickle of death will harvest in Prussia, in palaces as well as in
the houses of the poor, many will flee to England but to no
avail, for even there death will overtake them. In 1938 will
appear the Great Comet which will foreshadow these calamities."

156a. *Blessed Maria Taigi* (d. 1837)

"God will ordain two punishments: One, in the form of
wars, revolutions and other evils, will originate on earth; the
other will be sent from Heaven. There shall come over all the
earth an intense darkness lasting three days and three nights.
Nothing will be visible and the air will be laden with pestilence,

which will claim principally but not exclusively the enemies of religion. During this darkness artificial light will be impossible. Only blessed candles can be lighted and will afford illumination. He who out of curiosity opens his window to look out or leaves his house will fall dead on the spot. During these three days the people should remain in their homes, pray the Rosary and beg God for mercy.

"On this terrible occasion so many of these wicked men, enemies of His Church, and of their God, shall be killed by this divine scourge, that their corpses round Rome will be as numerous as the fish, which a recent inundation of the Tiber had carried into the city. All the enemies of the Church, secret as well as known, will perish over the whole earth during that universal darkness, with the exception of some few, whom God will soon after convert. The air shall be infected by demons, who will appear under all sorts of hideous forms.

"After the three days of darkness, Saints Peter and Paul, having come down from heaven, will preach throughout the world and designate a new pope (see 150). A great light will flash from their bodies and will settle upon the cardinal, the future Pontiff. Then Christianity will spread throughout the world. Whole nations will join the Church shortly before the reign of Anti-Christ. These conversions will be amazing. Those who shall survive shall have to conduct themselves well. There shall be innumerable conversions of heretics, who will return to the bosom of the Church; all will note the edifying conduct of their lives, as well as that of all other Catholics. Russia, England, and China will come into the Church.

156b. "France shall fall into frightful anarchy. The French people shall have a desperate civil war, in which old men themselves will take up arms. The political parties having exhausted their blood and their rage, without being able to arrive at any satisfactory understanding, shall at the last extremity agree by common consent to have recourse to the Holy See. Then the Pope shall send to France a special legate, in order that he may examine the state of affairs and the dispositions of the people. In consequence of the information received, His Holiness himself shall nominate a most Christian king for the government of France."

156c. "Religious shall be persecuted, priests shall be massacred, the churches shall be closed, but only for a short time; the Holy Father shall be obliged to abandon Rome."

157a. *Bro. Louis Rocco* (d. 1840)

"All over Europe there will rage terrible civil wars. God has long been patient with the corruption of morals. . . . He will destroy half of mankind. The poor will be rich and rich poor.

"Russia will witness many outrages; great cities as well as smaller towns will be destroyed and a bloody revolution will destroy half of the population; the royal family, the nobles and many of the clergy will be killed and the Russian Empire will be divided. Poland will become independent and develop into one of the principal Powers of Europe, whereas Hungary will disappear. In Constantinople, the cross will replace the half moon of Moslemism and Jerusalem will be the seat of a king. Vienna will be hated by all nations, suffer great devastation and become a waste place. A venerable monarchy will collapse after many battles, but its ruling dynasty will be preserved. The kings and lords of Germany will abdicate. The king of Prussia will suffer particularly. The German sections of Austria will join Germany, so also will the commercial cities of Belgium and Switzerland. A Catholic descendant of a German imperial house (Hapsburg?) will rule a united Germany with peace, prosperity and great power, for God will be with this sovereign (Great Monarch?).

"The Slavs of the South (Balkan states) will form a great Catholic empire and drive out of Europe the Turks, who will settle in Northern Africa and subsequently embrace the Catholic faith.

157b. "A Great Monarch will arise after a period of terrible wars and persecutions in Europe. He will be a Catholic; he will not be German (by birth?)."

157c. *La Salette* (1846)

The Blessed Virgin is quoted as saying that after a terrible European war, there will arise a great ruler and his reign will be marked by peace and marvelous progress in Christianity.

158a. *Mary Lataste* (d. 1847)

"Pray for France; pray much and never cease from praying. France shall not perish. When disorder and confusion are at their height in France, the merciful God will intervene in a marvelous manner, overthrow the evildoers and restore order. Afflictions shall come over the earth. Oppression shall reign in the city which I love, and where I have left my heart. She shall be in mourning and desolation, surrounded on every side by her enemies, like a bird caught in the net. During three years and a little more, this city shall appear overcome. (This may refer to the time of Anti-Christ.) But my Mother will come down to that city; she will take the hand of the old man sitting on the throne, and will say to him: Lo! the hour is come; rise up; behold thy enemies! I make them disappear, one after the other, and they shall disappear forevermore. Thou hast given me glory both on earth and in heaven (See 179c). Behold, men venerate thy name, venerate thy courage, venerate thy power: thou shalt live, and I will live with thee. Dry up thy tears, old man; I bless thee!" (this probably refers to Rome and the Pope).

158b. "Peace shall return to the world, because the Blessed Virgin Mary will breathe over the storms and quell them. Her name will be praised, blessed and exalted forever. Prisoners or captives shall recover their liberty; exiles shall return to their country, and the unfortunate or unhappy shall be restored to peace and happiness. Between the most august Mary and her clients there will be a mutual exchange of prayers and graces, of love and affection. From the east to the west, from the north to the south, all shall proclaim the holy name of Mary; Mary conceived without original sin, Mary queen of heaven and earth, Amen."

159. *Sister Rose Asdenti of Taggia* (1847)

"A great revolution will spread over all of Europe and peace will not be restored until the white flower, the lily (Bourbon) has taken possession of the throne of France. Not only religious communities, but also good lay Catholics, shall have their property confiscated. Many of the nobility shall be cast into prison. A lawless democratic spirit of disorder shall reign supreme throughout all Europe. There will be a general overthrow.

"There shall be great confusion of people against people, and nations against nations, with clashing of arms and beating of drums. The Russians and Prussians shall come to make war in Italy. They shall profane many churches, and turn them into stables for their horses. Some bishops shall fall from the faith, but many more will remain steadfast and suffer much for the Church.

"Many terrible calamities impend over Italy. Priests and religious shall be butchered and the earth, especially in Italy, shall be watered with their blood.

"The persecution in Italy is to begin by the suppression of the Jesuits; they shall be called back again; then a third time they will be suppressed and never more be revived.

"During a frightful storm against the Church, all religious orders will be abolished except two, namely, the Capuchins and the Dominicans, together with the Hospitaliers, who shall receive the pious pilgrims, who, in great numbers, shall go to visit and venerate the many martyrs in Italy, killed during the impending persecution." (See nos. 114e and 111.)

(Note: She also foretold the three days darkness and that England would return to the Unity of faith.)

160. *Joseph Goires* (d. 1848)

"The people will be united under a powerful monarch who will make new laws and banish corruption from the earth. To the Church will fall the task of rebuilding society. Before this man comes to save them, the people will realize how bitter it is to desert God."

161. *Father Bernard Maria Clausi, O.F.M.* (d. 1849)

"Before the triumph of the Church comes, God will first take vengeance on the wicked, especially against the Godless. It will be a new Judgment, the like has never been before and it will be universal. It will be so terrible that those who outlive it will imagine that they are the only ones spared. All people will then be good and contrite. This judgment will come suddenly and be of short duration. Then comes the triumph of the holy Church and the reign of brotherly love. Happy, indeed, they who live to see those blessed days. However, before that, evil will have made such progress that it will look like all the devils of Hell were let loose on earth, so terrible will be the persecution of the wicked against the just, who will have to suffer true martyrdom."

PROPHECIES FROM THE LATE NINETEENTH CENTURY

162. *Prophecy of Mayence* (1854)

"Woe to thee, great city (Paris): woe to thee, city of vice! Fire and sword shall succeed fire and famine. Courage faithful souls! The reign of the dark shadow shall not have time to execute all its schemes. But the time of mercy approaches. A prince of the nation is in your midst. It is the man of salvation, the wise, the invincible, he shall count his enterprises by his victories. He shall drive the enemy out of France, he shall march from victory to victory, until the day of divine justice. That day he shall command seven kinds of soldiers against three to the quarter of Bouleaux between Ham, Woerl, and Padenborn. (Westphalia.) Woe to thee, people of the North, thy seventh generation shall answer for all thy crimes. Woe to the people of the East, thou shalt spread afar the cries of affliction and innocent blood. Never shall such an army be seen. Three days the sun shall rise upwards on the heads of the combatants without being seen through the clouds of smoke. Then the commander shall get the victory; two of his enemies shall be annihilated; the remainder of the three shall fly toward the extreme East."

163a. *Cure of Ars* (d. 1859)

"After this victory their enemy (the Prussians) shall not quit entirely the occupied country. They shall come back (for a second invasion of France) ; but this time our army shall fight well everywhere. For during the first war our men would not combat well, but in the second war they will fight. O how they will fight!

"The enemy will allow the burning of Paris, and they will rejoice at it, but they shall be beaten; they shall be driven entirely from France. Our enemies shall return, and will destroy everything in their march. They shall arrive near Poitiers without meeting with any serious resistance, but there they shall be crushed by the defenders of the West, who shall pursue them. From other directions their provisions shall be cut off, and they shall suffer very serious losses. They will attempt to retire toward their country, but very few of them shall ever reach it. All that they took from us shall be returned, and a great deal more. "The Communists of Paris, after their defeat, shall spread themselves through all France, and will be greatly multiplied. They shall seize arms; they shall oppress people of order. Lastly, a civil war shall break out everywhere. These wicked people shall become masters in the north, east, and southwest. They will imprison very many persons, and will be guilty of more massacres. They will attempt to kill all the priests and all the religious. But this shall not last long. People will imagine that all is lost; but the good God shall save all. It will be like a sign of the last judgment. Paris shall be changed, also two or three other cities; God shall come to help; the good shall triumph when the return of the king shall be announced. This shall re-establish a peace and prosperity without example. Religion shall flourish again better than ever before. Paris shall be demolished and burnt in earnest, but not entirely. Events shall transpire more terrible than what we have seen. However, there shall be a limit beyond which the destruction shall not go. A great triumph will be witnessed on the feast of our Lady."

163b. I believe that the Church in England will return to her ancient splendor."

164. *Abbess Maria Steiner* (d. 1862)

"I see the Lord as he will be scourging the world, and chastising it in a fearful manner so that few men and women will remain. The monks will have to leave their monasteries, and the nuns will be driven from their convents, especially in Italy. . . . The Holy Church will be persecuted. . . . Unless people obtain pardon through their prayers, the time will come when they will see the sword and death, and Rome will be without a shepherd."

"The Lord showed me how beautiful the world will be after the awful chastisement. The people will be like the Christians of the primitive Church."

165. *Palma Maria d'Oria* (d. 1863)

"There will be an attempt of the sectaries to establish a republican government in France, Spain, and Italy; a civil war will, in consequence, break out in those countries, accompanied by other dreadful punishments, as pestilence and famine, the massacre of priests, and also of some dignitaries of the church. Rome shall have to endure severe trials from the malice of wicked men. But at the critical moment, when the rebellious Republicans shall attempt to take possession of the Holy City, they shall be suddenly arrested at the gates and froced to fly away in terror, crushed under the deadly blows of the exterminating angel, who, in behalf of the Israelites, destroyed 185,000 men of Sennacherib's army.

"There shall be a three days darkness, during which the atmosphere will be infected by innumerable devils, who shall cause the death of large multitudes of incredulous and wicked men.

"Blessed candles alone shall be able to give light and preserve the faithful Catholics from this impending dreadful scourge. Supernatural prodigies shall appear in the heavens. There is to be a short but furious war, during which the enemies of religion and of mankind shall be universally destroyed. A general pacification of the world, and the universal triumph of the Church are to follow."

166. *Mother Alphonse Eppinger* (1867)

"Many priests have lost their fervor for the honor of God and the salvation of souls. Their hearts hang too much on the phantoms of this life. God will, by chastisements, cure them thereof and so thereby change them. In many religious houses the spirit of poverty and simplicity is forgotten. They look only for convenience, they carry a scandalous splendor to satisfy their pride, therefore must God, through a salutary remedy, restore the true religious spirit. It is indeed a sad thing to see religious houses desecrated, but it will be necessary in order to eradicate pride and worldly luxuries and to bring all things back to simplicity.

"After God has purified the world, faith and peace will return. Whole nations will adhere to the teachings of the Catholic Church."

167. *Brother Anthony of Aix-la-Chapelle,* in 1871

"Some day war will break out again in Alsace. I saw the French in Alsace with Strassburg at their rear, and I saw Italians fighting with them. Suddenly great transports of troops arrived from the French side. A two-day battle ended with the defeat of the Prussian army. The French pursued the Prussians over the Rhine in many directions. In a second battle at Frankfort, the Prussians lost again and retired as far as Siegburg, where they joined a Russian army. The Russians made common cause with the Prussians. It seemed to me as if Austrians were aiding the French. The battle at Siegburg was more horrible than any before and its like will never occur again. After some days the Prussians and Russians retreated and crossed, below Bonn, to the left bank of the Rhine. Steadily pressed by their opponents, they retired to Cologne, which had been bombarded so much that only one-fourth of the city remained intact. Constantly in retreat, the remainder of the Prussian army moved to Westphalia, where the last battle went against them. The people greatly rejoiced because they were freed from the Prussians.

"Then a new emperor, about 40 years old, was elected in Germany, and he met the Pope. Meanwhile, an epidemic broke out in the regions devastated by the war, and many people died. After the battle in Westphalia the French returned to their country, and from then on there was peace between the French and the Germans. Industry and trade prospered, and many convents were founded. All exiles returned to their homes. When I begged God to take the terrible vision away I heard a voice saying: 'Prussia must be humiliated and in a manner that it never again will bring sorrow to the Church.' In the following year the Russians will war with the Turks, driving the latter out of Europe and seizing Constantinople. The new German emperor will mobilize for war, but the Germans will not go beyond their border. When afterward I was shown France and Germany I shuddered at the de-population that had taken place. Soon after the Russo-Turkish War England also will be visited by war."

168a. *Ven. Magdalene Porzat* (d. 1850)

"An enormous bird (Great Monarch) shall awake as from a sleep, and with its terrible bill and claws shall sever the ox's neck and shall eagerly devour the intestines of the wicked dragon. He shall drag to the mud the tricolor (revolutionary) flag of the French and restore to their dominions the legitimate kings. A just and pious man born in Gallicia shall be the Supreme Pontiff; then the whole world shall be united and prosperous. One faith only and one emperor shall reign over the whole earth."

168b. "Listen, my children, to what Mary our Mother charges me to announce to you. 'Behold the end of time! Behold the end of evil and the beginning of good. What is going to happen is not an ordinary event. It is a grand epoch which is going to commence. It is the third (era of the world).

Since the Father, who has created us, in order that we may know, love and serve him; since the Son, who has redeemed us; behold now the Father and the Son to console us, send to us the Triumphant Spirit, with Mary His spouse. This is a grand miracle.

"Mary comes from Heaven. She comes accompanied by a legion of angels. The elect living upon earth should through spiritual electricity elevate themselves in order to go forward before the messengers of God. Behold the host of the Lord! Many holy women, few St. John's. Behold the armor of God! No gun or musket, no club or truncheon, no bolt, no watchdog, no material force, no human means.

"After this Mary, all powerful, shall change all men into good wheat. All shall be good. The Pharisees will be the last to be converted; the great brigands will arrive beforehand. The Jews who have refused to receive Jesus Christ in his humiliation will acknowledge Him at the glorious arrival of Mary.

"The dove (the peace and grace of God through Mary) comes to us from Heaven, wearing on her breast a white cross, sign of reconciliation, and waving a sword of fire, symbol of love. She seats herself on a throne of solid gold, figure of Noah's ark; for she comes to announce the end of a deluge of evils. Behold, she comes, our Mother! The Church prepares everything for the glorious arrival of Mary. The Church forms for her a guard of honor to go before the angels. The triumphal arch is nearly accomplished. The hour is not far distant. It is Mary in person! But she has her precursors,—holy women, apostles, who shall cure the wounds of the body as well as the sins of the heart. Holy women, images of Mary, shall have power to work miracles. After them comes Mary to prepare the place for her Son in His triumphant Church. Behold the Immaculate Conception of the Kingdom of God that precedes the arrival of Jesus Christ. It is the mansion of God upon earth, which is going to purify and prepare itself to receive the Emmanuel. Jesus Christ cannot come into this hovel of the world.

It is necessary that God should send His spirit to renew the face of the earth by means of another creation, to render it a worthy mansion for the God made man. Behold here, the fire from below, for burning and changing everything. Behold here, the fire from above! The love of God comes to embrace and transfigure the world. I see the earth rendered level; its valleys are raised; its mountains are lowered; there is nothing more than gentle hills and beautiful vales (images of the Christian virtues regenerating fallen humanity). Since I am as I am, I see nothing else before us but union and universal fraternity. All men are in reciprocal love. One helps the other. They are all happy."

168c. "It is now twenty-six years since I announced to you the seven crises, the seven wounds and sorrows of Mary which should have to precede her triumph and our cure, namely: 1, Inclemencies of seasons and inundations; 2, Diseases to animals and plants; 3, Cholera over men; 4, Revolutions; 5, Wars; 6, An universal bankruptcy; 7, Confusion."

"The preceding evils have been mitigated through Mary's intercession, who detained the arm of her Son Jesus. Behold now the sixth calamity, the commercial crisis. Commerce marches to its ruin, because the axle, confidence, is shattered. There will be no respite between the sixth and seventh crises; the passage shall be rapid. The year 1798 upset France only; that which is coming shall cause the revolution of the whole world. The seventh crisis shall come to parturition. Men shall believe that all is lost and annihilated. Immense trouble shall be over the agitated sea of time. Whoever is not on the bark of Peter shall be ingulfed. The bark goes up and down. Peter, have confidence. The ark comes out of the storm and a calm ensues. Pius IX is the last pope of the Church oppressed. 'Cross of the cross.' To him sorrow, but also joy. After him comes deliverance. Lumen in Coelo. Light in Heaven. This is Mary's eye. (Leo XIII's coat of arms show a star appearing in the heavens.) In the Church, Christians will imagine that all is lost. Mary arrives. Behold there is confusion; confusion even in the sanctuary. Notwithstanding, it is to the Catholic priests that one shall have to go for absolution and blessing."

168d. "Pius IX is the last pope of an epoch. Do you think that Mary will come to destroy the work of her Son? The Pope holds the place of God upon earth; so does the bishop in every diocese, and the parish priest in every parish. Behold the representative of Jesus Christ, as the good and religious mother is the image of Mary. Go to your pastors who have been appointed by God. But woe! woe! to mercenaries who go to the side of the world! Look at that field where among bad weeds and every kind of damaged wheat there are some fine ears; that is a figure of how human society is now seated in wickedness. What should be done with it? Good souls should not be allowed to perish. The sound ears are good souls. Well! Mary comes to harvest the elect from the earth. . . . A grand event shall have to take place in order to terrify the wicked to their advantage."

168e. "In the year when Easter occurs on the feast of St. Mark (April 25), Pentecost on the feast of St. Anthony (June 13) and Corpus Christi occurs on the feast of St. John the Baptist (June 24), then the whole world will cry: WOE! WOE! WOE! (1943 is one such year; the next in 2038). (See no. 101, 123k).

168f. "Famine, pestilence, war and fraud shall prostrate the Italian Kingdom; and the ancient kings everywhere shall be expelled. The Supreme Pastor (Pope) shall hold the keys of heaven but will be deprived of earthly kingdom. Horrible spectacle: When the Red Ox (Communism? See 168a) shall give birth to the Hydra (Anarchy?), God will not extinguish the flames nor calm his anger until all these calamities shall have stricken the people of Italy. This state of affairs shall last about five years."

169a. *Pope Pius IX* (d. 1878)

"We expect that the Immaculate Virgin and Mother of

God, Mary, through her most powerful intercession, will bring it about that our holy mother, the Catholic Church, after removal of all obstacles and overcoming of all errors, will gain in influence from day to day among all nations and in all places, prosper and rule from ocean to ocean, from the great stream to the ends of the earth; that she will enjoy peace and liberty . . . that all erring souls will return to the path of truth and justice after the darkness of their minds has been dispelled, and that there will be then one fold and one shepherd."

169b. "Since the whole world is against God and His Church, it is evident that he has reserved the victory over His enemies to Himself. This will be more obvious when it is considered that the root of all our present evils is to be found in the fact that those with talents and vigor crave earthly pleasures, and not only desert God, but repudiate Him altogether; thus it appears they cannot be brought back to God in any other way except through an act that cannot be ascribed to any secondary agency, and thus all will be forced to look to the supernatural, and cry out: 'From the Lord is this come to pass and it is wonderful in our eyes!' . . . There will come a great wonder, which will fill the world with astonishment. This wonder will be preceded by the triumph of revolution. The Church will suffer exceedingly. Her servants and her chieftain will be mocked, scourged and martyred."

170. *Sister Mary of Jesus Crucified of Pau* (d. 1878)

"All states will be shaken by war and civil conflict. During a darkness lasting three days the people given to evil ways will perish so that only one-fourth of mankind will survive. The clergy, too, will be greatly reduced in number, as most of them will die in defense of the faith or of their country."

171. *Bishop Pie of Portiers* (d. 1880)

"At no time in the history of the world have we seen such universal rebellion against God as today. All grasp weapons against Him. Never has man dissolved so entirely every covenant with God and been so completely against Him.

'Go away from us, leave us;' that is what modern nations say. 'We don't want a God, we will do all against Him and do all without Him.' That is what the modern nations, with France in the lead, do. The State must be anti-cleric, atheistic, purely worldly.' And God takes them at their word and leaves them to their defiance and self will, until they, in their madness, tear one another to pieces and cover Europe with blood and ruin. Then God will come again, though armed: then will all see that He is the Lord of the world, created by Him, out of which they tried to expel Him."

172a. *Catherine Emmerich* (d. 1824)

"I wish the time were here when the Pope dressed in red will reign. I see the Apostles, not those of the past, but the apostles of the last times, and it seems to me, the Pope is among them."

"I was likewise told, if I remember right, that he (Satan) will be unchained for a time fifty or sixty years before the year of Christ 2000."

172b. "A pale faced man floated slowly over the earth and, loosening the cloths, which wrapped his sword, he threw them on sleeping cities, which were bound by them. This figure also dropped pestilence on Russia, Italy, and Spain. A red noose lay around Berlin, and from there it came to Westphalia. Now the man's sword was naked, bands red as blood hung from its hilt and blood trickled from it on Westphalia." (This could refer to the spread of communism chiefly in northern Germany, as well as the last battle).

172c. "The Jews shall return to Palestine and become Christians towards the end of the world."

173a. *St. John Bosco* (d. 1888)

"War comes from the south, peace from the north. French laws no longer recognize the Creator, but the Creator will make himself recognized and will visit her thrice with the rod of His wrath. In the first visit he breaks her pride by conquest, plundering ruined harvest and butchery of men and beasts.

"In the second visit the great Prostitute of Babylon, which makes decent people sigh and call the Brothel of Europe, will be left without a leader and will be a victim of disorder.

"Paris! . . . Paris! instead of arming yourself in the name of the Lord, you fortify yourself with Houses of Immorality. They will be destroyed by you yourself. Your idol, *The Pantheon*, will be burnt to ashes in order that this may come true: 'violence uttereth lies against me.' Your enemies will reduce you to want, to hunger, to fear, and will make you the abomination of the nations. Ah, woe to you, if you do not recognize the hand that strikes you! I want to punish immorality, the despising of, and the contempt for My law, says the Lord.

"In the third visit you will fall into the hands of foreigners. Your enemies standing afar off will behold your palaces in flames. Your homes will become a heap of ruins bathed with the blood of your heroes who are no more.

"But there will come a great warrior from the North carrying a banner and on the right hand that supports it is written: *"The Irresistible Hand of the Lord."* At that very moment there went out to meet him the Venerable Old Man of Lazio, holding aloft a brilliantly glowing torch. The banner then increased in size and turned from black to snow-white. In the middle of the banner, in letters of gold, there was written the name of Him who is able to do all things.

"The warrior with his men bowed and shook hands with the Venerable Old Man.

"Now Heaven's voice is addressed to the Shepherd of shepherds. You are now in conference with your advisors. The enemy of the good does not stand idle one moment. He studies and practices all his arts against you. He will sow discord amonst your consultors; He will raise up enemies amongst my children. The powers of the world will belch forth fire, and they would that the words be suffocated in the throats of the custodians of my law. That will not happen. They will do harm—harm to themselves. You must hurry. If you cannot untie the knots, cut them. If you find yourself hard pressed, do not give up but continue until the head of the hydra of error is cut off. This stroke will make the world and Hell beneath it tremble, but the world will be safe and all the good will rejoice. Keep your consultors always with you, even if only two. Wherever you go, continue and bring to an end the work entrusted to you. The days fly by, your years will reach the destined number; but the great Queen (Mary) will ever be your help, and as in times past so in the future She will always be the exceeding great fortress of the Church.

"Ah, but you, Italy, land of blessings! Who has steeped you in desolation? Blame not your enemies, but rather your friends. Can you not hear your children asking for the bread of faith and find only those who smash it to pieces? What shall I do? I shall strike the shepherds, I shall disperse the flock, until those sitting on the throne of Moses search for good pastures and the flock listens attentively and is fed.

"Over the flock and over the shepherds My hand will weigh heavy. Famine, pestilence and war will be such that mothers will have to cry on account of the blood of their sons and of their martyrs dead in a hostile country.

"And to you, Rome, what will happen? Ungrateful Rome, effeminate Rome, proud Rome! You have reached such a height that you search no further. You admire nothing else in your Sovereign except luxury, forgetting that you and your glory stands upon Golgotha. Now he is old, defenseless, and despoiled; and yet at his word, the word of one who was in bondage, the whole world trembles.

"Rome! to you I will come four times!

"The first time, I shall strike your lands and the inhabitants thereof.

"The second time, I shall bring the massacre and the slaughter even to your very walls. And will you not yet open your eyes?

"I shall come a third time and I shall beat down to the ground your defenses and the defenders, and at the command of the Father, the reign of terror, of dreadful fear, and of desolation shall enter into your city.

"But My wise men have now fled and My law is even now trampled under foot. Therefore I will make a fourth visit. Woe to you if My law shall still be considered as empty words. There will be deceit and falsehood amongst both the learned and the ignorant. Your blood and that of your children will wash away your stains upon God's law. War, pestilence, famine are the rods to scourge men's pride and wickedness. O wealthy men, where is your glory now, your estates, your palaces? They are the rubble on the highways and byways.

"And you priests, why have you not run to 'cry between the vestibule and the Altar,' begging God to end these scourges? Why have you not, with the shield of faith, gone upon the housetops, into the homes, along the highways and byways, into every accessible corner to carry the seed of My word? Know you not that this is the terrible two-edged sword that cuts down my enemies and that breaks the Anger of God and of men?

"These things must come one after another. They are inexorable.

"Things are happening too slowly.

"But the August Queen of Heaven is present.

"The power of the Lord is in His hands. He scatters His enemies as a cloud. The Venerable Old Man attires himself in all his ancient raiment.

"There will come again a violent hurricane.

"Iniquity is consummated. Sin will have its end. And before two full moons of the month of the flowers will have run their course, the rainbow of peace will rise above the earth.

"The Great Minister will see the bride of his King arrayed in festive fashion.

"Throughout the world the sun will appear so luminous that the likes of which never has been seen since the tongues of fire descended on the Cenacle until this day, nor will such a sun ever be seen again until the very last of days.

173b. "It was a dark night. Men could no longer tell which way to take in order to return to their homes. Of a sudden there appeared in the heavens a very bright light that illuminated the steps of the travelers as though it were mid-day. At that moment there was seen a host of men and women, of young and old, of nuns, monks and priests with the Holy Father at the head. They were going out from the Vatican and were arranging themselves in line for a procession.

"Then there came a furious storm which clouded that light somewhat and made it appear that light and darkness were engaged in battle. In the meantime they arrived at a little square covered with dead and wounded, some of whom cried aloud and asked for help.

"Very many were dropping out of the line of procession. After having walked for a time that would correspond to two hundred risings of the sun (200 days) they all realized that they were no longer in Rome. Struck with fear they all ran to the Holy Father to defend him personally and to attend his wants. Instantly two angels were seen carrying a banner, going they presented it to the Holy Father and said: 'Receive the banner of He Who fights and scatters the strongest armies of the world. Your enemies are dispersed. Your children with tears and sighs beg you to return.'

"Looking at the banner one could see written on one side, 'Queen conceived without sin'; and on the other side, 'Help of Christians.'

"The Holy Father joyfully took the banner, but looking closely at the small number of those who remained with him, he became very sad.

"The two angels added: 'Go quickly to console your children. Write your brothers dispersed throughout the world that there must be a reform in the morals of men. That cannot be obtained except by distributing to the people the bread of the Divine Word. Catechize the children. Preach the detaching of the heart from the things that are of the earth. 'The time has come,' concluded the two angels, 'when the poor shall evangelize the people. Vocations will come from among those working with the spade, the axe, and the hammer to the end that they fulfill the words of David: God has raised up the poor from the land in order to place them on the thrones of the princes of His people.'

"Having heard that the Holy Father began the march. The farther he went the greater did the procession behind increase. When finally he set foot in the Holy City, he wept bitter tears for the distress in which he found the people and the large number now missing. As he entered St. Peter's he intoned the 'Te Deum' to which a choir of angels replied singing: 'Glory to God in the highest and on earth peace to men of good will.'

"With the ending of the hymn there came an end to the thick darkness and the sun shone with a brightness all its own.

"The cities, towns, and villages were thinly populated. The land had been leveled down as if by a hurricane, by a tempest, and a hail storm. People went from one to another saying in tones of great emotion: 'there is a God in Israel.'

"From the beginning of the exile until the singing of the 'Te Deum,' the sun rose in the East two hundred times (200 days). The time that passed for the fulfilling of those things (all spoken of above) corresponds to four hundred risings of the sun."

173c. "After the World War there will follow another European war with great battles taking place on August 15th and September 15th" of a year not stated. "The Pope will die, and live again (Pius XI and Pius XII?) Belgium will undergo sufferings, but will rise again and become stronger than ever. Poland will get back her rights (See 148).

174. *Marie Julie Jahenny of La Faudais* (1891)

"There will come three days of continuous darkness. The blessed candle of wax alone will give light during the horrid darkness. One candle will last for three days, but in the houses of the Godless they will *not* give light. During those three days the demons will appear in abominable and horrible forms, they will make the air resound with shocking blasphemies. The lightning will penetrate the homes, but will not extinguish the light of the blessed candles; neither wind nor storm nor earthquake will extinguish it. Red clouds like blood will pass in the sky, the crash of thunder will make the earth tremble; lightning will flash through the streets at an unusual time of the year; the earth will tremble to its foundations; the ocean will cast its foaming waves over the land; the earth will be changed to an immense cemetery; the corpses of the wicked and the just will cover the face of the earth. The famine that follows will be great. All vegetation will be destroyed as well as three-fourths of the human race. The crisis will come all of a sudden and chastisement will be world wide."

175. *Ossolinski Library Prophecy* (1893)

After speaking of what corresponds with the first World War and Poland's precarious independence it goes on: "When the people suffer 30 years (1944?) there arises a great heart who works a miracle. When the Black Eagle disgraces the cross sign (swastika) and spreads its evil wings, two nations fall. Might surpasses right, but when this Eagle comes to the intersection of roads and looks to the east to diffuse its Teuton ways, it shall go back with a broken wing.

"The disgraced cross (swastika) shall fall together with the hammer (Russia) and the grasping powers shall retain nothing. Masuria and Danzig returns to Poland. In the difficult fight against the proud Teuton, the world will smell of blood, when the north threatened by the east creates for itself unity among four.

"The Western Lion, betrayed by its freed slave shall unite with the Cock and put a young man on the throne.

"This time the strength of the disturbers of Earth is broken for ever. Brother shall shake hands with brother and the foe retires to a distant country.

"At the sunrise the Hammer is broken, flames shall spread over the prairie and when the Eagle and Hammer invade foreign fields they shall perish on a river.

"Ruthenia and beyond the Dnieper shall be in Poland and its Eagle reaches its old haunts at the Black Sea.

"Witebsk, Odessa, Kiev and Czerkassy are the bulwarks of Europe. Forever shall the barbarian be banished in fear to Asia.

"Warsaw is become the earth's center, yet three capitols belong to Poland. The Asiatic abandons the far off marshes and the Dragon gains face anew.

"The Bear falls after a second expedition. The Danube shines again in splendor. When peace is made at Warsaw, three kings have their horses drink of its waters.

"Three rivers give three crowns to the Anointed One from Cracow. Four confederates from four boundaries swear allegiance to him.

"When the men of Hungary and Poland shake hands, three nations with Rumania shall join under Poland's throne in perpetual union.

"When the Crimean Tartar reaches the river he will not renounce his belief but will seek protection from Poland and remain faithful.

"Poland shall reach from sea to sea but that in half a century. The grace of the Lord shall always protect us, wherefore suffer and pray." (50 years from 1893 would be 1943. This would seem to foretell defeat of the lands of the Crooked Cross and the Hammer (Germany and Russia), and two United States in Europe, one Slav and one Scandanavian.)

176. *Marie Martel of Tilly* (d. 1899)

She saw in a vision great darkness, accompanying thunder and the destruction of nearly all of Paris through fire as well as the wiping out of Marseilles and other cities.

PUBLISHED PREDICTIONS FROM THE TWENTIETH CENTURY (1900-1936)

177. *Lucie Christine* (d. 1908)

"In the Old Testament men have mostly known and adored the Father. In the New Testament they have attached themselves to their Savior Jesus Christ. In the latter days the Holy Ghost will make His heat and light more strongly felt in the hearts of the faithful; they will find therein a renewal of faith and they will the better know and love the Father and the son, and especially Our Eucharistic Lord," (see no. 102b).

"I also thought I understood how the cult of the Sacred Heart, which offers us Divine Love in the Heart of the Man-God, prepares souls for that diffusion of the eternal and personal love of God which will in one supreme effort include the whole world in its all powerful embrace, and anoint souls for the conflict of those days which will be marked by all the fury of Hell.

"I understood that time had to be divided into epochs corresponding to the Three Persons of the Adorable Trinity."

178a. *Sister Marie Chambau* (d. 1907)

"The triumph of the Church will be hastened by devotion to the five wounds and Precious Blood of Jesus Christ."

178b. *Chesser Lortie* (1903)

"A great war will begin in the Eastern world. The next one which starts there commences it. It begins in an hour, gains strength in a day, increases in a month, and in a year from the month all shall become involved. According to the sign it shall occur during the reign of Pope Pius X. The principal powers involved: Japan, England and the United States against Russia, France and Germany. Other countries involved: China,

Austria, Spain, Italy and Turkey. Turkey shall be dismembered and England severely beaten.

178c. *Same* (1933)

"Anti-Christ is on earth at the present time. The two great prophets of the Lord are also right at hand. The War of Nations (noted above) is fought in two halves. The second half started in the war between Japan and China September 18, 1931. The Asiatic world will become involved, the European nations will again fight among themselves. South America, Mexico and the United States shall become involved.

179a. *Pius X* (d. 1914)

"I saw one of my successors by name fleeing over the corpses of his brethren. He will flee to a place for a short respite where he is unknown, but he himself will die a cruel death."

179b. "We hold that you are not ignorant thereof what an outrageous combat is everywhere going on in our time. In truth the heathens and self-conceited nations are rebelling against their Creator. The cry of God's enemies is: 'Depart from us.' In most people respect for God has disappeared both in public and in private life. They even go so far as to attempt to obliterate even the memory of God. When we consider these facts you must really feel that such wickedness is only the beginning of those evils which are to come before the end of the world, and that the Son of Perdition of whom the Apostles speak, is already among us (1903)."

179c. *The Prophecy of Fatima* (July 13, 1917)

"To save souls, the Lord desires that devotion to my (Blessed Virgin) Immaculate Heart be established in the world. If what I tell you is done, many souls will be saved and there will be peace. The war will end; but, if they do not cease to offend the Lord, not much time will elapse, and precisely in the next Pontificate (Pius XI) another and more terrible war will commence."

To prevent "the castigation of the world for its many transgressions" the vision asked the "consecration of the world to my Immaculate Heart[1] and Communion in reparation on the first Saturday of each month. If my requests are heard, Russia will be converted and there will be peace. Otherwise, great errors will be spread through the world, giving rise to wars and persecutions against the Church; the good will suffer martyrdom and the Holy Father will have to suffer much; different nations will be destroyed; but, in the end, my Immaculate Heart will triumph and an era of peace will be conceded to humanity."

180a. *Berry* (published 1920)

At the breaking of the fifth seal[2] St. John sees the souls of the martyrs beneath the altar where they enjoy eternal happiness in union with Christ, yet they cry out for justice. They beseech God to manifest His glory, His justice, and His mercy by the resurrection of their bodies, the punishment of His enemies and the general judgment of all men. The imagery of this vision seems to refer to the altar of holocaust which stood in the inner court of the temple before the Holy Place. In the Jewish ritual the blood of the victim was poured out at the foot of the altar. The life of the victim was said to be in the blood: 'the life of the flesh is in the blood,' and again, 'Beware of this that thou eat not the blood, for the blood is for the soul, and therefore thou must not eat the soul with the flesh.' Hence the life or soul of the victim was conceived as being under the altar. In like manner the souls of the martyrs are seen beneath the altar because they too have become victims to God through martyrdom and the voice of their blood cries out to God for justice. 'The voice of thy brother's blood crieth out to me from the earth.' The martyrs have received the white robes of eternal happiness and glory, but they must wait for the resurrection of the body until the number of their fellow martyrs has been filled up. They have but a short while to

---

[1]Pope Pius XII has consecrated the world to the Immaculate Heart of Mary.

[2]See Apocalypse quoted above in No. 32a.

wait since the whole course of ages is as a few moments when compared with eternity that follows: 'For a thousand years in thy sight are as yesterday which is past, and as a watch in the night.' This verse clearly foretells that there shall be martyrs other than those of the first ages of the Church. There shall be witnesses to God by their blood in every age, especially in the days of Anti-Christ and at the end of the world. The resurrection and general judgment shall not take place until after this last persecution."

180b. "On the opening of the sixth seal[1] we catch a glimpse of the last persecution and the destruction of the world. This is to show that the prayers of the martyrs have already been heard in the designs of God, and shall be answered in due time."

180c. "These verses make it clear that there is no question of real locusts such as those that ravaged Egypt in the days of Moses.[2] They are purely symbolic, and their ravages chiefly spiritual. Their sting burns and poisons the soul with false doctrines, but has no power to injure those who remain faithful to the graces received in Baptism and Confirmation. For a short time these locusts are permitted to harass and persecute without killing, but they cannot destroy the Church.

"In those days men seek death and find it not. The good would welcome death as an escape from the evils and miseries that surround them. Many who have been led astray by false doctrines would likewise welcome death as a relief from their doubts and remorse of conscience.

"The locusts resemble horses accoutred for war. Heresy and schism are ever fruitful sources of religious wars and persecutions. The crowns indicate that rulers,—emperors, kings, and princes will be arrayed against the Church as actually happened at the Reformation in the sixteenth century. The crowns merely resembled gold, because there was but a mere semblance

---

[1] See Apocalypse quoted above in No. 32a.
[2] See Apocalypse quoted above in No. 32b.

of real Christian charity in those days. The human faces prove that these locusts symbolize real persons.

"The hair of a woman probably signifies vanity and immorality; the teeth of a lion strength and cruelty. The breastplates of iron show preparedness for defense as well as for attack. The sound of their innumerable wings resembles the thunder of chariots rushing to battle. This indicates their great numbers and impetuosity. The scorpion-like sting is a symbol of heresy that stings and poisons the soul. Its location in the tail signifies deceit and hypocrisy.

"The king of these symbolic locusts is called the Destroyer (Exterminans). He is Lucifer, the angel of the abyss, the leader of the rebel angels. His minions on earth are the leaders of heresy, schism, and persecution."

180d. "The invasion of the locusts is the first woe predicted by the eagle.[1] The two yet to come will fill up the 'mystery of iniquity' with the appearance of Anti-Christ and his prophet.

"God sends a sixth angel to instruct and guide the Church. This mission will still further reveal the thoughts of many hearts. The wicked continue to be separated from the just.

"A voice from the golden altar commands the captive angels of the Euphrates to be released. As noted above, the altar is Christ who makes trials and tribulations a means of sanctification for souls and an increase of fervor and holiness in the Church. They also serve to spread the blessings of the Gospel for as Tertullian says: 'The blood of martyrs is the seed of Christians.'

"Christ Himself gives command to release the captive angels thus showing that the enemies of the Church have no power against her unless God permits. The Church can say to her enemies as Christ said to Pilate: 'Thou shouldst not have any power against me, unless it were given thee from above.'

---

[1] See Apocalypse quoted above in No. 32b.

"The captive angels are demons who will arouse new enemies and increased enmities against the Church. In a figurative
sense they represent the new enemies thus aroused against the
Church, whether they be nations, individuals or secret societies
hostile to her. Four, the number of universality, indicates how
widespread will be their influence.

"With the prophets of old the region of the Euphrates was
ever the country whence came the enemies of God's people.
Its mention here indicates that these new enemies will arise
among nations already hostile to the Church. In a secondary
sense the term may be taken literally to represent peoples from
that region who are hostile to the Church.

"The four angels of the Euphrates, now ordered to be released, may be the same as those whom Christ forbade to injure
the earth until the Church could be firmly established after the
persecutions.

"Even the time for the manifestation of these evil spirits and
their minions has been accurately fixed in the designs of Providence. The very day and hour has been determined.

"Great numbers will be done to death in the religious wars
and revolutions stirred up by these angels from the Euphrates.
The prophecy may also mean that large numbers will be led
into new errors and schisms. Both interpretations are fully
justified by the history of the pretended Reformation and the
wars that followed it.

"These scourges shall be more terrible than any yet predicted. The first plagues were brought to earth by four horsemen. Then we saw four charioteers, the four winds, ready to
scourge mankind. Here we find a vast array of cavalry. The
chastisements sent upon the world increase with the growth
of iniquity and the approach of Anti-Christ.

"The description of horses and riders in this vision gives
some idea of their boldness, strength, and cunning ferocity.
They inflict upon men the plagues of fire, smoke and sulphur.
The fire is persecution and war. Smoke symbolizes the obscur-

ing of doctrine and the weakening of faith; sulphur, the moral depravity which follows.

"The fire, smoke and sulphur issue from the mouth of the horses. From the mouth should proceed words of wisdom; instead there come forth heresies, and incitements to revolt and revolution. It should be noted that Luther openly preached revolt and revolution to the peasants of Germany, but when they put his words into practice, he turned to the princes and urged them to stamp out the revolt with fire and sword.

"The horses of this vision inflict injuries with their tails which resemble serpents. Amongst all peoples the serpent is a symbol of lying and hypocrisy. These vices have ever characterized the enemies of the Church.

"There is no question here of real artillery as some have imagined. St. John is giving only the broad outlines of the Church's history. He is not concerned with the material means employed by men to wage war against her.

"The vision of locusts and the vision of cavalry horses are not two representations of one and the same event. They foreshadow two distinct events that follow one another in the order of time. The one is the great revolt against the Church brought about by the fallen star. The other consists of wars and disturbances which follow in the wake of that revolt.

"After these plagues have passed there still remain many who worship idols, and many guilty of robbery, murder, and immorality. This is verified today. Although nineteen hundred years have elapsed since the first preaching of the Gospel, whole nations are still steeped in idolatry, and Christendom seems hopelessly divided by heresy and schism."

180e. "An angel coming in clouds of grace and glory brings to St. John a book of further prophecies.[1] The rainbow about his head symbolizes mercy, while the brightness of his countenance expresses the power of his teachings to en-

---

[1]For Text of Apoc., see above No. 32c.

lighten souls. The feet as of fire indicate that he shall lead the
Church in the ways of truth and justice as the pillar of fire
guided the Israelites in the wilderness.

"The book is open to signify that the prophecies therein
revealed to St. John are intelligible and shall be understood in
due time according to the needs of the Church. The angel places
one foot upon the sea, the other upon the land to express God's
supreme dominion over all things.

"The voice like the roar of a lion is the voice of the Gospel
which shall penetrate to the very ends of the earth teaching
divine truth, condemning error, and threatening persecutors
with the vengeance of God. Here, as elsewhere, the thunders
may symbolize the anathemas of the Church against all wickedness and error; but it would be useless to comment on their
exact meaning since St. John was commanded to seal up their
words. In like manner Daniel was ordered to seal up the words
of his prophecies until the time appointed by God for their
publication. The words of the seven thunders may also have
been such as St. Paul heard—'secret words which it is not granted to man to utter.'

"Lifting his hand to heaven the angel calls upon the God of
all creation to witness the truth of his words that time shall be
no more. This does not mean that the end of the world is
at hand, but that the time for judgment against obstinate sinners
and persecutors has arrived.

"This judgment shall be the great persecution of Anti-
Christ and its attendant evils. Then shall be accomplished the
'mystery of God' which has been announced (evangelized) by
the prophets of old. To evangelize is to announce good tidings,
hence this 'mystery of God' is probably the plenitude of the
Redemption applied to all nations of earth. After the destruction of Anti-Christ and his kingdom all peoples shall accept
the Gospels and the Church of Christ shall reign peacefully
over all nations."

"Eating the book symbolizes an intimate union with the
Holy Ghost by which the mind of the Apostle is illuminated

with the spirit of prophecy. St. John finds the book sweet to the taste because it announces mercy to the elect and the final triumph of the Church. It is bitter in so far as it predicts dire persecutions for the Church and terrible punishments for the wicked."

180f. "The followers of Anti-Christ have been warned of defeat and eternal punishment;[1] the faithful have been encouraged by promise of victory here and eternal happiness hereafter. The time of judgment is at hand; the final conflict now begins. The separation of the good from the bad will be still further accomplished. As on the last day, Christ sends forth His angels to gather the wheat into the barns while the cockle is being bound into bundles for the fire. The gathering in of the good through martyrdom is represented as a harvest. The destruction of the wicked is depicted as the vintage of God's wrath. The realization of this judgment will be found in the complete destruction of the kingdom of Anti-Christ in subsequent chapters.

"The reaper sitting upon a bright cloud, is an angel who comes in the name of Christ to execute His orders. Hence he bears the resemblance of Christ and is surrounded by a cloud of glory. He also wears a crown of gold, the emblem of royalty, because as representative of Christ he exercises dominion over all peoples.

"The cloud of glory and the crown of royalty might lead one to accept the reaper as Christ Himself. Yet the context makes it plain that the reaper cannot be identified with Christ since he is commanded by an angel to thrust in his sickle. Furthermore, Christ has told us in the Gospel that angels shall be commissioned to separate the wheat from the cockle.

"The voice from beneath the altar, commanding the vintage to be gathered is the voice of a martyr whose blood cries to heaven for vengeance. This martyr who has "power over fire" is probably Elias who will destroy Anti-Christ by sending

---

[1] For text of Apoc., see above No. 32d.

down fire from heaven. The prophet Joel also describes the judgments of God against unholy nations as a vintage and a treading of the wine-press.

"The wine-press of divine wrath shall be trodden outside the city of Jerusalem. Final victory over Anti-Christ will be won through great slaughter and bloodshed in a battle near the Holy City, perhaps in the Valley of Josaphat. The prophecy of Joel may refer to this event instead of the last judgment; 'Let the nations come up into the Valley of Josaphat: for there I will sit to judge all nations round about . . . in the valley of destruction: for the day of the Lord is near.' "

181. *Benedict XV* (d. 1922)

"The return of the Jews to Palestine is the will of God, hence they will have to leave many countries."

182. *X. B. Markiewicz* (before 1922)

Due to a second world war "two great plagues and many other evils will come. The true Christian civilization will be restored through the heroic action of Polish men and women, and the correct road to true peace and happiness will be shown them."

183. *Père Lamy* (d. 1931)

"The prayer of the children must be the foundation of everything. . . . (What a different world this would be) if only we did not place obstacles in the way of (Our Lady's) empire over our souls. . . . She told me she desired a new congregation. . . . The dispersal of the congregations (or religious) was more a punishment for the people than the individuals concerned. . . . The monasteries will flourish again and the convents will once more be filled. After these (not specified) calamities many souls will come to dwell in them. . . . Prayer offered in union with Our Lady has great power. . . . Our Lady requires the sanctity of family life. She requires that disorder should cease and that people should observe order once more. God asks only this so that he may grant them pardon. . . . If people had heeded Her the war (1914-1918) would not

have come. . . . I will not tell you a tenth part (of what I
know of the future). There are some things it would not be
well to say even in 40 years' time. Besides this is perhaps the
least suitable epoch that has ever existed for revelation. I do
not mean that small fraction of the people who are fervent
Catholics. It is just those who do not need revelations. . . .
Penance, penance, penance, terrible times are coming. The times
we are living in now (1914-1918) are as nothing to what
we are soon to see. . . . How Our Lord must have suffered! And
yet Christians are always seeking pleasure! If it were thus in
the green wood, how shall it be in the dry. . . The (first)
world war had three causes, blasphemies, work on Sundays and
desecration of marriage. . . . When we are not in the state of
grace (our guardian angels) would like to help us but they
cannot. They often save us from accidents. Our Lady was
weeping over the world (1929). There are few devout souls
nowadays. . . . The Jews are scattered all over the world, but
they will not be abandoned. God never forsakes his own . . .
As to the Apostles of the latter days, I only know one thing:
Our Lord has said in His Gospel that this day is known to
nobody. . . . One should never order one's life according to
visions, especially according to the visions of others. In material
things we must use common sense. And in spiritual things we
need common sense, too. . . . We must be careful of mysticism.
The devil stands behind the Mother of God; if you let her
pass you by, you find the devil.

"Lucifer is playing his last card; he thinks the game is in
his hands, in which he is mistaken. . . . We must pray con-
fidently, in spite of his blustering. . . . People will appreciate
still more the gentle goodness of Our Blessed Lady. . . . Peace
will be restored to the world, but I shall not see that, and other
things will come to pass of which I shall not see the end.

"When peace has been established in the world many things
will be changed. . . . The manufacture of aeroplanes, the ex-
ploitation of mines, iron works, all this will diminish. There

will be no more of these great factories where morality suffers and dies. Workers will be obliged to go back to the land. Work on the land will receive a great impetus. . . . Industry will be reduced to smaller proportions and it will remain so. But still old workmen will insist on dying in the towns. . . . When peace has been restored to the world, it will be necessary to re-evangelize it, and that will be the work of a whole generation. . . . There will be many difficulties. . . .

"The state of the early Christians will come back again; but there will be few men on the earth then! And there will be another magnificent revival of Orders and Congregations."

184. *Countess Francesca de Billiante* (d. 1935)

"Great tribulations are coming; however, before this God will send a light of the Church, so that those who follow the light will be given a clear understanding of right and justice. Albertus Magnus will be elevated to the throne of sainthood and recognized as a Doctor of the Church. God will shame the professors of theology with whom he is displeased due to their pride. He will elevate to sainthood the ignorant Brother Konrad and the unknown Brother Jordan Mai. Likewise God will cause Don Bosco to be canonized (these things have come to pass). In these days the Rosary will bring down untold blessings. We will even know the true Christian by his Rosary.

"I see a land with a hooked cross (swastika). In this nation there will arise proud statesmen who will seek to throw Christ from His throne. They will even attack the power of reproduction in the mother's womb. Many in this land will carry the hooked cross on their forehead and breast, not suspecting that this is a sign of Satan. In these times many priests and monks will suffer in prison. They will be designated as criminals and most of their wealth will be confiscated. When the hooked cross glitters on the top of church steeples, they will be at the zenith of their power.

"When the land with the great fleet enters the Mediterranean (England or United States?), then Europe will tremble. God will save Rome from the worst, due to the intercession of the Holy Father Pius X and the holy martyrs. France and Spain will sink deeply and will be saved only at the intercession of the Immaculate Conception, from the worst.

"I see yellow (Japanese?) and red (Communists?) warriors marching against Europe and Europe will be covered by a yellow fog. The cattle in the fields will die from this yellow fog. The nations, who have risen against Christ, will be destroyed by flames. Famine will annihilate those who remain, so that Europe will be too large. In those days there will be many saints. Then the sons of St. Francis and St. Dominic will pass through the world and lead it back to Christ. Then the Holy Father will gather the remnant in an open field under the Cross. The hooked cross will be branded on the forehead of the criminals.

"The beginning of these days I shall yet see. I am sick from what I have seen. May God grant my little children a perseverance in the true faith."

185. *A Bernadine Sister* (before 1938) was shown in spirit the vast devastation caused by the devil throughout the world, and at the same time she heard the Blessed Virgin telling her that it was true, hell had been let loose upon the earth; and that the time had come to pray to her as the Queen of Angels and to ask of her the assistance of the heavenly legions to fight against these deadly foes of God and of men. "But my good Mother," she replied, "You who are so kind could you not send them without our asking?" "No," Our Lady answered, "because prayer is one of the conditions required by God Himself for obtaining favors." Then the Blessed Virgin communicated the following prayer, bidding her to have it printed and distributed.

"August Queen of Heaven! Sovereign Mistress of Angels! Thou who from the beginning has received from God the power and mission to crush the head of Satan: we humbly beseech thee to send thy holy legions, that under thy command, and

by thy power, they may pursue the evil spirits: encounter them
on every side: resist their bold attacks and drive them hence
into the abyss of eternal woe. Amen."

186. *Priest in Rome* (before 1936)

According to information from a reliable source, the following prayer was disclosed to a devout priest in Rome during
the Holy Sacrifice of the Mass, when it was revealed to him that
those who say the prayer with devotion and faith would be
spared from the great sufferings that are soon to come into the
whole world:

"O Jesus, Divine Savior! be merciful, be merciful to us and
to the whole world. Amen. Powerful God! Holy God! Immor-
tal God! Have compassion upon us and upon the whole world.
Amen. Eternal Father, show us mercy, in the name of the
Precious Blood of Thy Only Son, show us mercy we implore
Thee. Amen."

187. *Theresa Neumann* (September 6, 1936)

"The provocations have in these days attained their height.
The furies of Hell rage now. The chastisement of God is inevitable. Every future petition to help them, to spare them, dis-
pleases Me. If you petition Me for the conversion of dying
sinners in the last hour, I will hear you. No! do not petition
Me to prevent this chastisement. Until now victims (many
of whom existed in many parishes) have offered their merits
to expiate for the crimes of mankind, which held back the wrath
of God, but now their expiations are not enough and the chastisement is now certain and unpreventable. It will happen
suddenly. Fortunate are those who already are in their graves.
I have warned them and have postponed, as I did with Sodom,
but Sodom would not listen to Me, nor do the people listen to
Me nowadays, nor heed My warnings, therefore they will incur
the sad experience of My wrath which they deserve."

188a. *Pope Pius XI* (d. 1939)

"The churches are destroyed, ruined from base to steeple,
the religious and the consecrated virgins are expelled from their

habitations, delivered to insults and bad treatment, and condemned to prison, multitudes of children and young women are torn from the bosom of the Church, their mother; they are incited to deny and blaspheme Christ; they are pushed to the worst excesses of luxury; the entire people of the faithful is terrorized, lost, under the constant menace that they must deny their faith or perish, at times, under the most atrocious form of death: It is a spectacle so appalling that one might see in it already the dawn of the beginning of sorrows that will bring 'the man of sin' arising against all which is called God and is honored by worship."

188b. *Pope Leo XIII,* in ordering the prayers after Mass, is said to have been prompted by a vision of St. Michael driving Satan back into hell. The principal intention of these prayers was changed by Pope Pius XI in 1934 to be "for the return of Russia to God." Therefore their efficacy in restraining the devil is, as it were, placed secondary or rather directed to hasten the conclusion of his work in Russia. Prayer to St. Michael: "St. Michael, the archangel, defend us in battle, be our protection against the malice and snares of the devil. We humbly beseech God to command him, and do thou, O prince of the heavenly host, by thy divine power thrust into hell Satan and the other evil spirits who roam through the world seeking the ruin of souls."

189a. *Pius XII* (See appendix for additional matter)

"the Virgin Mother of God, invoked by such prayers (for peace) will obtain from the Divine Savior liberation from present anxieties, the peace of hearts and fraternal concord among peoples."

189b. "For God or against God—this once more is the alternative that shall decide the destinies of all mankind. . . . (prayer and penance) . . . are the inspirations that will dispel and remedy the first and principal cause of every revolt and every revolution—the revolt of man against God."

189c. (My Christmas 1942 blessing goes) "to all those who, like the Crusaders, will fight for this and for a better Christian world. . . . a new danger has arisen—the subordination of everything to politics and the heresy of a national state which subordinates all to human law. . . . Communism and National Socialism: these orders conflict with those of God. It is useless to fight without faith in God.

"Do you, crusader-volunteers of a distinguished new society, lift up the new banner of moral and Christian rebirth, declare war on the darkness which comes from deserting God, on the coldness that comes from strife between brothers."

SOME CONTEMPORARY PROPHECIES

(The first two are merely students' observations. The rest, all anonymous but one, are said to result from private revelations. I have reason to believe that the authors are not deceivers. It is not within my power to determine whether or not they have been deceived):

190. *Franciscan Father of Arizona*

"Don Bosco's prophecy 'The Pope will die and live again' refers to the peculiar circumstances surrounding Pius XI and Pius XII: when the former died, 'Fides Intrepida' died, but when Pius XII, his Secretary of State, was elected, 'Fides Intrepida' lived again." Pius XII according to this would not be the Pastor Angelicus, at least not the one who would rule with the Great Monarch."

191. *The so-called Pyramid prophecy*

"A period of very great trial and distress for millions of humanity will occur over the 17-year period September 16, 1936 to August 20, 1953. This will be a period during which the whole earth is to be cleansed of its iniquity."

192. *Rev. Theophilus Reisinger, O. M. Cap.* (d. 1940)

"The Great Monarch was destined to have been Archduke Franz Ferdinand of Austria (his assassination was the spark that started the first world war), but, because of the many 'souls of atonement,' the reign of Anti-Christ was postponed, and hence, also that of the Great Monarch."

193. *New York Laywoman*

"God wants a new world. This (war) is the judgment of nations. Rome will be invaded. A German ruler will be converted and an English one assassinated. Another Englishman once great now small will become a member of the Church and will be all powerful. There will be much suffering before this war ends and it will end as a religious war with terrible persecution everywhere. Thereafter will be a crusade which will be victorious under Mary's banner."

194a. *Phoenix, Arizona, Mother*

Vision: "A terrific wind seemed to blow from earth to heaven. It rent the blue sky as tho it were a canvas. The opening was at first in the form of a cross. The wind kept up and blew back the four triangular flaps whose edges formed the cross and in this kite-shaped opening there appeared a happy young mother with a child on her arm. This was in the south-west sky." The vision faded. Eleven months later after being warned to remember the vision described above "there opened to my view a scene beyond description. My only thought was that could it be reduced to canvas it would convert all men. Since that time it is no credit to me that I love God." (Suggested meaning of the visions: Through Our Lady's intercession God will do something that will make men understand their relations to Him. This something will follow terrific commotions on earth). (See 150 also.)

194b. "When intellectual Christianity will have suffered long enough it will find its heart, and the whole world will see it: then will come the peace of Christ. This peace will come first to the United States."

195. *Chicago Mother*

"The present Pope will spend his last year in exile. A severe plague will strike in middle Europe so deadly that it will take months to bury the dead. In 1943 Russia will defeat Germany. God's anger at men's indifference will not be averted this time."

196. *Chicago Layman*

"Those who lord it over the parts of the world today and who condone or propagate evil in national laws, press and schools as well as private lives and who think they can restore peace to nations and reform society and bring happiness to men, these err greatly. The gifts they think they can disburse are the property of God alone. Infidels, even though Christian in name, shall not dispense them lest the recipients say: See, I have received happiness from so and so or such a nation or such a government or such a form of government. No, irrespective of the sincerity of any individual involved misery will grow, war will come. Communism will rule and the Anti-Christ will arrive. Success will come only when man reverts to a system laid down by God himself as he laid it down to the Hebrews before the days of the Kings."

197a. *The "Mystic" in the Earling Case*

In urging universal and perpetual adoration before the Blessed Sacrament this person is said to state that this is the Heaven desired means of atoning for the sins of the world.

197b. Further, in urging exposition from dawn to midnight in United States churches generally, and nocturnal adoration in convents and other convenient American Chapels, this person is said to state that this method of adoration, even though practiced only in our country, and especially if Novenas for peace and prayers to the Blessed Virgin be added, then for a certainty, when enough atonement be offered, God shall work the wonder which is necessary to end the war and to bestow peace on the world.

198. There is a movement among Polish Catholics to have the picture of Our Lady of Jasna Gora declared the Catholic Action Banner. To Our Lady under this title is attributed both the 1683 Victory over the Turks and the 1920 Victory over the Communists. Another Polish source that I have not been

able to identify, says that the Victory flag in this war will have a White Eagle crowned with gold on one side and on the other a picture of Our Lady.

199. *Monessen (Pa.) Layman*

"Russia will defeat Germany and Communism will dominate the governments from Sweden to China inclusive. Soon after an Anti-Christ appears. We will be at war again in 1952 and that war will last 3½ years. This one will end in Europe in 1943 and in Asia in 1944. I feel certain that this is the meaning of the visions."[1]

There are appended *two prophecies* said to be old but I have found no reference to them prior to 1915. This is neither in their favor nor against them:

200. "And it shall come to pass that . . . the Earth shall become like unto this Garden (Eden). . . . Behold, this last hour (of evil) is at hand (1850-1950). . . . Now is it come to pass that the hearts of men and nations are hardened like flint upon the face of the earth. For this is the last hour of self-righteousness and of the hypocrite; when men of smug face and smooth tongue gather into their snares all the people of simple mind, to pour upon them the force of hatred and jealousy and lead them into slaughter.

"Behold, the whole Earth is filled with turbulence and discontent. The rulers use their vast powers for greater domination and the struggling multitude uncoils itself like a serpent seeking its prey. They seize nations against their neighbors and waste their strength to break one another. The victors are too far spent to shout, and the defeated utterly despoiled . . . For the last half of the hour is wombed with the most terrible period of the Earth's history. . . .

"And it came to pass that when the last quarter of the last hour arrived . . . the yellow hordes in the place of the Rising

---

[1] These living seers have much more to say that I haven't deemed wise to publish, and there are several others in the United States but I have not been able to have samples, as yet, of their oracles.

Sun, and the white hosts of the middle kingdom have joined hands. . . . And behold, they pour out their terrifying wrath upon the inhabitants of the island kingdom which is swelled with victory and grown fat upon the commerce of sea and land.

. . . "Behold, saith the Lord: 'I will turn thee inside out, who in the folly of thine hypocrisy imagined a vain thing in thine heart. Thou art an harlot among the vain people of the earth. Thou hast lain in the beds of divers nations, and by charm and deceit, by beguilements thou hast brought under thy dominion the uttermost parts of the earth. But I shall make thee over. . . . Thy seamen and thy pilots and all men of war that are within thee, with all thy company, shall fall into the heart of the sea. And I will break thee in pieces as thou hast broken many before thee. For the nations from the ends of the earth, and of the middle kingdom, which I have pitched against thy strength, are cruel beyond endurance whose might thou canst not overcome . . . Thou and thy companions shall be brought down to earth and it shall be a day of repentance. . . . On that day, when the day of thy repentance is full, when remorse hath broken thy heart, and thy cry is raised unto Me, I shall remember and send thee thy deliverer.' "

201a. (Said to be Ancient Irish: If so it is likely merely a form of other Irish prophecies given above.) What resembles the first world war is described and then the text continues "A number of years must elapse before the second and more terrible part of this war begins. It shall come out of Asia and shall require the aid of every occidental on earth to put down. England will again injure the Irish. This will be a sign for the frightful punishment of England. She has betrayed all nations. . . . When the world is appalled by the anguish of Britain, the leaders of the dispersed Irish in all parts of the world shall call upon them (their followers?) to kneel in supplication to God for mercy on their fallen enemy. 'We forgive her,' they will say, 'Why not you?' And God astonished (so to speak) at finding in any race of men so God-like a quality, rescinds His judgment (of utter annihilation) against them (the English).

"England suffers the same degradation as she meted out to her neighbor, and for the same length of time. Not the smallest fraction of time in this long period shall be remitted. Often shall she attempt to rise, but each attempt shall fail. Never shall world power be hers again, but she shall do very much for the Faith, once she makes submission to Rome.

"Ireland's progress in peace and plenty shall intrigue the world. Many shall come from afar to see that land so blessed. To the end of time no enemy shall ever again set foot on her soil."

201b. "France restores order in England after her own recovery from a violent revolution."

201c. "The close of the war finds a Celt in the Chair of Peter. He is the most perfect of all the popes—chosen miraculously amidst chaos. An angel in human form, he shall be called "Papa Angelorum." This Celt is not an Irish Celt but one born in Galicia, and the only Celt to occupy Peter's throne.

"He shall, like Peter of old, take his staff and his scrip, and with a few companions start out to reconcile the nations. They shall walk over mounds of dead and find the rivers choked with the bodies of the dead. The pope will die in exile." (This last sentence apparently refers to his death while away from Rome.)

Holy Spirit, all divine,
Dwell within this heart of mine;
Cast down every idol throne,
Reign supreme, and reign alone.

See, to Thee I yield my heart;
Shed Thy life through every part:
A pure temple I would be,
Wholly dedicate to Thee.

APPENDIX I

Some Significant Statements of Pius XII

MARCH 3, 1939

"We speak of that peace which Our predecessor of blessed memory urged so insistently upon men, . . . and for which he made to God a spontaneous offer of his life.

". . . the peace of families united and harmonized by much love of Christ.

"Before Us is a vision of the enormous evils afflicting the world, for the correction of which may Our Blessed Lord send help to Us, unarmed but confident. . . . We are sure that you Our children, Our Brothers (meaning the Cardinals), will not render this Our wish in vain. After the Grace of God, it is in your good will that Our soul so greatly trusts."

AUGUST 24, 1939

". . . through Our voice you may hear the voice of . . . Christ . . . in a crisis in which His word alone is capable of mastering all the tumultuous disturbances of the earth.

"We . . . speak to you in the Name . . . of the Holy Ghost, . . . the inexhaustible source of love in the hearts of men.

". . . Today . . . the tension of minds seems to have arrived at such a pass as to make an outbreak of the awful scourge of war appear imminent, We . . . appeal to those in power . . . that, laying aside accusations, threats and causes of mutual distrust, they may attempt to resolve their present differences with the sole means suitable thereto, namely by reciprocal and trusting agreements; . . .

". . . empires which are not founded on justice are not blessed by God.

"Statesmanship emancipated from morality betrays those very ones who would have it so.

". . . Nothing is lost with peace; all may be lost with war.

". . . May the strong hear Us that they may not become weak through injustice. May the powerful hear Us if they desire that their power be not destruction, . . .

". . . Christ . . . has made His solemn commandment, love of one's brother. . . . promise of salvation for individuals and for nations.

". . . human efforts are of no avail without Divine assistance."

DECEMBER 24, 1939

"The indescribable disaster of war, which Pope Pius XI, with profound and extreme regret, foresaw . . . has broken out . . .

". . . We of the Christian brotherhood have been obliged to see a series of irreconcilable acts, . . . acts which show in what chaotic and vicious circles has the sense of justice been deviated from useful consideration.

"Atrocities and illegal use of means of destruction even against noncombatants, refugees, old people, women and children and disregard of human dignity, liberty and life are acts which cry for the vengeance of God—as does ever more extensive and methodical anti-Christian and even atheistic propaganda, mostly among young people.

". . . We . . . contemplate the . . . spiritual ruin . . . accumulating because of confusion of ideas which, more or less voluntarily, shades and distorts truth in the souls of many people, whether they be involved in war or not.

"We, therefore, must regard with alarm the tremendous amount of work that will be necessary when a world tired of fighting wishes to restore peace——to break down the walls of aversion and hatred which have been built up in the heat of the strife.

". . . We attempted . . . to the last moment, to prevent the worst and to persuade men in whose hands power lay . . . to abstain from armed conflict and so to save the world from incalculable disaster.

"These efforts . . . failed . . . chiefly because of deep and apparently irremovable distrust . . . which had grown in recent years and which had raised insurmountable spiritual barriers.

". . . 'How can exhausted or weakened economy, at the end of the war, find means for economic and social reconstruction among difficulties which will be enormously increased, and of which the forces and artifies of disorder, lying in wait, will seek to make use in the hope of giving the final blow to Christian Europe?'

"First. A fundamental condition of a just and honorable peace is to assure the right to life and independence of all nations, large or small, weak and strong. . . .

"Second. That order, reestablished in such a manner may be tranquil and durable . . . nations must be liberated from the heavy slavery of the race for armaments. . .

"Third. In any reordering of international community life it would conform to the rules of human wisdom for all parties concerned to examine the consequences of the gaps and deficiencies of the past; . . .

"And since it is . . . almost impossible for human weakness to foresee everything . . . at the time of the drafting of treaties of peace . . . the establishment of juridical institutions . . . to revise . . . is of decisive importance.

"Fourth. A point which should draw particular attention . . . concerns the real needs and just demands of nations and of peoples as well as of ethnical minorities: . . .

"Fifth. But even better and more complete settlements will be imperfect and condemned to ultimate failure, if . . . peoples . . . do not allow themselves to be penetrated always more and more by that spirit from which alone can arise life, authority and obligation for the dead letter of articles in international agreements . . . by that hunger and thirst for justice which is proclaimed as a Beatitude in the Sermon on the Monut . . .

"We wait for and hope that all those who are united to Us by the bond of Faith, each at his post within the limits of his mission, will keep both mind and heart open, so that, when the hurricane of war ceases and is dispersed, there will rise up in every nation and among all peoples far-sighted and pure spirits, animated by courage, who will know how and will be able to confront the dark instinct of vile vengeance with the severe and noble majesty of justice——the sister of love and companion of all true wisdom.

". . . 'O Emanuel, Our King and Our Law-maker, the awaited of the Gentiles and their Saviour, come to save us, Lord Our God.' "

NOVEMBER 24, 1940

". . . we feel . . . that the present hour is a phase in the solemn story of humanity predicted by Christ. . . .

"But if the din of war seems to overcome and drown Our voice, We turn Our gaze away from earth to Heaven, to the Father of Mercies . . .

Who . . . commands the flow of the ocean: 'Hitherto thou shalt come, and shalt go no further' . . .

". . . Our heart, imploring from Him better days . . .

"Grant us, O Lord, peace in our days!

"God . . . will hear us—at the moment and in the manner which He will have disposed—if we send up to the seat of His throne with one voice a trusting and fervent prayer enriched by the humiliation of penance; . . .

". . . May whirlwinds, that in the light of day or in the dark of night scatter terror, fire, destruction and slaughter on humbel folk, cease. . . . "

DECEMBER 24, 1940

". . . the peoples will be obliged to dedicate themselves to the task of repairing the deep-seated evils which will be their bitter social and economic heritage; when disorganized nations find themselves, at the war's conclusion, with spiritual wounds which will certainly demand assiduous and watchful care, that their pernicious effects may be forestalled or minimized.

". . . a quasi-universal opinion . . . contends that . . . Europe as well as its political structure are now undergoing a process of transformation of such a nature as to signal the dawn of a new era.

"Indispensable prerequisites for such a new order are:

"One, triumph over hate . . .

"Two, triumph over mistrust . . .

"Three, triumph over the . . . principles that utility is a basis of law and right, and that might makes right; . . .

"Four, triumph over . . . too strident differences in the field of world economy; . . .

"Five, triumph over the spirit of . . . egotism . . . "

APRIL 13, 1941

"In this tempest . . . our most powerful and safest haven of trust and peace is found in prayer to God, in Whose hands rests not only the destiny of men but also the outcome of their most obdurate dissensions. . . .

". . . We are saddened to note that there seems to be as yet little likelihood of an approximate realization of peace that will be just, in accordance with human and Christian norms.

"Thus Our supplications to Heaven must be raised with ever increasing meaning and fervor, that a new spirit may take root and develop in all peoples . . . the spirit of willingness, devoid of sham and artifice, that is ready to make mutual sacrifices in order to build . . . a new edifice of fraternal solidarity among the nations . . .

"Nothing can . . . restrain Us from doing all in Our power in order that, in the tempest of surging waves of enmity among the peoples of the earth . . . the Church of Christ may be held firmly by the anchor of hope under the golden rays of peace . . ."

. . . the virtuous man is neither exalted by worldly well-being nor humbled by temporal misfortune; the evil man on the other hand, being corrupted in prosperity, is made to suffer in adversity.

". . . upon the manner in which you deal with those whom the fortunes of war put in your hands may depend the blessing or curse of God upon your own land.

"Contemplation of a war . . . inspires in the heart of the Common Father . . . words of comfort and encouragement for the pastors and faithful of those places where the Church, the Spouse of Christ, is suffering most; where fidelity to her, the public profession of her doctrines, the conscientious and practical observation of her laws, moral resistance to atheism and to de-Christianizing influences deliberately favored or tolerated, are being openly or insidiously opposed and daily in various ways made increasingly difficult."

JUNE 1, 1941

"What problems and what particular undertakings, some perhaps entirely novel, our social life will present to the care of the Church at the end of this conflict . . . is difficult at the moment to trace or foresee.

"Our planet . . . is not . . . without habitable regions and living spaces now abandoned to wild natural vegetation and well suited to be cultivated by man . . . it is inevitable that some families migrating from one spot to another should go elsewhere in search of a new homeland. Then . . . the right of the family to a living space is recognized. When this happens emigration attains its natural scope . . . the more favorable distribution of men on the earth's surface . . . that surface which God created and prepared for the use of all. . . .

"Do not let yourselves be misled by the manufacturers of errors and unhealthy theories, . . . Oh, lamentable ignorance of the work of God! Professing themselves to be wise they become fools.

". . . you . . . must not ever be satisfied with this widespread public mediocrity in which the majority of men cannot, except by heroic acts of virtue, observe the Divine precepts which are always and in all cases inviolable.

". . . tomorrow, when the ruin of this world hurricane is cleared, at the outset of that reconstruction of a new social order, (social justice) will infuse new courage and a new . . . growth in the garden of human culture.

"Keep burning the noble flame of a brotherly social spirit . . . do not allow . . . it to (be) overcome by the dust and dirt carried by the whirlwind of the anti-Christian or non-Christian spirit."

JUNE 29, 1941

"All men are as children before God; all, even the most profound thinkers and the most experienced leaders of peoples. They judge events with the foreshortened vision of time, which passes and flies past irreparably; God, on the other hand, sees events from on high from the unmoved center of eternity. They have before their eyes the limited view of a few years; God has before Him the all-embracing panorama of the ages.

"Trust in God means the abandonment of oneself . . . in spite of all the doubts suggested by appearance to the contrary, to the wisdom, the infinite love of God. It means believing that nothing in this world escapes His Providence. . . . It means believing that God can permit, at times here below, for some time the preeminence of atheism and of impiety, the lamentable obscuring of a sense of justice, the violation of law, the tormenting of innocent, peaceful, undefended, helpless men. It means believing that God at times thus lets trials befall individuals and peoples, trials of which the malice is the instrument in a design of justice directed toward the punishment of sin, towards purifying persons and peoples through the expiations of this present life and bringing them back by that way to Himself; but it means believing at the same time that this justice always remains here below the justice of a Father inspired and dominated by love.

". . . It means believing finally that the fierce intensity of the trial, like the triumph of evil, will endure even here below only for a fixed time and not longer; that the Hour of God will come, the hour of mercy, the hour of holy rejoicing, the hour of the new canticle of liberation, the hour of exultation and of joy, the hour in which, after having let the hurricane loose for a moment on humanity, the all-powerful Hand of the Heavenly Father, with an imperceptible motion, will detain it and disperse it and, by ways little known to the mind or to the hopes of men, jutsice, calm and peace will be restored to the nations.

". . . . suffering stands at the threshold of life."

December 24, 1941

"Such large-scale disbursements, giving rise as must to a contraction of the forces of production in the civil and social field, cannot but be the basis for serious anxiety on the part of those who turn their thoughts with preoccupation towards the future.

"No! Christianity, whose force derives from Him Who is the Way, the Truth and the Life and Who is with it and shall remain with it until the consummation of the world, has not failed in its mission but men have rebelled against that Christianity which is true and faithful to Christ and His doctrine.

"In its place they have fashioned Christianity to their liking, a new idol which does not save, which is not opposed to the passions of carnel desires nor to the greed for gold and silver which fascinates, nor to the pride of life; a new religion without a soul or a soul without religion, a mask of dead Christianity without the spirit of Christ. And they have proclaimed that Christianity has failed in its mission!

"A religious anemia, like a spreading contagion, has so afflicted many peoples of Europe and of the world and has created in their souls such a moral void that no spurious and pharisaical religious organization and no national or international mythology will serve to fill this emptiness. Is it not true that for decades and centuries past men have directed their every thought, word and deed to their sworn objective of tearing from the hearts of our young and old alike their faith in God, the Creator and Father of all, Rewarder of good andAvenger of evil, and have they not striven for the accomplishment of this goal through a process of radical change in education and instruction, opposing and oppressing by every art and means the diffusion of the spoken and printed word, and by the abuse of scientific knowledge and political power, the religion and the Church of Christ?

". . . it has happened that the spirit and the tendency with which technical progress was often (but by no means necessarily) put to use have brought it about that in our time technology must expiate its error and be, as it were, its own avenger by producing instruments of destruction which destroy today what it had erected yesterday).

"Now the destruction brought about by the present war is on so vast a scale that it is imperative that there be not added to it also the further ruin of a frustrated and deluded peace. In order to avoid so great a calamity it is fitting that in the formulation of that peace there shall be assured the cooperation, with sincerity of will and energy, with the purpose of a generous participation, not only of this or that party, not only of this or that people, but of all people; yea, rather of all humanity. It is a universal undertaking for the common good which requires the collaboration of all Christendom in the religious and moral aspects of the new edifice that is to be constructed.

"Within the limits of a new order founded on moral principles there is no room for the violation of the freedom, integrity and security of other States; . . .

". . . no place for open or occult oppression of the cultural and linguistic characteristics of national minorities, . . .

". . . no place for that cold and calculating egoism which tends to hoard the economic resources and materials destined for the use of all . . .

". . . once the more dangerous sources of armed conflicts have been eliminated, there is no place for a total warfare or for a mad rush to armaments. . . .

"Means must be found which will be . . . efficacious in order that the norm 'pacts must be observed' . . .

". . . no place for the persecution of religion and of the Church.

". . . priceless . . . will be the contribution of statesmen who show themselves ready to open the gates and smooth the path for the Church of Christ so that, free and unhindered, it may bring its supernatural influence to bear in the conclusion of a peace amongst nations and may cooperate with its zeal and love in the immense task of finding remedies for the evils which the war will leave in its wake.

". . . in some parts of the world countless legislative dispositions bar the way to the message of the Christian Faith while free and ample scope is given to a propaganda that opposes it, . . .

"At the dawning of that day with what great joy will nations and rulers, freed in mind from the fear of the insidious dangers of further conflict, transform the swords, nicked and jagged from constant use against their fellow man, into ploughs with which to furrow the fertile breast of the earth under the sun of Heavenly Benediction and to wrest from it their daily bread, dampened now by the sweat of their brows but no longer bathed in blood and tears of sorrow? In expectation of that happy day, and with this longing prayer upon Our lips, We send Our greeting and Our blessing to all Our children of the entire universe."

MAY 13, 1942

"Let us rekindle in ourselves the spirit of love; let us hold ourselves ever ready to collaborate with our faith and our hands, after the most extensive, disastrous and bloody cataclysm of all history, to reconstruct from the pile of material and moral ruins a world that the bonds of brotherly love will weld in peace, a world in which, with the help of the Almighty, all may be new hearts, words and works."

NOVEMBER 1, 1942

"Queen of the Most Holy Rosary, Refuge of the Human Race, Victress in all God's battles, we humbly prostrate ourselves before thy throne, confident that we shall receive mercy, grace and bountiful assistance and protection in the present calamity, not through our own inadequate merits, but solely through the great goodness of thy Maternal Heart.

"To thee, to thy Immaculate Heart, in this, humanity's tragic hour, we consign and consecrate ourselves in union not only with the Mystical Body of thy Son, Holy Mother Church, now in such suffering and agony in so many places and sorely tried in so many ways, but also with the entire world, torn by a fierce strife, consumed in a fire of hate, victim of its own wickedness.

"May the sight of the widespread material and moral destruction, of the sorrows and anguish of countless fathers and mothers, husbands and wives, brothers and sisters, and innocent children, of the great number of lives cut off in the flower of youth, of the bodies mangled in horrible slaughter, and of the tortured and agonized souls in danger of being lost eternally, move thee to compassion!

"O Mother of Mercy, obtain peace for us from God and above all procure for us those graces which prepare, establish and assure the peace!

"Queen of Peace, pray for us and give to the world now at war the peace for which all peoples are longing, peace in the truth, justice and charity of Christ. Give peace to the warring nations and to the souls of men, that in the tranquillity of order the Kingdom of God may prevail.

"Extend thy protection to the infidels and to all those still in the shadow of death; give them peace and grant that on them, too, may shine the sun of truth, that they may unite with us in proclaiming before the one and only Saviour of the World 'Glory to God in the highest and peace to men of good will.'

"Give peace to the peoples separated by error or by discord, and especially to those who profess such singular devotion to thee and in whose homes an honored place was ever accorded thy venerated icon (today perhaps often kept hidden to await better days): bring them back to one fold of Christ under the one true shepherd.

"Obtain peace and complete freedom for the Holy Church of God; stay the spreading flood of modern paganism; enkindle in the faithful the love of purity, the practice of the Christian life, and an apostolic zeal, so that the servants of God may increase in merit and in number.

"Lastly, as the Church and the entire human race were consecrated to the Sacred Heart of Jesus, so that in reposing all hope in Him, He might become for them the sign and pledge of victory and salvation: so we in like manner consecrate ourselves forever also to thee and to thy Immaculate Heart, Our Mother and Queen, that thy love and patronage may hasten the triumph of the Kingdom of God and that all nations, at peace with one another and with God, may proclaim thee blessed and with thee may raise their voices to resound from pole to pole in the chant of the everlasting Magnificat of glory, love and gratitude to the Heart of Jesus, where alone they can find truth and peace."

DECEMBER 24, 1942

". . . the road from night to full day will be long; but of decisive importance are the first steps on the path, the first five milestones . . . the following maxims:

"He who would have the star of peace shine out and stand over society should cooperate for his part in giving back to the human person the dignity given to it by God . . .

"He . . . should reject every form of materialism which sees in the people only a herd of individuals . . . to be lorded over and treated arbitrarily; . . .

"He . . . should give to work the place assigned to it by God

"Is it not true that deep thinkers see ever more clearly in the renunciation of egoism and national isolation the way to general salvation, ready as they are to demand of their peoples a heavy participation in the sacrifices necessary for social well-being in other peoples?

"May this Christmas Message of Ours, . . . encourage and increase the legions of these social crusades in every nation. And may God deign to give to their peaceful cause the victory of which their noble enterprise is worthy.

"He . . . should collaborate towards a complete rehabilitation of the juridical order.

"He . . . should cooperate towards the setting up of a State conception and practice founded on reasonable discipline, exalted kindliness and a responsible Christian spirit."

APPENDIX II

BIBLIOGRAPHY

A. *Scripture, the Fathers and Commentaries Thereon*

The Holy Bible (Vulgate and Douay-Rheims Versions)
The New Testament (Westminster and Spencer Versions)
a Lapide: Commentaria in S. Scripturam and partial English translation of the same by Mossman and Cobb
Migne (editor): Scripturae S. Cursus Completus
Berry: The Apocalypse of St. John
Holzhauser: Apocalypseos D. Joannis Expositio
Parker and the Rivingtons (printers): A Library of the Fathers of the Holy Catholic Church
Roberts and Donaldson: The Ante-Nicene Fathers
Pohle-Preuss: Eschatology
Hermann: Institutiones Theologiae Dogmaticae
Lindberg: Gog—All Agog
de Journal: Enchiridion Patristicum
Denzinger: Enchiridion Symbolorum
Thomas Aquinas (St.): Summa Theologica (2:2:171-174)

B. *The Apocrypha*

Charles: Apocrypha and Pseudepigrapha of the Old Testament
James: The Apocryphal New Testament

C. *Collections of Private Prophecies*

Antoine: Le Grand Pape et le Grand Roi
Beck: Great European Monarch and World Peace
Bembord: Spielbachn
Benedictine Sisters: Armenseelenfreund
Beykirch: Prophetenstimmen
Boswell: Prophets and Portents
Bricaud: Le Guerre et les Propheties Celebres
de Busto: Rosarium Sermonum
Celtic el Nobi: La Voix des Prophetes
Collier: Something to Hope For
The Christian Trumpet—Anon. (Donohoe: Boston)
Curicque: Voix Prophetiques
Dalgairns: The German Mystics of the Fourteenth Century
Daniel: Serait-ce Vraiment La Fin Des Temps
Delattre: Le Second Avenement de Jesus Christ
Deniers avis Profetiques—Anon.
Dollinger: Fables of the Middle Ages
    The Prophetic Spirit and the Prophecies of the Christian Era
Dompierre: Comment Tout cela va Finir
Dornstetter: Das endzeitliche Gottesreich nach der Prophetie
Forman: The Story of Prophecy
I Futuri Destini degli Stati e delle Nazioni—Anon.
Godard: Le Prophetisme et le temps Nouveaux
Honert: Prophetenstimmen
Josserand: Recueil Complet des Propheties
Konzionator: Der Kommende Grosse Monarch
    Die Zukmft Englands
    Die Zukumft Frankreichs

Lanslots: The End of the World and of Man
Lilly: A Collection of Ancient and Modern Prophecies
Luetzenburg: Vita Antichristi
Michel: The Last Things
Naquet: Europe Delivree
Novaye: Demain
Peladan: Le Derniere Mot des Propheties
Pelletier: La Chef des Temps
Plancy: La Fin des Temps
Prophecies—Sadlier & Co., New York City
Rademacher: Der Weltuntergang
Reed: Prophecies about the War in Europe
Spirago: Antichrist
    Der Weltuntergang
    Die Zukumft Deutschlands
Stenay: L'Avenir devoile
Stern: Die Offenbarung
Thomas Das Weltende nach der Lehre des Glaubens und der Wissenschaft
Thurston: The War and the Prophets
Timbs: Things not generally known
Zalinski: Noted Prophecies

D. *Matter on Specific Private Prophecies*

Jerome of Prague: Book of Visions and Instructions—Bl. Angela of Foligno
St. Bede: In die Judicii
Roux: Examen de la Prophetie de Blois
Don Bosco in the West: issue for Nov.-Dec., 1939
Poulain (editor): The Spiritual Journal of Lucie Christine
O'Kearney: The Prophecies of St. Colum-Cille et al.
Emmerich: The Dolorous Passion
Wegener-McGowan: Sister Anne Katherine Emmerich
Spirago: Katherine Emmerich
The Life and Revelations of St. Gertrude (Burns, Oates & Washbourne, publishers)
St. Hildegard: Scivias
Steele: Life and Visions of St. Hildegard
Venerabilis Servi Dei Bartholomaei Holzhauser Opuscula Ecclesiastica—Published in "Graduel" (Paris: 1861)
Luca of Cosenza: Expositio Magni Prophetae Abbatis Joachim
Biver: Pere Lamy
Stenay: Le Prophete David Lazzaretti
Lortie: Is the Pope of Rome Infallible?
"Ressehc": Leviathan
Maitre: La Prophetie des Papes attribuee a Saint Malachie
    Les Papes et la Papaute de 1143 a la fin du monde
Spirago: Die Malachias-Weissagung
Paton: Prophecies of Merlin
Spirago: Klarheit ueber Konnersreuth
Von Lama: Therese of Konnersreuth
Ratcliffe Thompson: The True Prophecies of Michael Nostradamus
Modern Library: Oracles of Nostradamus
The Southern Messenger: issues of Jan. 7 and 14, 1943

APPENDIX

Allen: Window in Provence (Nostradamus: Good)
Lamont: Nostradamus Sees All
McCann: Nostradamus
Boswell: Nostradamus Speaks
Jeantin: Croniques historiques sur l'Abbaye d'Orval
Smith: The House of Glory
    Miracle of Ages
Konzionator: La Salette
Lola: La Grand Nouvelle de la Mere de Dieu
Parent: Le Secret Complet de la Salette
Baker: Mother Shipton and Nixon's Prophecies
Harrison: Mother Shipton Investigated
Providence-Sligo: Life of Ven. Anna Maria Taigi
Thompson: Life of Ven. Anna Maria Taigi
Dixon: St. Vincent Ferrer
Portentosa vida y Milagros de S. Vincente Ferrer—Madrid, 1856

E. *Manuscripts*

Philip Beecher of St. Louis, Mo.: The Private Prophets
The Works of Mother Rafols translated from the Spanish text bearing the
"Nihil Obstat" of the Assessor of the Cong. of Rites
Various letters and manuscripts in which information on the contemporary
    seers is given.

Books and pamphlets noted above, if not out of print and obtainable in
this country, may be ordered through the "Thomas More Library and Book
Shop," 22 W. Monroe St., Chicago, Ill.

Important Notes

Leaflets on Universal Atonement are advertised as obtainable from
Loretta Laney, 3154 College Ave., Berkeley, Cal. The same on prayers to
the Queen of the Angels and on the prayer said to be revealed to the Roman
Priest are listed as obtainable from Betty Kelly, 1008 Riverside Avenue,
Baltimore, Md. Prayers to the Holy Ghost is a third leaflet put out by Holy
Ghost Fathers, 1615 Manchester Lane N. W., Washington, D. C. Paul
Husted, 6531 So. Union Ave., Chicago, Ill., is advertised as the source
whence priests may obtain information on a plan of social reform which is
said to have some mystical connections. Beck's booklet noted above is published by Our Sunday Visitor. The Prayer revealed by Our Lady of Fatima
is: "O, my Jesus, forgive us; deliver us from the flames of Hell and have
mercy on the souls in Purgatory, chiefly those most abandoned." This to be
said after the "Gloria Patri" which folows each decade of the Rosary. (Fon-
seca: Nossa Senhora de Fatima, p. 23.)
Whether any faith be put in the private pamphlets quoted herein or not,
there is one pamphlet which should not go unread in these times, namely
"Pius XII and Peace" put out by the N. C. W. C., 1312 Massachusetts Ave.
N. W., Washington, D. C. It may be expected that the pope will have
much more to say. Follow his words carefully. The prayers and conditional
prophecies in the works of Pius XII are most valuable. The prophecies
give no appearance of revelations. They are rather external truths applied
to our times. Finally, "Principles of Peace," published by the N. C. W. C.
contains the mature thought of the last five Popes on the subject of peace.

Come, Holy Ghost, Who ever one
Art with the Father and the Son,
Come, Holy Ghost, our souls possess
With Thy full flood of holiness.

In will and deed, by heart and tongue,
With all our pow'rs Thy praise be sung,
And love light up our mortal frame,
Till others catch the living flame.

O Comforter, to Thee we cry,
The heav'nly gift of God Most High,
Thou fount of life and fire of love
And sweet anointing from above.

Praise we the Father and the Son,
And Holy Spirit with them one;
And may the Son on us bestow
The gifts that from the Spirit flow.

INDEX TO PROPHETS AND PROPHECIES

(reference to numbers not pages)

Adso, Abbot of Montier-en-Der: 79
Ageda, Bishop Christianos: 98
Agreda, Sister Mary of: 130
Alacoque, St. Margaret Mary: 128b
d'Ally, Cardinal: 110
Alphonsa Eppinger: see "Eppinger"
Amadeus, Blessed John, de Sylva: 116 and 117
Amos: 15
Anthony of Aix-la-Chapelle: 167
Anonymous: 92 and 200
Apocalypse: St. John: 32; of Thomas: see "Thomas"
Apostles, Epistle of the: 57 and 58
Apostolic Constitutions: see "Didache"
Ars, Cure of: 163
Asdente, Sister Rose Columba, of Taggia: 159
Asher: 56
Augustine, St., of Hippo: 35
Aystinger the German: 91
Bacon, Roger: 99
Bartholomew, Venerable, da Saluzzo: 142
Baourdi, Marie: 144
Baruch: 10 and 41
Bearcan, St.: 68
Becket, St. Thomas a: see "Thomas"
Belez, Nursing Nun of: 152
Benedict, Pope, XV: 181
Bernardine Sister: 185
Bernhardt Rembordt: see "Rembordt"
Berry, Rev. Dr. E. Sylvester: 180 ff
Billiante, Countess Francesca de: 184
Birch-Tree Prophecy: 89 (See "Peter Schlinkert")
Blois, Prophecy of: see "Gaultier"
Bosco, St. Don John: 173
Bobolo, St. Andrew: 148
Bourg, Mother Josefa von: 145
Bridget, St., of Sweden: 106
Bufalo, Blessed Caspar del: 154
Busto, Bernardine von: 119
Caesar, St.: 67
Calliste, Father: 156 (Recorder for Bl. Anna Maria Taigi)
Canori-Mora, Elizabeth: see "Mora"
Capistran, St. John: 113

Capuchin Friar: see "Franciscan Friar"
Caspar del Bufalo: see "Bufalo"
Cataldus, St.: see "Kataldus"
Catherine Mattei, Blessed, of Racconigi: 121
Catherine, St., of Sienna: 107
Chambau, Sister Marie: 178
Chrysostom, St. John: 36
Chicago layman: 196
Chicago mother: 195
Clausi, Father Bernard Maria: 161
Chesser Lortie: see "Lortie"
Cleft-Rock, Brother John of the: 104
Colomba, Sister Rose: see "Asdente"
Columcille (Columba), St.: 70
Cristine, Lucie: 177
Cyril the Hermit (St.): 108
Daniel: 12
Daniel, Book of (Apocryphal): 52-54
Deuteronomy: 2
Didache (Apostolic Constitutions): 33
Dionysius of Luxemburg (Letzenburg): 132
Dionysius Ryckel: see "Ryckel"
Dolcino: 109
Earling Mystic: 197
Ecclesiaticus (Sirac): 7
Edward, St., of England: 80
Emmerich, Venerable Anne Catherine: 172
English, Old: 85
Enoch: 44
Eppinger, Mother Alphonsa: 166
Ezechial: 11 and 47
Ezra: 48 (Apocryphal)
Fatima, Prophecy of: 179c
Ferrer, St. Vincent: 111
Fluh, Blessed Nicholas: 118 (Known also as "Brother Klaus")
Francesca, Countess, de Billiante: see "Billiante"
Francis, St., de Paul: 114
Franciscan Father of Arizona: 190
Franciscan Friar: 139
Gameleo: 124

Gaultier, Sister Marianne: 144 (Known also as "Sister Marianne")
Geckner, Rudolph: 131
German, Old: 88
Gertrude, St.: 102b
Gora, Jasna: see "Jasna Gora"
Goires, Joseph v.: 160
Gregory, Pope St., the Great: 37
Grignon: see "Montfort"
Hampole: see "Rolle"
Herman, Monk, of Lehnin: 103
Hermes, Pastor: 34
Henoch, Book of: 44
Hilarion, Monk: 81 and 115
Hildegard, St.: 84
Holzhauser, Venerable Bartholomew: 129
Italian, Old: 93
Irish, Old: 75
Isaias: 8; Testament of: 43
Jahenny, Marie Julie, of La Fraudais: 174
James, The Epistle of: 59 (Apocryphal)
Jane Le Royer: 141 (Known also as "Sister Mary of the Nativity")
Japanese Prophecy: 126
Jasna Gora: 198
Jeremias (Jeremiah): 9
Jerome, St.: 39
Jesuit Founder: 120
Joachim, Blessed, of Fiore: 97 (Known also as "Merlin Joachim")
Joel: 14
John, St., the Evangelist: Gospel: 21; 1st Epistle: 29; 2nd Epistle: 30; Apocalypse: 32; Baptist Vianey see Ars; Capistran: 113
John, Brother, of the Cleft-Rock: see "Cleft-Rock"
Josefa von Bourg: see "Bourg"
Jubilees, Book of: 46
Judah, Book of: 50
Jude, Epistle of: 31
Kataidus, St.: 64
Klaus, Brother: see "Fluh"
Korzeniecki, Father: 148
Lactantius: 38
Lamy, Pere: 183

Lang, Matthew: 149
La Roque, Cardinal: see "Roque"
Lataste, Sister Marie: 158
Latin, Old: 94
Lavinsky, Father: 134
Lehnin, Prophecy of: see "Herman"
Leo XIII, Pope: 188b.
Leo the Philosopher: 78
Levi, Book of: 49
Leviticus: 1
Lortie, Chester: 178b
Lucie Christine: see "Christine"
Luke, St. (Gospel): 20
Luxemburg: see "Dionysius"
Machabees, Book of: 18
Maeltamlacht, St.: 74
Madgeburg, Chronicles of: 90
Malachy, St.: 82
Maurus Rabanus: see "Rabanus"
Markiewicz, X. B.: 182
Margaret Mary St.: see "Alacoque"
Martel, Marie, of Tilly: 176
Mary of Earling: see "Earling"
Mary, Sister, of Jesus Crucified: see "Baourdi"
Matthew Lang: see "Lang"
Matthew, St. (Gospel): 19
Mayence, Prophecy of: 162
Merlin: 72
Methodius, St.: 40
Micheas: 16
Monessen layman: 199
Montfort, Blessed Louis Marie Grignon de: 135
Mora, Elizabeth Canori: 150
Nativitas: see "Jane"
Nectou, Father, S. J.: 137
Nepthali: 55
Neumann, Therese: 181
New York laywoman: 193
Nicholas, Blessed, of Fluh: see under "Fluh"
Nostredamus (Nostradamus); Michael: 123
Odile, (Odilia), St.: 76
Oria, Palma Maria: see "Palma"
Orval Prophecy: 102
Osee: 13
Ossolinski Library Prophecy: 175
Otrante: see "Werdin"
Padua, Monk of: 136

Palma Maria Addolorata Matarelli d'Oria: 165
Parallelipomenon: 3
Pastor Hermes: see "Hermes"
Paul, St.: 22-27
Paul, St. Francis de: see "Francis"
Peter, St.: 28
Peter, Apocalypse of: 61
Philosopher, Leo the: see "Leo"
Phoenix mother: 194
Pie, Cardinal: 171
Pius IX, Pope: 169
Pius X, Pope: 179
Pius XI, Pope: 188a
Pius XII, Pope: 189, and Appendix I
Poreaus, David: 127
Porsat, Venerable Magdalena: 68
Premol, Prophecy of: 65
Psalms: 4
Psalms of Solomon: 45
Pyramid Prophecy: 191
Rabanus Maurus, Blessed: 77
Racconigi: see "Catherine"
Rafols, Mother Maria: 147
Reisinger, Father Theophilus: 192
Rembordt, Bernhardt: 140
Remigius, St.: 66
Ressehc—pen name for Lortie q. v.
Ricci, Father Laurence: 138
Richard Rolle: see "Rolle"
Richter, Bishop Jean Paul: 146
Rocco, Louis: 157a
Rock, Blessed John of the Cleft: see "Cleft"
Rolle, Richard, of Hampole: 105
Roger Bacon: see "Bacon"
Roman, Old: 95
Roque, Cardinal La: 155
Royer, Jane: see "Jane"
Ryckel, Dionysius: 118b

Saluzzo: see "Bartholomew"
Saxon, Old: 87
Schlinkert, Peter: see "Birch-Tree"
Scotch, Old: 86
Senatus, St.: 69
Shepherd of Hermes: see "Hermes"
Shipton, Mother: 122
Sibylline Oracles: 63
Sibylla Tiburtina: 96
Sienna, St. Catherine of: see "Catherine"
Silva, Amadeus: see "Amadeus"
Sirac: see "Ecclesiasticus"
Solomon, Psalms of: see "Psalms"
Souffrand, Abbe: 151
Spielbahn: see "Rembordt"
Steiner, Abbess Marie: 164
Strassbourg Prophecy: see "Mayence"
Taigi, Blessed Anna Maria Giannetti: 156
Talmud: 62
Telesphorus of Cosenza: 125
Testament of Isaias: 43
Thomas, Apocalypse of: 60
Thomas, St., a Becket: 83
Tobias: 6
Tobit: 42
Ultan, St.: 71
Vatiguerro, John of: 100
Vianney, St. John Baptist: see "Ars"
Vincent, St. Ferrer: see "Ferrer"
Votin, Father Jerome: 112
Wallraff, Helen: 143
Welsh, Old: 73
Werdin, Abbot, d'Otrante: 101
Werl, Monk of: 133
Wisdom, Book of: 5
Wittman, Bishop George Michael: 153
Zabulon: 51